Playing the Ukulele

by David Hodge

A member of Penguin Group (USA) Inc.

This book is dedicated to Claudia and Sean Barry, who continually help others to bring music and joy into their lives.

ALPHA BOOKS

Published by Penguin Group (USA) Inc.

Penguin Group (USA) Inc., 375 Hudson Street, New York, New York 10014, USA • Penguin Group (Canada), 90 Eglinton Avenue East, Suite 700, Toronto, Ontario M4P 2Y3, Canada (a division of Pearson Penguin Canada Inc.) • Penguin Books Ltd., 80 Strand, London WC2R 0RL, England • Penguin Ireland, 25 St. Stephen's Green, Dublin 2, Ireland (a division of Penguin Books Ltd.) • Penguin Group (Australia), 250 Camberwell Road, Camberwell, Victoria 3124, Australia (a division of Pearson Australia Group Pty. Ltd.) • Penguin Books India Pvt. Ltd., 11 Community Centre, Panchsheel Park, New Delhi—110 017, India • Penguin Group (NZ), 67 Apollo Drive, Rosedale, North Shore, Auckland 1311, New Zealand (a division of Pearson New Zealand Ltd.) • Penguin Books (South Africa) (Pty.) Ltd., 24 Sturdee Avenue, Rosebank, Johannesburg 2196, South Africa • Penguin Books Ltd., Registered Offices: 80 Strand, London WC2R 0RL, England

International Standard Book Number: 978-1-61564-185-7
Library of Congress Catalog Card Number: 2011945183

16 15 14   8 7 6 5 4 3 2

Interpretation of the printing code: The rightmost number of the first series of numbers is the year of the book's printing; the rightmost number of the second series of numbers is the number of the book's printing. For example, a printing code of 12-1 shows that the first printing occurred in 2012.

Printed in the United States of America

Note: This publication contains the opinions and ideas of its author. It is intended to provide helpful and informative material on the subject matter covered. It is sold with the understanding that the author and publisher are not engaged in rendering professional services in the book. If the reader requires personal assistance or advice, a competent professional should be consulted.

The author and publisher specifically disclaim any responsibility for any liability, loss, or risk, personal or otherwise, which is incurred as a consequence, directly or indirectly, of the use and application of any of the contents of this book.

Most Alpha books are available at special quantity discounts for bulk purchases for sales promotions, premiums, fundraising, or educational use. Special books, or book excerpts, can also be created to fit specific needs.

For details, write: Special Markets, Alpha Books, 375 Hudson Street, New York, NY 10014.

Publisher: *Marie Butler-Knight*

Associate Publisher/Acquiring Editor: *Mike Sanders*

Executive Managing Editor: *Billy Fields*

Development Editor: *Susan Zingraf*

Senior Production Editor: *Janette Lynn*

Copy Editor: *Megan Wade*

Cover Designer: *Kurt Owens*

Book Designers: *William Thomas, Rebecca Batchelor*

Indexer: *Angie Bess Martin*

Layout: *Brian Massey*

Senior Proofreader: *Laura Caddell*

Contents

Introduction

Making music is fun. Sure, people take up instruments for all sorts of reasons, but the reason most musicians make music is because it's one of the most fun and rewarding things you can do.

Few instruments just shout out "fun" like the ukulele! It's both readily portable and incredibly versatile. Sure, you can play "Tiptoe Through the Tulips" on it (if you're in a silly or nostalgic mood), but you can also rock out on songs like "All Along the Watchtower" or "While My Guitar Gently Weeps," lay down some jazz standards like "All of Me" or "Autumn Leaves," or even belt out some traditional blues. The ukulele sounds as much at home playing classical music as it does playing traditional Hawaiian melodies or the folk songs of almost any culture around the globe.

Not only does the uke provide so much musical potential, it's also, as you'll soon discover, remarkably easy to learn. Most beginners pick up the basics of the ukulele fairly quickly. Before you know it, you will be playing simple melodies and then strumming chords, and then hopefully sitting in a ukulele group having the time of your life. By the time you get through this book, you'll be discovering first-hand the joys of creating and sharing music with others.

Why This Book Is for You

Whether you have never played a musical instrument before or you are taking up the ukulele as an additional instrument to those you can already play, you'll find *The Complete Idiot's Guide to Playing the Ukulele* a valuable guide. Those of you who have read any of my other books in the *Complete Idiot's Guide* series (*The Complete Idiot's Guide to Guitar*, *The Complete Idiot's Guide to Playing Bass Guitar*, and *The Complete Idiot's Guide to Playing Rock Guitar*) know that I am first and foremost a teacher. My job, if you will, is to help you start creating music in your life. *The Complete Idiot's Guide to Playing the Ukulele* has been designed to get you playing music right away, even if you've never held a ukulele before in your life.

Like my other *Complete Idiot's Guides*, this one is also designed to give you the necessary tools to become a musician. Instead of just showing you some chord charts and saying "strum this way" and having you simply copy what I do on the audio CD that accompanies this book, my goal is to make sure you know as much about the whys of playing the uke as you do the hows. My goal as a teacher is to ensure you can continually grow and evolve as a ukulele player and as a musician.

This book will guide you step-by-step through the process of learning to play the ukulele. Learning any musical instrument is rarely done in linear fashion, but this book will start you out on the basic skills and then help you build on that foundation so that you will find yourself able to create music for yourself as well as make music with others in a group setting.

That last bit is especially important. While playing the ukulele for your own entertainment is certainly fun, sitting in with other musicians—whether they are playing ukes or other musical instruments—is an even more enjoyable experience. *The Complete Idiot's Guide to Playing the Ukulele*, unlike any other ukulele tutorial, teaches you about how to play in a group. You will also learn important musical tools like transposing, which will allow you to play any ukulele you'd like, whether it's a soprano, concert, tenor, or baritone.

What You'll Find in This Book

The Complete Idiot's Guide to Playing the Ukulele is 23 chapters arranged in 6 general parts. They are as follows:

Part 1, Gearing Up to Play, gives you an introduction to the ukulele, including a bit of its history as well as a description of the various sizes of the instrument. You'll get a rundown on the uke's basic parts and also some audio samples so you can hear the differences between the various types of ukuleles. Then you'll learn to get your instrument in tune and start playing single note lines to get your fingers used to the ukulele's small neck and fretboard and to get ready to strum and play chords. Additionally, you'll learn how to read ukulele tablature and basic music notation. The warm-up exercises and simple, familiar song melodies will help you get your fingers limber for the chapters in Part 2.

Part 2, Chords and Strumming Made Easy, takes you to the next step—strumming and changing chords. You'll learn how to read chord charts, but you'll also learn how chords are formed so that you'll be able to find ways of playing chords all up and down the neck of your uke. You'll discover how easy it is to keep a steady rhythm and still create interesting and creative basic strumming styles.

Part 3, Expanding Your Horizons, introduces you to early intermediate techniques for both rhythm and single note playing. You'll discover playing arpeggios and strumming with percussive and rolling strums; you'll also learn various slur techniques such as hammer-ons and pull-offs as well as the basics of finger-style playing. After working through these chapters you'll be able to play songs of all styles, from pounding rock songs to lilting waltzes to swinging jazz and blues tunes. Plus, as a bonus, you'll also get a taste of alternative tunings and a primer on transposing, as well as a guide to playing the baritone ukulele.

Part 4, Going Solo, expands on the skills and techniques learned in Part 3. You'll learn how to play jazzy chord melodies and how to apply the basics of music theory to create fills and solos to spice up your ukulele playing. You will also learn how to combine all the various single note techniques with strumming, making you sound like you've been playing the uke for years!

Part 5, All Together Now!, examines the nuances of specific musical genres and prepares you to play all kinds of music on your ukulele. In addition to a quick rundown on blues, jazz, rock, pop, Hawaiian, and classical music, you'll also learn about playing in groups. You'll find that everything you learned earlier in the book will give you the skills and confidence you need to make cool music with other musicians.

Part 6, The Adventure Continues, helps you choose the right ukulele for you and provides tips on keeping your instrument in its best condition. You'll find out how easily you can do simple main-tenance, like changing your strings, and learn about the day-to-day things you can do to give your ukulele a long, healthy life.

At the end of the book are four helpful appendixes: a track listing for the CD that accompanies this book; a handy reference for reading music notation; rhythms and ukulele tablature; charts for ukulele chords; and a list of books, websites, and other tutorial material that you'll probably find useful in your ongoing ukulele (and musical) education.

Practice, Practice

At the end of most of the chapters, you'll find a section marked as "Practice, Practice" where you will get advice and tips to help you get the most out of the techniques and ideas discussed in that particular chapter. You'll also find a lot of tips in Chapter 18 and Chapter 23 devoted to putting together your own personal practice plans and schedules.

Sidebar Icons

You will also find more advice, tips on various techniques, suggestions on how to avoid common bad playing habits, and other useful bits of information in the numerous sidebars found throughout *The Complete Idiot's Guide to Playing the Ukulele*. Four types of sidebars occur in this book:

DEFINITION

These provide definitions and details about various musical terms and specific ukulele-playing techniques.

SMOOTH STRUMMING

These give you advice on the various topics and techniques you'll be reading about, from fingering the frets to strumming and working out rhythms to playing different musical parts in a group setting.

FRET LESS!

These offer guidance to help you steer clear of developing any potential bad habits that will hinder your playing abilities in the future.

UKE LORE

These contain interesting facts and stories about the ukulele, its history, and the people (and music) who have played and promoted this incredible instrument.

Using the CD

Throughout this book you will find an icon that looks like this:

This indicates that the example in question is on the audio CD included in this book. The first track demonstrates the sounds of the various types of ukuleles. Then you will hear a tuning track (to get your instrument in tune) as well as audio examples for most of the exercises in this book. Many of the CD's tracks are devoted to the various songs used as examples for the various rhythms, techniques, and other lessons you'll be learning in this book.

With the exception of the first few tracks, each track on the CD is introduced by its corresponding label in the book. So for instance, the first example in Chapter 3, which is marked "Chapter 3, Example 1" in the book, will be announced as "Chapter 3, Example 1" on the CD as well. In addition to the various exercises and examples of ukulele techniques, there are more than two dozen songs for you to play. Because the ukulele is quite often used as accompaniment for a vocalist, it makes more sense for you to hear it played in a real-world scenario, meaning with a vocalist as opposed to another uke (or another instrument) playing the melody. A number of audio examples are simply a single ukulele (I use a tenor ukulele in most of the examples to give you the clearest possible sound), but there are also quite a few vocal numbers. The vocals are all performed by my good friend Nick Torres, who deserves a lot of praise for his efforts. The song arrangements in this book were written to teach specific techniques and ideas, and Nick's ability to create wonderful vocal interpretations (whether the song in question was in his singing range or not) is both impressive and inspiring. Just as with *The Complete Idiot's Guide to Guitar*, this book is greatly enriched by his contribution.

As with my other *Complete Idiot's Guides*, I have to give thanks to Todd Mack and Will Curtiss of Off The Beat-n-Track Studio in Sheffield, Massachusetts, for their invaluable assistance in putting together, mixing, and mastering the CD. This book is the fourth *Complete Idiot's Guide* I've recorded with Will and Todd, and the talent and effort they have put into each one is nothing less than astounding. I can't thank them enough for their work, advice, and support in helping produce the music for this book.

But Wait! There's More!

Have you logged on to idiotsguides.com lately? If you haven't, go there now! From quick articles on picking the right sized ukulele for you to step-by-step performance notes on almost all the songs here in this book, you can check them all out at your leisure online. Point your browser to idiotsguides.com/ukulele, and enjoy!

A Thank-You to Our Technical Editor

Speaking of help and support, I'd like to thank Greg Nease for being my technical editor for *The Complete Idiot's Guide to Playing the Ukulele*. His patience and ability to explain complex, technical matters to everyday folks (meaning me!) have been essential for making this book the useful guide that it is.

Let Me Know What You Think

Feel free to contact me directly with any questions, comments, or suggestions you may have about this book at my email address: dhodgeguitar@aol.com. Although I do try to answer every email I receive, sometimes I fall a bit behind due to my teaching schedule. But rest assured that every email gets read and I will do my best to reply to you as soon as possible. As a teacher, and as a writer, your thoughts and opinions are not only appreciated, but usually quite helpful.

Above all, I hope that you find playing the ukulele—not to mention simply making and sharing music with the world—as much fun as I do. I also hope that one day I have the honor of hearing you play!

Looking forward to hearing from you.

Peace

Acknowledgments

Any book is the result of a lot of work by a lot of different people. I thank my agent, Marilyn Allen, and Mike Sanders of Alpha Books for choosing me to write it. Special thanks also go to Marie Butler-Knight and Billy Fields as well as to Susan Zingraf, Janette Lynn, Megan Wade, Kurt Owens, Angie Bess Martin, Brian Massey, and Laura Caddell, and to all the rest of the Alpha team who contributed their time and talents on this project.

My thanks also go to Paul Hackett, the creator of Guitar Noise (www.guitarnoise.com). Through Guitar Noise, Paul introduced my writing and teaching to the world, and it's only through him that I've managed to have my teachings read by people in more than 150 countries all over the world. And to all of my Guitar Noise readers, I thank you for continually making me both a better teacher and a better writer.

For this book I must also thank Claudia and Sean Barry, Fred Schane, Lisa Parris, Bob Mothers (along with the West Yorkshire Mandolin and Ukulele Society), ukulele guru Jim Beloff, and a very, very big thank you to Phyllis and Dale Webb of the Magic Fluke Company of Sheffield, Massachusetts, for their time, advice, and expertise.

Finally, any thanks would be incomplete without acknowledging my youngest brother, Tom, and my good friends Laura Pager and Greg Nease, all of whom have been a lifelong source of encouragement, advice, and support.

And speaking of lifelong support, I offer thanks to my "partner in everything," Karen Berger, who not only took the photos for this book but also put up with me turning our home into a ukulele warehouse and patiently listened while I tinkered and noodled and crafted the song arrangements and exercises for this book. Thankfully she loves music!

Trademarks

All terms mentioned in this book that are known to be or are suspected of being trademarks or service marks have been appropriately capitalized. Alpha Books and Penguin Group (USA) Inc. cannot attest to the accuracy of this information. Use of a term in this book should not be regarded as affecting the validity of any trademark or service mark.

Gearing Up to Play

To get things started, we will explore a brief history of the ukulele, its various sizes and styles, its anatomy, and how to tune it.

Then you'll get basic instructions on holding the uke and how to strum with one hand and finger the frets with the other. You'll also learn all about notes, and how to read ukulele tablature and basic music notation, which will include playing some warm-up exercises with familiar melodies. By the time you're finished with this part, your fingers will be warmed up and ready to tackle what comes next—forming chords and strumming.

A Big Sound in a Small Package

In This Chapter

- A brief history of the ukulele
- Ukulele anatomy
- The four basic ukulele sizes
- Some variations on the ukulele
- A quick listen to various ukes

Type the word *ukulele* into your favorite search engine and you'll immediately see that you have a lot of company when it comes to enjoying or playing this musical instrument. Google alone lists more than 29 million results, from online stores selling ukuleles to online ukulele tuners to essays on the uke's history to video performances.

Speaking of videos, click over to YouTube and you'll see a search on "ukulele" will net you close to 20,000 videos. There are performances by well-known ukulele virtuosos like Jake Shimabukuro playing "While My Guitar Gently Weeps" or "Bohemian Rhapsody" or wonderful original songs by Zach Condon and his band Beirut. Or you could take in any of the delightful concert clips from the Ukulele Orchestra of Great Britain. You can see the late George Harrison play "Ain't She Sweet," with his face all smiles because he's truly enjoying himself and his ukulele.

You also could view thousands of other videos by enthusiastic ukulele players from all over the world covering just about every style of music from almost any era you choose. You'll find songs made famous by Frank Sinatra and hear music by the Ramones. You'll find uke (that's the traditional nickname of the ukulele) players performing traditional songs like "Greensleeves," that's more than 400 years old, and songs by twenty-first century artists like Outkast and Pearl Jam's Eddie Vedder. Whatever type of music you're into, you're likely to find someone playing it on the uke.

While you can play almost any type of music on a ukulele, it still has its own distinct voice. No other instrument truly captures the sound of a uke, and that's what makes it so special and unique.

A Little History

Although it has been around for fewer than 150 years, the ukulele has brought music to people all over the world. In many ways, it is an ideal instrument for a lot of people. Its small size allows you, and encourages you, to take it almost anywhere. You can play it in the park or in your car in a parking lot.

You can make music on a boat or in a tree house. A uke is the musical equivalent of Dr. Seuss's *Green Eggs and Ham*—you can play it *anywhere*. Its portability helped the ukulele, as we know it today, come into being.

In the mid-1800s, many Portuguese people left their homeland to seek better lives. While many sailed west to Brazil and New England, others—mainly from the Portuguese Archipelagos (islands) of Madeira and the Azores—traveled east, around Cape Horn, and across the Indian and Pacific Oceans to find work and new homes in Hawaii. These immigrants often came with their families and whatever they could manage to carry with them on the boats.

One such boat, the *Ravenscrag*, reached Honolulu in late August of 1879. Some of these new arrivals from Madeira brought along their *machêtes* (small four-stringed guitar-shaped instruments) and delighted their new friends with evening performances. The Hawaiians were very much taken with the instrument and rechristened it the *ukulele* (pronounced "oo-*koo*-ley-ley" in Hawaiian). Madeiran cabinet makers Manuel Nunes, Augusto Dias, and Jose de Espirito Santo, who were immigrants on the *Ravenscrag*, soon found themselves in huge demand as Hawaii's first ukulele *luthiers*—simply put, the ones making the ukes.

 DEFINITION

A **luthier** is a maker of stringed instruments (whether the instruments have frets or not), such as violins, violas, cellos, guitars, banjos, and (as you might guess from the name itself) lutes (a plucked string instrument popular during the fourteenth to seventeenth centuries).

It wasn't long before the ukulele's popularity won it the support from Hawaii's royalty. King David Kalakaua, an active proponent of the island's traditions and cultures, liked the ukulele so much that it became the featured accompanying musical instrument for hulas and other performances at royal events. His sister Queen Lili'uokalani, who ascended the throne after his death, was renowned for her musical talent, both as a performer (in addition to the ukulele she played piano and guitar) and as a songwriter. Her song titled "Aloha Oe" is a standard among uke players even today.

America Discovers the Uke

In 1915, the Panama Pacific International Exposition was held in San Francisco. It was here at this World's Fair–style event, meant to celebrate both the completion of the Panama Canal and the city's recovery from the earthquake of 1904, that the mainland got its first taste of the ukulele. Visitors to the Hawaiian Pavilion couldn't get enough of George E. K. Awai and his Royal Hawaiian Quartet, an ensemble of guitar and ukuleles.

From here, the uke's popularity spread across America. During the 1920s and 1930s, Tin Pan Alley churned out songs about Hawaii and songs with a distinctive Hawaiian feel, usually brought out musically by using Hawaiian steel guitars and ukuleles in the accompanying band. Hawaiian bandleader Johnny Noble, through mainland tours, recordings, and radio broadcasts, rearranged hundreds of traditional Hawaiian songs for the ukulele as well as wrote many original hit songs.

At the time, ukulele tutorials were selling almost as well as the instruments themselves! Sheet music of the popular songs of the day, published primarily for piano players, often included chord charts for ukulele so that everyday folks could entertain each other and make music together.

Becoming Mainstream

Like all instruments, the ukulele has gone through periods of popularity and decline, and not just in America. The uke was all the rage in Japan in the early 1930s and, according to Jim Beloff's terrific book *The Ukulele: A Visual History*, Japan is still very much the second home of ukulele virtuosos today.

And while America had uke ambassadors such as Cliff "Ukulele Ike" Edwards, Arthur Godfrey, and later Tiny Tim, England had George Formby and his banjolele (more on this in a moment) wowing the British music hall patrons and making a huge impression on youth, which would later lead the British Invasion of rock music in the early 1960s.

Nowadays, thanks especially to the internet and digital recording devices, ukuleles are seemingly everywhere. And great uke players like Paul Luongo, Jake Shimabukuro, Julia Nunes, Paula Fuga, James Hill, Kalea Gamiao, Derick Sebastian, Jim Beloff, Brittni Paiva, Deb Porter, and many more can be found with the click of a button. Check them out!

> **SMOOTH STRUMMING**
>
> When you listen or watch other ukulele players, you're bound to have one or two reactions: you'll either find yourself inspired and excited about playing or wonder why you think you should even try to learn to play. Just remember that every person who plays ukulele started out in the same exact spot you're in right now—being an absolute beginner who perhaps has never even held a uke before. Think of learning to play as the first steps of a lifelong musical adventure and you'll soon find every new technique a joy, and that there are always new things to learn!

All About the Uke

As you'll soon learn, ukuleles come in different sizes, but they all share the same basic components. The following illustration details the essential anatomy of a ukulele:

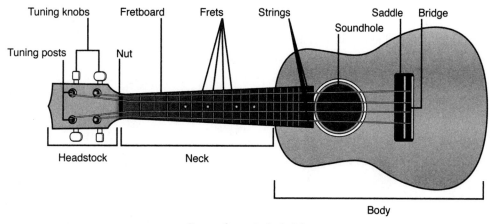

Parts of a typical ukulele.

Your instrument has three main sections:

The **headstock** is the end of the ukulele where the strings are attached to the tuning posts. The headstock ends at the nut (a hard piece of plastic with slots for each individual string), which separates the headstock from the neck of the ukulele.

The **neck** is the area between the headstock and the body. This is the area where you'll be placing your fingers on the strings to create notes and chords. The side of the neck where your uke's strings are is called the *fingerboard*, or *fretboard*, which makes sense because it's where the *frets* are located.

DEFINITION

The term **fret** has two meanings. First, a fret is any one of the raised metal wires on the neck of the ukulele. It's also the act of placing one's finger in the spaces between the frets on the neck of the ukulele.

The **body** is the wider guitar-shaped area of your instrument. It's essentially a hollow resonating chamber that projects the sound of the vibrating strings. On the body is where you will find the bridge and saddle, which is where the strings are attached at this end of the ukulele.

SMOOTH STRUMMING

The "front" side of the ukulele, which is the side that faces your listeners as you hold it, is also called the top.

To produce a note on your ukulele, you simply pluck a string. If your ukulele has four strings (most do, but some have six or even eight) you can play up to four notes at a time. Each string is stretched from the bridge/saddle area of the body to the tuning mechanisms in the headstock and, depending upon the string's diameter and on how tightly it is stretched, is set to the pitch of a specific note (you'll learn more about tuning your ukulele in Chapter 2). Placing a finger on the string along the fingerboard changes the length of the vibrating string, stopping it at the fret immediately closest to the finger on the body side of the fingerboard and raises the pitch of the string to a new note.

Meet the Family

Ukuleles usually come in one of four sizes. From smallest to largest they are soprano, concert, tenor, and baritone.

Despite their differences in size, the soprano, concert, and tenor ukuleles are usually all tuned to the same notes. You'll read all about how these ukes are tuned in Chapter 2. The strings of the baritone ukulele, as you'll learn in Chapter 14, are tuned to different notes.

From left to right: soprano, concert, tenor, baritone.

Soprano

The soprano ukulele is the "original sized" uke—the size they were at the beginning. It may be the runt of the litter, but it enjoys the most history and prestige. When most people envision a ukulele, it's more likely than not a soprano uke they see in their mind's eye.

Concert

As the ukulele gained in popularity, people came up with ways to "improve" it, meaning make it louder. The concert size was created in the 1920s. Being slightly larger than the soprano, it is a slightly louder instrument with a slightly fuller, deeper sound. Plus, because it has a slightly longer neck, it has slightly more room to place fingers along the frets.

Tenor

The tenor ukulele takes the idea of the concert ukulele one step further. Almost twice the body size of the soprano, the tenor gives you a lot of volume and a much fuller overall tone. Most of the examples on the CD included with this book were recorded on a tenor ukulele to give you the clearest sound possible to help you learn.

Baritone

The baritone ukulele is the biggest of the bunch, but it's the youngest, having been created in the 1940s. As you learned earlier, the strings of the baritone ukuleles are tuned to different notes than the strings of the other three basic types of ukes. Being bigger, the neck is longer and the strings are longer (and thicker), making the notes of a baritone uke quite a bit lower than those of the soprano, concert, and tenor. In fact, the strings of the baritone ukulele are typically tuned to the same notes as the four highest strings of a regular guitar, giving the baritone a deeper, more resonant quality than the other ukes.

FRET LESS!

Despite what you might have heard or read, the basic skills you learn to play on any one type of ukulele can be used to play them all. True, it will require a little bit of thinking on your part, but with the information you'll get in this book you'll be more than able to handle switching from soprano to baritone ukulele whenever you feel the urge to do so.

Other Relatives

Ukulele players weren't content to simply make the ukulele larger—after all, you'd eventually just end up with a four-string guitar! So while many of the initial tweaks to the ukulele were concerned with making the instrument louder, another logical progression was a hybrid ukulele, which gave us the banjolele and the resonator ukulele.

On the left, a banjolele. On the right, a resonator ukulele.

Both banjoleles and resonator ukuleles usually come in either soprano or concert size, with the former being more common than the latter. The resonator uke, like its resonator guitar counterpart, uses a resonator (a cone-shaped device) built in to the body to give more oomph to the instrument's volume.

Banjo resonators work on a different principle than guitar-style resonators—they're basically a structurally rigid, nonvibrating cover affixed to the rear of the instrument to form a resonating chamber that reinforces low frequency loudness. Not all banjoleles have a resonator. Those without get their sound from the vibrations of the banjo-like top of the instrument (usually a drum head). While both resonator ukuleles and banjoleles belong to the uke family, they have a distinct sound all their own, as you'll discover in a moment.

UKE LORE

British comedian/singer-songwriter George Formby had a hugely successful career as a comedian and entertainer playing Britain's music halls, starring in dozens of films in the 1930s and 1940s, and recording more than 200 songs. At shows he would usually accompany himself on the banjolele, introducing the instrument (and the ukulele itself) to the British public.

One of the more recent additions to the ukulele family is the Tahitian ukulele. Unlike the more traditional ukes, all three parts of the Tahitian (the body, neck, and headstock) are usually carved out of one single continuous piece of wood. Instead of a sound hole, a cone-shaped hole is bored through the entire body with the smaller side of the hole (about 2 inches in diameter) in the back and the larger side (a little bigger than 6 inches) in the front. The front hole is covered with a very thin piece of wood on which the ukulele's bridge is glued. The saddle, where the strings are attached to the body, sits at the bottom of the body.

Tahitian ukuleles often look like prehistoric electric guitars!

Front view of an eight-string Tahitian ukulele (left). Back view of a Tahitian ukulele (right).

Instead of the usual four strings, Tahitian ukes have eight, giving their sound more of a mandolin-like quality. The strings are usually light-gauge fishing line (30 lbs.). So if you happen to break one, you would need to run to a sporting goods store to get a replacement!

Today, ukulele manufacturers are still coming up with new and exciting ideas for the instrument. Some are inspired by the history of other instruments, such as the mandolin-style ukulele that uses F-holes (much like a mandolin or violin) for the sound hole. And others, such as the folks at The Magic Fluke Company in Sheffield, Massachusetts, create entirely new styles, such as their Fluke and Flea ukuleles.

The back and sides of the Fluke and Flea are molded plastic, fitted to a top of either pine or birch. And although they might seem a little high tech, they still have the wonderful sound of the traditional ukuleles.

Ukuleles by The Magic Fluke Company. The Fluke (left) and the Flea (right).

Sound Check

It's one thing to see the various types of ukuleles available. Hearing the differences is a whole other matter. To help you, the first track of the included CD gives you a sound comparison of the four basic types of ukes as well as a few of the other relatives of the ukulele family, playing the same basic chord progression with a few single notes tossed in for good measure.

Track 1

You truly shouldn't worry if you don't hear all that much of a difference between the soprano and the concert or between the concert and the tenor. Likewise, you might not make out a lot of variation between the banjolele and the resonator ukulele. The contrast between the ukes can be fairly subtle. But rest assured that, just as with everything else about learning to play, your ears will improve with practice.

The Tahitian ukulele, with its double strings and slightly different tuning (the two inner strings are higher than the outers; you'll read about this tuning in Chapter 13), will probably stand out from the others quite easily.

Later in Part 5, you learn songs played in ensemble style will have different ukuleles playing different parts of the arrangement. So it's good to start listening for the sounds of the different ukuleles. Again, it's all a matter of practice.

Which Uke for You?

If you don't already have a uke, skip ahead to Chapter 21 for guidance and tips on buying your first uke. You will also want to check out the Quick Guide, "Choosing the Ukulele That is Right for You" at idiotsguides.com/ukulele.

Although most people start out on soprano ukuleles, you should check out all your options before settling on one. Remember the soprano, concert, and tenor ukuleles are all tuned to the same notes, so if you feel more comfortable holding a tenor uke, for instance, or if you find yourself digging the sound of a particular concert uke, go for it!

You might find that your fingers seem a little less clunky on the slightly longer necks of the concert and tenor ukes—quite a few people do. But remember that at this point you have not really played your instrument at all. As you learn more and get more acclimated to your own personal ukulele, you'll find yourself gaining confidence and getting better at placing your fingers along the frets.

And if your heart is set on a baritone ukulele, then jump ahead to Chapters 13 and 14, learn about transposing (it won't take long!), and then come right back and learn the basics taught in the first two parts of this book.

Also, you probably should realize that your first ukulele is going to be just that—your *first* one. If you're like most ukulele players, it's going to be the first of many! When you find that you love the instrument and you love playing it, you are likely to end up with a complete set of ukes.

Practice, Practice

Even though you're literally just starting out as a ukulele player, there are still things you can do to help yourself. First and foremost is to listen to ukulele music. Not just songs played by single ukulele players (although that's obviously a great place to start), but ensemble pieces and other music where the ukulele might be a supporting instrument instead of the featured one. Listen first to the solo players and make notes about what you like about their various styles of play.

If you're watching videos, notice how the uke player holds the instrument and how he strums or picks the strings. You should try to absorb as much as you can so you have some basic ideas of how it looks to be playing your ukulele.

You might find yourself writing a wish list of songs to learn, or of techniques you are worried might pose a bit of a challenge, or of ukulele players you would like to emulate.

Also, listen to music you already know and enjoy and want to learn to play, whether they have ukuleles in their arrangements or not. Try to imagine what your favorite songs might sound like when played on a single ukulele or how your favorite band might go about adding a ukulele part to a song. Consider all these pointers a part of your practice for becoming a uke player.

A quick story before you start learning in earnest … in November 1997, a concert honoring the late folksinger/songwriter Steve Goodman took place in Chicago. As you might imagine, some big names performed—artists like Emmylou Harris, Lyle Lovett, Kathy Mattea, Jackson Browne, Iris DeMent, Todd Snider, and John Prine. They each played one of Goodman's songs as well as another one of their choice.

And, of course, Arlo Guthrie was there and, of course, he sang Goodman's "City of New Orleans." Then things got interesting. He came back out onstage, carrying a very beat-up looking soprano ukulele. The audience thought it was a joke, but he then went on to explain how great songs were great songs, regardless of how and on what instruments they were played. He proceeded to sing Bob Dylan's "All Along the Watchtower" accompanied only by his ukulele. And while some in the theater found it hilarious, eventually everyone got mesmerized by the urgency of Guthrie's performance and at how right the little ukulele sounded for his interpretation of the song.

Although this story's moral might be as familiar as "don't be fooled by appearances," the idea you should take to heart is that you can play just about any song on any instrument. This especially applies to you as a new ukulele player. As you grow as both a ukulele player and a musician, let your imagination as well as your uke make any song your own. Be fearless, and above all, have fun!

The Least You Need to Know

- The ukulele is a relatively new instrument, yet it has a rich history.
- The four basic sizes of ukuleles are soprano, concert, tenor, and baritone.
- The soprano, concert, and tenor ukuleles differ primarily in size and body depth. The strings of these three ukes are usually all tuned to the same notes.
- The baritone ukulele is the largest of the four basic ukes and its strings are normally tuned quite lower than those of the soprano, concert, and tenor.
- Listen to and watch videos of ukulele music and players to help you learn, and remember that any song you like can be played on the uke.

Getting In Tune

In This Chapter

- Understanding notes
- Learning the "standard tuning" of the ukulele
- Using a tuner, piano, or yourself to tune
- Developing ear training

Before you start playing your ukulele, you need to get it in tune, meaning each of your instrument's four strings is matched with specific notes. If your ukulele is not tuned, you'll think it sounds funny or strange, or just flat out awful! Even people who have never played any musical instrument before can tell when one is out of tune.

It is even more important to be in tune when you are playing with other musicians, no matter what instruments they are playing. Very few things put an audience's ears on edge than hearing the sound of instruments that aren't quite in tune with each other.

Tuning your ukulele might seem like a daunting challenge, but it can be an easy task to learn, especially when you have a digital tuner to help you. With a little practice (and trust me, you'll be getting a *lot* of practice on this!), getting your instrument in tune can become almost automatic to you.

Additionally, the time you spend tuning your ukulele, and listening to the notes as you do so, is a great way to start developing your musical ear. You might think you don't have much of a musician's ear right now. But after spending a couple of months tuning your uke each time you pick it up, you'll be surprised at how quickly you're able to tell whether your uke is in tune.

The ABCs of Notes

As you read in Chapter 1, you play individual musical *notes* on your ukulele by striking any single string. The *pitch* of the note you play is determined by the gauge (diameter) of that string and by the tension exerted on the string. By turning a string's tuning knob, you are adjusting the string's tension, which changes the string's pitch. Tightening the tuning peg raises a string's pitch. Loosening the tuning peg lowers a string's pitch.

Although you can raise or lower a string's pitch to any point you like using the tuning knobs, to learn the basics of playing ukulele you need each string of your instrument to be tuned to what is known as standard tuning. After your ukulele is in standard tuning, you have a point of reference for everything, from playing single-note melodies or cool riffs from your favorite songs to strumming out chords for those songs.

It will help, however, to know a little more about the names of notes and how they relate to each other to make tuning your ukulele easier to understand.

DEFINITION

Notes are musical sounds or tones. They also are the symbols used to indicate such tones. For the uku-lele, as well as most musical instruments and music of Western music (meaning music of the Western Hemisphere), there are 12 musical note names. The **pitch** of a note is its relative position to other notes, usually described as "high" or "low" in terms of sound. Notes can share a name, but can also be different in pitch, as in the two "do" notes at the end of the "do re me fa sol la ti do" scale.

Notes in music are given names of the first seven letters of the alphabet, going from A to G as you go higher in tone. When you reach G, the note names cycle around again, so A is the note again after G, but that A is at a higher pitch (greater vibration frequency) than the A that started the sequence:

A   B   C   D   E   F   G   A   B ...

You can begin counting off notes anywhere as long as you keep them in order. For instance, you could begin with C, like this:

C   D   E   F   G   A   B   C   D ...

Of course, it would be too good to be true if that were all there was to tell! Life, and music, just doesn't seem to work that way. Besides these seven notes, there are five additional notes that fall between some of the notes. These additional notes are called *accidentals* and are labeled as *sharps* (♯) or *flats* (♭). Also, each accidental has two different, yet correct, names because they fall in between notes. For instance, the accidental between C and D can be called either C♯ or D♭.

When you raise a note (increasing the pitch a little higher), you are making it sharp; when you lower a note (decreasing the pitch a little lower), you're making it flat.

DEFINITION

To make any note **sharp** is to raise that note a half-step in tone. When you lower any given note by a half-tone, you make it **flat**. An **accidental** is a note that has been made either flat or sharp. Some accidentals share the same note but can be called by one of two names. For example, the note that is a half-step between G and A is called G♯ because it is a half-step higher than G. That same note also can be called A♭ because it is a half-step lower than A.

Adding these five accidentals to the original seven notes (A–G), they are arranged, from low to high, like this:

C	C♯/D♭	D	D♯/E♭	E	F	F♯/G♭	G	G♯/A♭	A	A♯/B♭	B	C

Each of these notes is a musical half-step away from its neighbor, either up or down. Going from C to D involves two half-steps, moving from C to C♯ and then from C♯ to D. The notes E and F are a half-step from each other, as are the notes B and C.

This relationship of half-steps is important to remember because each of the frets on the neck of your ukulele also is a musical half-step away from the note of the adjoining fret. Knowing this relationship, as you will read in the next chapter, can help you find any note you want on your uke's fretboard.

Don't worry too much about all of this right now because we cover it again in more detail in future chapters.

Tuning Options

Your ukulele has four strings. Although that seems simple enough, naming and numbering the strings at first often causes confusion. The first string is the one that sits closest to the floor when you are holding your uke, and the fourth string is the one sitting closest to the ceiling.

Many players (especially if they already have knowledge of guitar, violin, or other stringed instruments) think of the numbering or ordering of strings in terms of pitch. The first string (the one nearest the floor) is usually the highest note. And they usually tune the strings from the lowest in pitch to the highest.

However, unlike other fretted instruments such as the guitar or mandolin, or even fretless stringed instruments such as the violin or viola, the strings of a ukulele are not always tuned from the lowest pitched note to the highest. A big part of the uke's signature sound comes from the fact that it is not tuned in the same manner as a guitar or other stringed instruments.

Traditionally, a ukulele is tuned in what is called standard tuning. But because each string can be tuned to many different notes, numerous other tuning choices are available to you (you learn more about these in Chapter 13). For now, let's get acquainted with the typical tunings of your uke.

Standard Tuning

In standard tuning, the strings of your ukulele are tuned to the following notes:

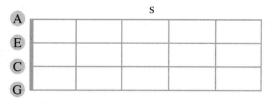

Notes of ukulele strings in standard tuning.

But here's the twist: Although the A string is higher in pitch than the E, which is in turn higher in pitch than the C, the G string is higher in pitch than both the E and C strings. In other words, given a range of notes starting with G and continuing on through two C notes, the strings of the ukulele use these underlined notes in relation to each other:

Note:	G	A	B	<u>**C**</u>	D	<u>**E**</u>	F	<u>**G**</u>	<u>**A**</u>	B	C
String:				3rd		2nd		4th	1st		

The A note of the open A string (an "open" string is a string played without it being fretted on the neck of the ukulele) is one full musical step higher than the note of the open G string. That means if you play the note at the second fret of the G string, provided you are in tune, it should sound the same as the note of the open A string.

> **SMOOTH STRUMMING**
>
> It is important you know your string names so you can follow any instructions you receive about playing either single strings or combinations of strings (chords). Some people find it helpful to come up with mnemonic phrases to remember the strings, like "**G**oofy **C**ats **E**at **A**sparagus" (strings 4, 3, 2, 1) to remember which notes to tune to. There is no definitive mnemonic phrase for the ukulele yet, so see what you can come up with.

Because the G string is higher in pitch than the C and E strings, it has become convention to write out the ukulele's standard tuning in the following manner:

gCEA

Using the lowercase *g* indicates that this note is a higher pitch than the *G* one would expect in a traditional guitar-style tuning.

Having both the outer strings at higher pitches than the inner strings is called re-entrant tuning. This tuning is *the* standard tuning of the ukulele. It's important to stress that this tuning of the ukulele gives the instrument a lot of its tonal color. And, as you'll read in later chapters, the ukulele's standard tuning allows you to play many interesting and fun flourishes other instruments like the guitar can't play—at least not without totally changing its strings!

Two Common Alternatives to Standard Tuning

Speaking of which, a string change would be necessary to get your instrument into one of the more common alternate tunings for ukulele. It is called low G and at first glance you might think it is the same as standard tuning because it's typically written out like this:

GCEA

But notice that this *G* is a capital one, not lowercase. This means the G of the fourth string is lower in pitch than the C of the third string. Using the chart from our earlier tuning, you'd be using these notes for the strings:

Note:	<u>**G**</u>	A	B	<u>**C**</u>	D	<u>**E**</u>	F	<u>**G**</u>	<u>**A**</u>	B	C
String:	4th			3rd		2nd			1st		

You most likely would need a thicker string than the one you have on your ukulele to achieve this tuning. Some people who enjoy playing in both gCEA and GCEA solve the problem by having two ukuleles, one in each tuning.

Fortunately, a second common alternative ukulele tuning doesn't require a change of strings. All it involves is tuning each string up one whole step (two musical half-steps) higher than standard. This alternative tuning, called *D tuning*, is written out like this:

aDF♯B

D tuning was used a great deal by ukulele players during the instrument's heydays of the 1930s. As you'll read in Chapter 13 (and later in Chapter 20), D tuning can also make playing with guitarists and other fretted instrument players a little easier.

Your Friend the Tuner

Getting your uke in tune is easy if you have a tuner. A tuner is a small battery-operated device that lets you know which note you are playing when you pluck any string. Knowing where you are on the scale lets you know which direction you need to go in tuning—up or down—and the tuner will tell you how far to go to get to the note you want.

Any guitar tuner works well on a ukulele. You just turn it on, strike a string, and then see how that string compares to the note you want to tune to.

Many tuners nowadays are chromatic tuners. With a chromatic tuner, you strike a string, the display screen shows you the name of the note you're playing, and then you can adjust according to whether you are flat or sharp of your target note. So if you are trying to tune this fourth string to g, for instance, and the screen says you're on "F♯" or "g♭," then you are too low and need to turn the tuning peg so that you're tightening the string. Conversely, if your tuner reads "g♯," "A♭," or even "A," then your string is higher than the desired note and you need to loosen the string by turning the tuning peg in the appropriate direction.

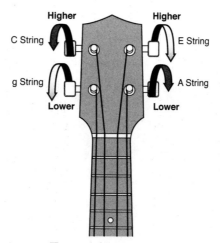

Turning the tuning pegs.

When you tune your strings it is best to tune them up (tightening the string) to the proper note. If you tune down (loosening the string) to get a note, the natural tendency of the string is to continue to loosen—not a lot but enough to put it out of tune eventually. So if you find a string is higher than it should be, first tune lower than your target and then raise it back up to the proper note by tightening the tuning peg. This will help the string stay in tune.

For your convenience, Track 2 on the CD in this book is a tuning track. On the recording, you will hear each string, from the fourth to the first, played one at a time (three times each) so that you can make sure you're in tune.

 Track 2

But you should get a tuner because carrying around the CD all the time, not to mention something to play it on, isn't the easiest or best thing to do at your first gig or open mic!

> **SMOOTH STRUMMING**
>
> You might find it wise to buy a clip-on style of tuner that picks up the notes from the vibrations of the strings through the neck (as opposed to doing so through an in-board microphone). Because these tuners rely on vibration to work, they won't be affected by the sounds of other instruments tuning up and at the same time. And if you ever find yourself in a roomful of uke players who are all trying to tune at the same time, you'll be incredibly glad you have a clip-on tuner!

Tuning to a Piano or Keyboard

If you have a piano or electronic keyboard at home, or are playing someplace where there is one, you can tune your ukulele to that instrument, as long as you know where the notes you want to tune to are on it.

To help, here is an illustration showing how the notes of the open strings of your ukulele correspond to those on the piano:

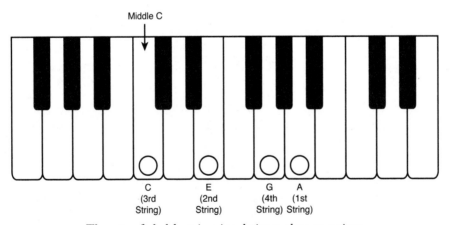

The notes of ukulele strings in relation to those on a piano.

This method of tuning is not always as accurate as using a tuner because not all pianos are in tune, but if you are using an electronic keyboard, you should be good to go.

FRET LESS!

If you find yourself tuning to a piano (as opposed to an electronic keyboard), remember the piano might not necessarily be in tune. Check the notes of the piano with a chromatic tuner if you suspect it is not in tune. And if you have to play with the piano in question, tune your ukulele to the middle C of the piano and then tune to yourself for the other notes. You and the piano might be slightly off, but it shouldn't be bad enough to offend anyone's ears.

Tuning to Yourself

If you know that one of your strings is in tune, then you can tune the others by means of relative tuning. Each note of your uke (except for some of the highest notes on your first string and some on the first three frets on your third string) can be found in multiple places on the neck.

Remember the chart of all 12 notes from earlier in this chapter. Here it is again:

C	C#/D♭	D	D#/E♭	E	F	F#/G♭	G	G#/A♭	A	A#/B♭	B	C

Remember that each of these notes is a musical half-step away from its neighbor, and that each fret of your ukulele marks off a half-step. So when you place a finger on the first fret of your in tune G string, you have changed the note from G to G♯ (or A♭, if you prefer that name). The note at the second fret is A, and so on.

Here is a fretboard map to show you the notes along the neck of your uke:

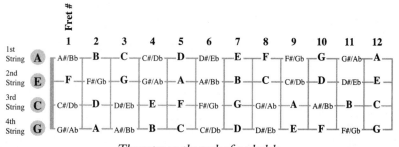

The notes on the neck of a ukulele.

After you have your third string tuned to C, you can then match the tone of the other open strings to the corresponding fret of the C string. E will be on the fourth fret, G on the seventh, and A on the ninth.

Practice, Practice

You should get into the habit of tuning each time you pick up your ukulele. And you also should get into the habit of working on your *ear training* each time you play. Initially this will take a little work, but it will be worth the effort to get your ears trained to hear differences in musical pitches.

DEFINITION

Ear training is the skill to hear and identify different aspects of music, whether specific notes; relative pitches and intervals (which you'll learn about in Chapter 6); or harmonies, chords, rhythms, or bass lines.

To get your ukulele in tune, use a tuner or Track 2 of your CD. After your ukulele is in tune, play each string individually, from the G down to the A one at a time and listen closely to how your instrument sounds when it is in tune.

Then deliberately detune one string—either G, E, or A. Not by a lot! Just give any single tuning peg a slight turn in one direction or another. Now play each string again and listen. Can you hear a difference from before? And can you tell which string is out of tune and whether that string is now flat or sharp in contrast to the way it was earlier?

Chances are likely that you might not catch the difference the first few times you try this, especially if you haven't put the string in question that much out of tune to start with. But with repeated practice, you will begin to pick up on when a string is out of tune.

Because you have not changed the tuning of the C string, use the method described in the "Tuning to Yourself" section of this chapter to get the detuned string back to its proper note. Then check it against the tuner to see how good of a job you did. Again, the more you put your ears to use the easier it will become.

After you learn the four basic chords in Chapter 5, you can try playing a C chord or a G chord before you tune your uke to hear if you can tell whether or not the uke is in tune (or close to it) and try to determine which string(s) might not be in tune.

The ability to listen and to hear is probably the most important skill any musician can have, whether you are playing on your own or in a group or simply listening to music and not playing. And like any skill, you can develop your musical ear through practice and repetition. So each time you tune your ukulele, make the most of the opportunity to improve your listening skills.

The Least You Need to Know

- Including the accidentals, there are 12 different notes on the ukulele, and in Western music in general.
- In standard ukulele tuning, the strings, from the fourth string to the first, are tuned to the notes gCEA.
- Having a tuner, preferably a chromatic tuner, and using it each time you pick up your instrument will help you keep your ukulele in tune.
- Learning to tune your ukulele is important because being in tune ensures your ukulele sounds its best and helps you develop your musical ear.

Putting Your Hands to Work

In This Chapter

- Holding your uke while sitting or standing
- Positioning your right and left hands for playing
- Strumming with your thumb, fingers, or a pick
- Introducing you to ukulele tablature
- Doing some warm-up exercises

After your uke is in tune, it is time to get ready to play! Getting ready to play involves placing both yourself and your ukulele into the best position possible to make music happen.

The whole idea of warming up or preparing for playing your uke might seem silly, but it is important. Playing the ukulele is not like playing, say, the piano. Yes, playing the piano isn't easy, but making any given note certainly is—all you do is plunk your finger down on a key and you have a note! You can also play the piano, albeit not all that well, with one hand tied behind your back.

The ukulele, like other stringed instruments, requires some coordination and cooperation from both of your hands. One hand places fingers on the fretboard along the neck to create notes, while the other hand picks or strums the strings down on the body of the ukulele. And there's even more to it than just that! Playing the uke involves your whole body, from head to toe.

Thinking Small

Your whole body also includes your brain, by the way. You can psych yourself out of playing any musical instrument, and the ukulele is no exception given its own built-in hazards. First, it's quite a small instrument—small body, small frets—and you might have huge hands and fingers. Also, the uke's smallness might make you think of it as a toy, and that's not good. You might worry you can't hold it without breaking it, or you might think your ukulele sounds nothing at all like the ones you've heard or seen.

Remember that playing the uke is entirely new to you. Even if you've played the guitar or another instrument before, the uke is going to be different. Although this might seem obvious to you, it is important to keep in mind. It is easy to think that you should be able to pick up your ukulele and *instantly* make incredible music, but nothing could be further from the truth.

Playing any instrument is going to involve practice, patience, and persistence. You might want to make that your mantra right now. If you can enjoy each phase of your musical journey, you'll find yourself both having fun and learning, not to mention improving as you go. Treat learning music, as well as your ukulele, with curiosity and respect and you will get much farther along, more quickly than if you think of your uke as a small, unplayable toy.

FRET LESS!

Frustration is the biggest setback most people experience when they take up a musical instrument, and frustration is more of a mindset than anything else. Don't let your brain put you into a negative frame of mind. Never use the word *can't* in a sentence (like "I can't play this note or this chord") unless you end that sentence with the word *yet*!

Be patient with yourself. You are going to be learning a whole lot of things from this point on, from making single notes to playing chords to strumming rhythms to creating your own musical arrangements of songs. Start off on the right foot by enjoying each small step you make, no matter how small. After all, you are just setting out on a whole lifetime of making music.

Left- or Right-Handed?

Speaking of "right foot," this is probably the best place to address the age-old question: do you play your ukulele left- or right-handed? If you are right-handed, the choice is fairly obvious—play right-handed (if that feels right to you). If you are left-handed, you have a choice to make.

That choice has to be based on which hand, left or right, you can count on to best fulfill its appointed task. If you play right-handed, your right hand does the strumming and your left hand frets the notes. If you play left-handed, the reverse is true.

For most people, the choice of hand comes down to playing rhythm. Think about it. Why don't right-handed players play left-handed when their right hand (their dominant hand) would be handling all the fretting of the notes? Usually it is because their right hands are better at finger picking and strumming and keeping rhythm. At least, right-handed players believe that to be true.

UKE LORE

Tiny Tim (born Herbert Khaury) and his soprano ukulele arrived on the American music scene in 1968, hitting #7 on the Billboard Album Charts with his first album, *God Bless Tiny Tim*, and the smash single "Tiptoe Through the Tulips." His 1969 album *For All My Little Friends*, a collection of children's songs, earned the left-handed ukulele player a Grammy nomination.

If you feel comfortable either way, my advice would be to play right-handed. If you decide to play with your left hand, you don't need to buy a left-handed uke. You will need to swap the strings around (actually just your C and E strings as the g and A strings are so close to the same that they're interchangeable) so that you can follow how to play chords and scales. Even though you are holding the instrument backwards, you still need the strings tuned gCEA when you strum down toward the floor. Changing strings is fairly easy to do; you can jump ahead to Chapter 22 to learn how.

For whatever it might be worth, I am left-handed and I play the ukulele left-handed, as I do other stringed instruments. But for the sake of clarity, this book is written under the assumption you are playing right-handed. Quite simply, most of you will be playing right-handed. If you are a lefty, it is simple to make the necessary adjustments as you're reading, and it will only help you learn!

Holding Your Ukulele

Whether you play left-handed or right-handed, the first thing to do when you are getting ready to play is to relax. Being relaxed and loose will help you get into the best possible position for playing (standing or sitting), and that makes all the difference in the world when it comes to producing clean, clearly ringing notes versus making clunky, off-beat sounding ones.

Start by rolling your shoulders and shaking your arms and hands to get loose. You should try to be as tension free as possible, even though you're probably more than a little worried about playing your first notes. Pay attention to your posture. Whether sitting or standing, try to be straight and not slouched and keep your hands and arms loose and free.

Sitting

Whether you sit or stand, angle the neck of your ukulele so anyone looking at you would think the headstock was pointing at the two o'clock position of a clock. Holding the neck at this angle ensures your fretting hand will be about chest high, giving you free and easy movement about the neck.

Sitting with your ukulele.

When playing while seated, most players set their uke on the right leg, high on the upper thigh. Keep the neck of the uke elevated, and give your left arm enough room so your left wrist stays relatively straight while holding the neck.

Standing

When you play standing up, you still need to make certain your fretting hand has the best possible chance for playing the strings. Cradle the uke in your right arm, holding it just about chest high, still angling the neck so the headstock points to two o'clock.

Standing with your ukulele.

SMOOTH STRUMMING

Soprano and concert ukuleles are easier to hold while standing than larger ukes such as the tenor and baritone. If you own a tenor, you might find it worth purchasing a strap to hold it when you play standing up. Having your uke on a strap can be helpful when you are playing in a sitting position as well.

The Right Hand

Your right hand takes care of all the picking or strumming so keep your right arm free and loose to handle the rhythm chores. Depending on the length of your arm (not to mention the size of your ukulele), your right hand could naturally place itself anywhere from just about over the sound hole to where the neck of your uke meets the body. The shaded area in the following illustration demonstrates where most uke players tend to strum the strings.

It is important your right wrist has as much freedom of movement as possible. In Part 2, you will read over and over again how your wrist and forearm control most of your strumming motion, so you should have your right arm free enough to strum or pick the strings with ease and still hold on to your uke while playing.

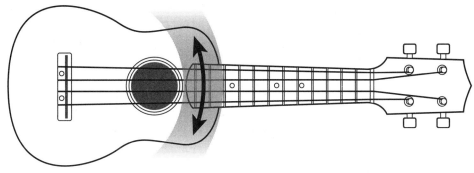

Where to strum your ukulele.

Using Thumb and Fingers

There is not a singular "right" way to strum your ukulele, or a "wrong" one for that matter. Many players use only their thumbs, strumming both downstrokes and upstrokes with the side of the thumb.

Strumming with your thumb.

Generally, you should keep your strums fairly short and controlled. Start by laying your thumb parallel along the edge of the g string (the one closest to the ceiling). Use your wrist to flick your thumb in a downward motion toward the floor. Your thumb should stay relatively straight. If you place your uke flat on your lap so that you're looking at the top of it while strumming, your thumb will be moving from a nine o'clock position (pointing in the same direction as the headstock) to an almost twelve o'clock position.

SMOOTH STRUMMING

The strumming motion comes from your wrist and forearm. When you strum, your upper arm should hardly move at all. Think of the motion you make when turning a key in a lock or an ignition and you'll have the right idea. Remember the less movement you exert when strumming, the more control over your dynamics (changes in volume) you will have.

Some players prefer strumming with the index finger, flicking it downward for a downstroke and then sweeping back across the strings for the upstoke.

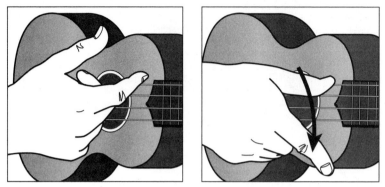

Strumming with your index finger.

Strumming in this manner, the nail of the index finger striking the strings gives a bit of bite to the downstroke. Some of the rhythms you will be learning later on make use of combining single notes struck with the thumb with these "finger flick" strums.

You can also use both your thumb and index finger (or a combination of fingers) to strum, holding them in this manner:

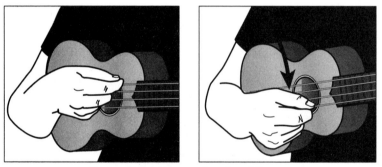

Strumming with your thumb and fingers.

Experiment with each of these methods of strumming. Take the time to listen to what you are doing and decide what you like. Eventually you are going to want to be able to switch smoothly from one mode of strumming to another at a moment's notice.

Using a Pick

Although traditionally a ukulele player uses his thumb and fingers to strum the strings, you can use a *pick* (also called a *plectrum*). However, there are good reasons not to use a pick. Unlike guitars, most ukuleles do not have a pick guard, which is a hard plastic surface along the lower edge of the sound hole that protects the wood of the top of the ukulele from being scratched by the pick.

DEFINITION

Picks, or **plectrums,** are small, usually rounded-triangular-shaped pieces of plastic, felt, or other material used to strike the ukulele's strings instead of using one's fingers.

Some players use picks made of felt that has been layered and compressed into a relatively solid form suitable for picking strings. Although felt picks don't scratch your ukulele's finish, they do tend to shed if you're strumming fairly rigorously. You can end up with a fine coating of felt dust all over your uke, not to mention any surrounding furniture.

However, it is not impossible to develop a light enough touch to play a ukulele with a pick. It is a matter of practice. If you truly want the finesse and confidence needed to use picks without a second thought, you might want to get a cheap uke to practice your picking on.

Most ukulele players who use picks tend to hold one in this manner:

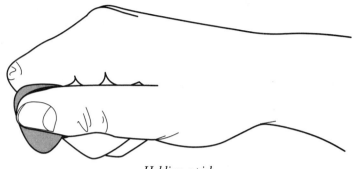

Holding a pick.

First, hold your right hand as if you were holding a key. Your thumb should rest right along the edge of your index finger. Lift your thumb and place the pick so it is pointing in the same direction as your index finger and its tip extends just slightly, not even as much as a quarter-inch beyond the tip of your index finger. Place your thumb on the pick with just enough pressure to keep it in place. Now you're good to go!

Keep your pick perpendicular to the strings when striking, using as little motion as possible. As you practice and gain confidence in your abilities, these small pick movements will lead to greater pick speed and accuracy in your playing.

FRET LESS!

Digging in toward the body of the uke with the pick or sweeping it outward (like flicking your wrist away from the body of the uke) results in a twangy tone from the string you might or might not like. More importantly, flicking the pick out places it a good distance away from the string, meaning you have to waste time getting back in place for your next pick strike.

You need a firm, but flexible hold on your pick, neither too tight nor too loose. Additionally, try to choke up on the pick so that only a quarter-inch or so sticks out beyond your finger. You have less control over the pick's movements and it is likely to get caught up and tangled in the strings when you leave too much of it exposed in your fingertips. Ultimately, it is up to you to control your pick and not the other way around!

Both methods of strumming, either with fingers or with a pick, produce their own unique sounds. At some point you will definitely want to try both styles of strumming to explore the different sounds and feels each provides.

The Left Hand

While your right hand is busy strumming or picking the strings, your left hand's job is to fret (hold down) the strings along the neck of your ukulele. The key is realizing it is the tips of your fingers—the space between your nail and the whorl of the fingerprint—that give you the cleanest sound when fretting notes. Your first priority is to position your left hand and fingers so the fingertips can dance freely along the fretboard.

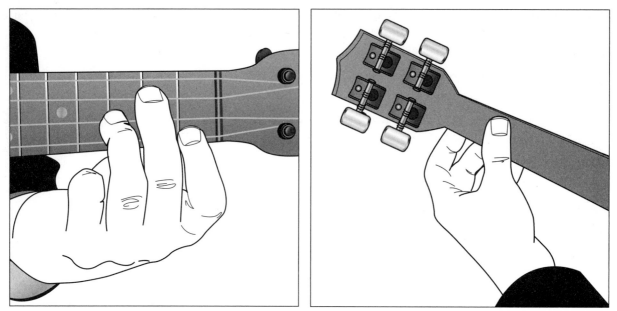

Placing your fingers on the fretboard (left), and your thumb position on the back of the neck (right).

This is especially important given the small size of the ukulele's neck. You might get away with slightly angling your left hand's fingers when you are playing single notes one at a time. But when you're playing chords or rapid successions of single notes, your fingers should be arched and on their tips to ensure you are not blunting or muting adjacent strings.

Avoid Gripping the Neck

Most ukulele players hold the uke by grasping the neck in their fretting hand. This is normal and expected, given the small size of the instrument; however, it is not the best way to hold the uke. If you can feel the lower edge of the neck of your uke along your palm, your fingers are not getting optimal placement. They are being pulled down to fret the notes, and ultimately, this will negatively affect both speed and accuracy when fretting notes.

SMOOTH STRUMMING

Do your best to keep your left hand's hold of the ukulele's neck relatively fluid. You need to be able to shift your wrist and fingers from side to side with practically no friction at all. Relax and let your thumb rest against the back of the uke's neck without locking it up in a death grip.

Keep the neck angled so your fretting hand is about chest high. Having an easy, relaxed hold on the neck will put your fingers in an optimal position to cleanly fret the notes while keeping them arched and on their tips.

FRET LESS!

Your fingers have the important job of fretting the notes cleanly. Get them into position first and then let the neck of the uke rest against the thumb. Your fingers will (and should) decide where your thumb will be. Don't let your thumb dictate where your fingers go.

Fretting Notes

When you put your finger *on a fret*, it actually means placing your finger in the middle between two frets, not on the actual fret. When fretting a note, place your finger(s) slightly closer to the body-side of your ukulele, as shown in the previous illustration.

Apply just enough pressure to press the string straight onto the fingerboard. You'll be surprised at how little pressure you need. Push the string straight onto the neck of the ukulele with your fingertips. Too much pressure pushes the string to one side or the other, which deadens the note or can even bend the string slightly, giving you a note that is out of tune.

A Quick Look at Ukulele Tablature

Your ukulele is in tune and you can hold it while sitting or standing. Now you need a little more musical information; then you will be playing! Actually, you can already play notes, but it would be good to have some idea which notes you want to play, and for that it is time to learn a bit about *tablature*.

DEFINITION

Tablature is a system for writing and reading music for fretted instruments such as ukuleles, guitars, and banjos. Horizontal lines represent the strings of your instrument and numbers written on those lines indicate which fret to play with your fingers.

Tablature, along with standard music notation (which you will read about in the next chapter), is one of the two main ways of reading ukulele music. In ukulele tablature, the notes are written on a staff of four lines (one for each string) as a series of numbers (which, depending on the type of uke you play, will usually be from 0 to 12), like this:

 Track 3

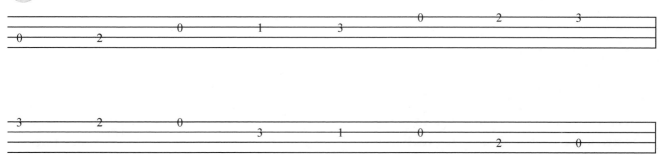

Chapter 3, Example 1.

The four lines represent the strings of your ukulele. The top line is your first string, the A. The lowest line is your fourth string, the G. The numbers tell you which fret to place your finger on. 1 is the first fret, 2 the second, and so on. 0 means to play that string without any fingers on it—this is called an *open string*.

You read tablature from left to right, regardless of on which string a number appears. In the first line of this example, you start by playing the open C string, which is indicated by the leftmost 0 sitting on the third line. Do this by picking the C string with either the thumb or any finger of the right hand.

Then place a finger on the second fret of that same string (for now, use any left-hand finger you like) and then pick the C string again with either the thumb or a finger of your right hand.

Next, pick the open E sting. Then place a finger of your left hand (the index finger will do nicely) on the first fret of the same string and pluck the E string a second time, again using either your thumb or your finger to do so. Now place another left-hand finger on the third fret of the E string and pluck the string once more with your right hand. Congratulations! You have played the first five notes of this example.

Next (following the tablature), play the open A string. Then place a finger of your left hand on the second fret of the A string and pick the string with your right hand. Finally, place a left-hand finger on the third fret of the A string and pluck the string one more time with your right hand. You've now played the entire first line of this example. If you have done this correctly, it should sound like the "Do Re Mi" scale from *The Sound of Music*. And the second line does it all in reverse, going from the highest note to lowest. You can listen to it (and play along!) on Track 3 of the CD to ensure you have it right.

FRET LESS!

The tablature numbers indicate which fret to play, not which fingers to use when playing the notes.

In this exercise, focus on both reading and understanding the instructions of the tablature as well as in making clean and clear-sounding notes. Do not worry about speed; right now, it is all about accuracy.

Warming Up

With this little bit of tablature under your belt, you can start with some simple warm-up exercises:

Track 4 (0:00)

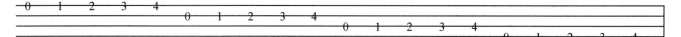

Chapter 3, Example 2.

Start by striking the open A string. Then place your index finger (labeled 1 on the tablature) on the first fret of that string and play the new note (which you know to be A♯ from your earlier reading in this chapter); then move on to the middle finger (labeled 2) at the second fret, the ring finger (3) at the third fret, and the pinky (4) at the fourth. Finally, move on and repeat this process with the remaining three strings.

Again, do not worry about speed. Concentrate on producing clean, clear, ringing notes each time you finger a fret. Listen carefully as you play. If you hear any buzzing, it is likely you are too close to, or on top of, a fret. Muted or clunky sounding notes usually indicate you are not on your fingertips and are likely pressing the string sideways along the fretboard.

Practice, Practice

The whole purpose of these warm-up exercises (which are usually called *one finger one fret* exercises) is to get your hands used to the mechanics necessary to making music on your ukulele. There are lots of variations you can do; here are some more:

 Track 4 (0:18)

Use index finger on "1"   Use middle finger on " 2"
Use ring finger on "3"   Use pinky on "4"

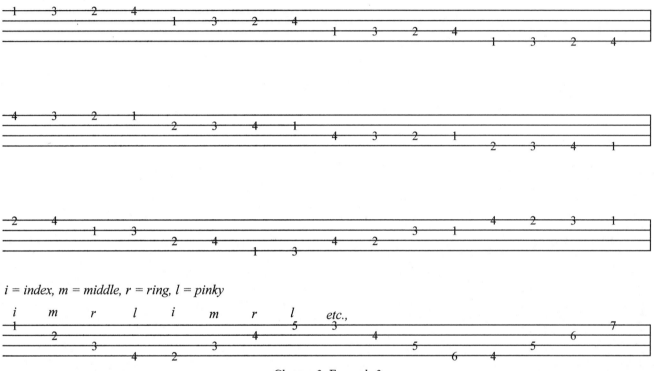

Chapter 3, Example 3.

The important thing is to be accurate and be sure to use each finger of your fretting hand correctly. Ultimately you are going to be using all the fingers on your left hand to play, so be sure you do so now with these exercises.

Think of these warm-up exercises as a way for your fingers to get used to your ukulele. When you do these exercises, be accurate with both hands. Make sure you pick the string you need, and be sure you are fretting each note so it rings out cleanly and clearly. Also, explore and create some warm-up exercises of your own.

The Least You Need to Know

- Both your right and left hands are needed to play the ukulele. When playing right-handed, your right hand takes care of the picking and strumming while the left hand fingers the notes on the frets.

- Use good posture and relax when holding your uke.

- Keep your right arm and hand free to comfortably strum or pick the strings. Avoid gripping the ukulele's neck too tightly with your left hand.

- Tablature is a method of reading music that uses numbers to indicate on which fret to play notes.

- Use warm-up exercises to get your fingers acclimated to playing. Be deliberate both in picking the correct strings and in fretting the correct notes.

Getting to Know Your Fretboard

In This Chapter

- Learning the basics of music notation
- Understanding the rhythmic values of notes
- Combining notation and ukulele tablature
- Exploring options for playing notes on your ukulele
- Playing and practicing some simple melodies

Although ukulele tablature is certainly helpful, it is far from sufficient for the needs of any uke player. Remember the second line of the first ukulele tablature example from the last chapter, the one that sounded like the "Do Re Mi" scale except backwards? Well, what if I told you that example was supposed to sound like the first line of the Christmas carol "Joy to the World?" Go back a few pages, try it out, and see if you can't make it sound like that. Pretty wild, isn't it?

This happens because all notes of music operate on two levels. First, there is the note itself, meaning its pitch or the name we give it, such as A, B, C♯, E♭, and so on. But every note also has a rhythmic value, a length if you will. Tablature tells you which notes to play, but it does not tell you how long any given note should last. So our first example *could* be the first line of "Joy to the World" for all you know because there's no rhythmic value in the tablature.

Rhythm is a vital part of all music, and ukulele players have to focus on playing in rhythm. The easiest way to grasp the concepts of rhythm is to learn to read a bit of standard music notation. Fortunately, learning to read the rhythm aspects of notation so you can strum along with any song is not as hard as it might initially seem to be. Not only is learning to read music fairly easy, but the ukulele itself can make the learning a lot of fun!

In this chapter, you will get an overview of the elements of music notation that provide the rhythmic value to notes.

Deciphering the Dots

If you took piano lessons as a kid, you will recognize *standard music notation* from the sheet music you toted to and from your lessons. At first glance, it looks a little like tablature in that it is laid out on a set of lines. However, it has five lines instead of four and instead of having numbers on those lines it has some interesting symbols—kind of like slightly squished dots, usually with a pole attached to them at one side or the other.

These dots are called *notes*, which should give you a good idea of what they represent from what you learned in Chapter 2! The notes are read in two ways: where a note is placed on the set of lines, or in the spaces between those lines, tells you which note it is and the type of note symbol used indicates its rhythmic value.

DEFINITION

Standard music notation is a method of reading and writing music. It uses a **staff** of five horizontal lines and various symbols for notes. The symbols themselves indicate the note's rhythmic value. Where the symbol is placed on the staff, whether on a particular line or in a particular space between those lines, indicates which note it is. **Ledger lines** are freestanding lines above and below the staff to indicate notes, such as the note for your C string.

Meet the Staff

The five lines used in standard music notation are called a *staff*. Although it looks a bit like tablature, one big difference from tablature is that the spaces between the lines are equally important as the lines themselves because those spaces are notes as well:

The staff in standard music notation.

At the far left edge of the staff is a symbol called a *clef*. The clef indicates which kind of staff you are dealing with and where the notes on that staff will be. Unless you come across some incredibly strange anomaly, ukulele music is almost always written in the treble clef or G clef, such as the one shown in the previous example (and every example in this book).

Naming Names

It is called a *G clef* for a reason. Any note placed on the second line up from the bottom is G, the same note as your open G (fourth) string. Here is where all the notes on the staff are located:

C   D   E   F   G   A   B   C   D   E   F   G   A

Where musical notes are on the staff.

Notice the first two notes, C and D, are below the bottom line of the staff. D is in the space just below the last line, and C is on a kind of freestanding line below the space the D note occupies. This freestanding line is called a *ledger line*. As you can see, it is possible to have ledger lines above the staff. Uke players rarely need to read notes higher than the high A note (at the far right end of the example) because the instrument probably goes only as high as that—unless it's a concert or tenor ukulele.

    FRET LESS!

When it comes to reading standard notation for the ukulele, you really need to learn only 13 notes. The A note at the twelfth fret of the A string is about as high as most ukuleles can go. This means that if you can memorize one note a day, you will be able to read music in less than two weeks! It is an incredibly small investment for something that will help you as you progress as a ukulele player and a musician. Plus, the skill of reading music is transferable to many other musical instruments.

Here are the notes of the four open strings on the ukulele:

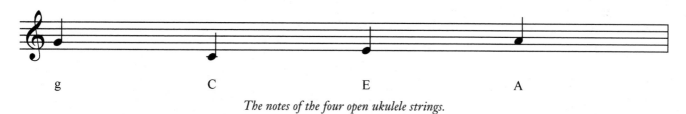

g   C   E   A

The notes of the four open ukulele strings.

Accidentals

Accidentals, as you learned in Chapter 2, are the notes that are either flats (♭) or sharps (♯). But there is a third accidental symbol, one used to "cancel out" a flat or sharp and return a note to its normal or "natural" state—that is neither flat nor sharp. The symbol, ♮, is called a "natural sign." You won't initially run into it a lot but you will be seeing them later throughout the book.

C   E   F♯   G♯   E♭   A♭   A(natural)   G(natural)

Examples of accidentals.

Matters of Timing

Although knowing which notes are which is important, it is perhaps even more important to know the rhythm of a song's strumming pattern. In other words, when people listen to music, the stray wrong note might escape detection, but a glitch in the rhythm is usually heard, or felt, by everyone!

Rhythm, in music, is counted out in beats. That's the "one, two, three, four" you might hear a musician say before launching into a song. Beats are grouped together in sets called *measures* to make keeping count of the rhythm both easier and equal. In music notation, measures are easily identifiable—they are represented by the vertical dividing lines in music, such as these:

Examples of measures in music notation.

Although a measure can have any number of beats in it, typically most songs are written with four beats per measure. The *time signature*, which is a pair of numbers stacked one atop the other at the start of a piece of music, tells you how many beats will be in the measures throughout the song:

Examples of time signatures in music notation.

As a beginner, your main concern with time signatures is the number on top. Usually it is a four, which means each measure will have four beats. Occasionally, as you will discover in Chapter 9, there might be another number on top such as three or six; even two, five, seven, nine, and twelve are used from time to time. Whichever number is on top is the number of beats in any given measure for that song. If the time signature is 3/4, for instance, then the song will have three beats per measure. But don't worry about that at this point. You will mostly be playing four beats per measure as a beginner.

Whole Notes and Half Notes

Whole notes have a rhythmic value of four beats, while half notes last two beats in duration. In music notation, whole notes and half notes look a little alike in that they share the same "body type" of a hollowed-out note. The half note, though, has a stem on it, either on one side of its body or the other. This stem differentiates it from the whole note, which has no stem, as you can see here:

*whole notes
(4 beats each)*

*half notes
(2 beats each)*

Examples of whole notes and half notes.

> **FRET LESS!**
>
> You will see stems of notes go either up or down from the note head. Often it is a matter of the music notation software used or the way the music writer wants it to look on a page, which determines the stem's direction. For now, worry more about where the note is in terms of the lines and spaces on the staff and not about whether its stem is up or down.

Quarter Notes and Eighth Notes

A quarter note, which has a rhythmic value of one full beat, looks like a half note except that the body of the note is solid. An eighth note, which has a rhythmic value of one-half of a beat, looks like a quarter note except it has a flag on its stem. When two or more eighth notes are joined together, the flags are joined into a *"beam"*:

*quarter notes
(1 beat each)*

*eighth notes
(1/2 a beat each)*

Examples of quarter notes and eighth notes.

Dots and Ties

Sometimes a note has a rhythmic value other than whole, half, quarter, or eighth. A note could be three beats in length, for instance, or maybe a beat and a half. On the other hand, the rhythmic value of a note might extend from one measure to the next, such as a note of a melody might start on the fourth beat of a measure and then continue through the first three beats of the following measure.

Standard music notation covers these instances by using dotted notes and tied notes. When a note is followed by a dot, as seen in the following examples, the rhythmic length of the original note is given an additional 50 percent of its value.

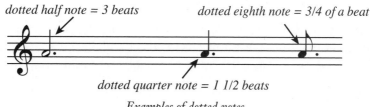

dotted half note = 3 beats

dotted eighth note = 3/4 of a beat

dotted quarter note = 1 1/2 beats

Examples of dotted notes.

So a dotted half note has a rhythmic value of three beats (two beats for the half note plus one beat for its dot), while a dotted quarter note is one and one-half beats (one beat for the quarter note plus a half beat for its dot).

Tied notes are notes of the same pitch—that is, notes having the same position on the musical staff—which are connected by a slightly curved line, as shown here:

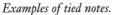

Examples of tied notes.

In this example, the first measure starts with a dotted half note, which takes up the first three beats of the measure. It is followed by a quarter note tied to a half note (in the next measure). To play this, you would strike the note of the open A string once on the fourth beat of the first measure and let it ring for a total of three beats (one beat for the quarter note and two beats for the half note).

This first set of tied notes is followed by a second set consisting of an eighth note and a quarter note. Tying these two notes together gives you a note of one and one-half beats in rhythmic value. This set is followed by three notes, an eighth note and two whole notes, tied together. This last set would have a rhythmic value of eight and one-half beats.

Rests

It might seem strange, but not playing notes is an important part of playing music. Songs sound better when they have spaces in them—pauses where the music takes a rest.

Although these rests have no note value in terms of a note name, they do have a time (or length) value, so music notation uses different symbols to indicate the rhythmic value of rests. They are as follows:

Examples of whole, half, quarter, and eighth rests.

Differentiating between whole rests and half rests might take a little practice. A trick to help you can be to think "whole = hole" and "half = hat" in terms of the respective rest's placement on the line of the staff. The quarter rests and eighth rests are pretty easy to recognize.

The Notes on Your Ukulele Strings

Now that you have a grasp on both the note names as well as the rhythmic value of those notes in standard music notation, it is time to see what it means to you as a ukulele player. Here is where the notes in music notation correspond to the numbers of ukulele tablature for just the first three strings:

Where the notes in notation are in terms of ukulele tablature.

In this last example, only the natural notes (meaning no notes with flats or sharps) are shown. However, you are going to be playing both flats and sharps, too, so let's add them to the mix:

Where the flat and sharp notes are in ukulele tablature.

Remember that each flat or sharp can go by one of two names. F♯, for example, is the same as G♭.

The Notes on the G String

The G string of the ukulele is what gives the instrument much of its unique voice. Being tuned one full step lower than the A string, you will find it has all the same notes of the A string. However, they are all two frets higher up on the neck on the G string, as you can see here:

Notes on the A (first) string

Notes on the G (fourth) string

Where the notes in notation are on the G and A strings.

Making Noteworthy Decisions

Having two strings using almost the same set of notes gives you a lot of options as a ukulele player. Suppose, for example, you want to play the song "Twinkle, Twinkle, Little Star." You might find it written in notation like this:

"Twinkle, Twinkle, Little Star" in notation.

You might also find it in tablature like this:

Track 5 (0:00)

Chapter 4, Example 1.

This is one of the reasons it is important to you as a ukulele player to have a rudimentary grasp of music notation and how it relates to ukulele tablature. And you might be very happy with this arrangement. But you also could realize that the 3 on the second line from the top in the tablature, which is the note at the third fret of the E string, is G—the same note as the open G string. This means you could play "Twinkle, Twinkle" like this:

Track 5 (0:18)

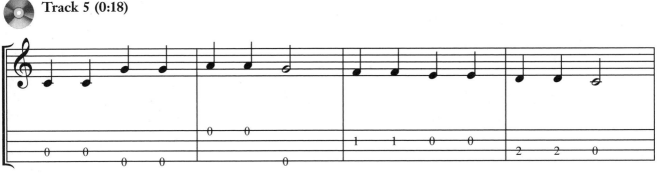

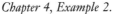

Chapter 4, Example 2.

Both ways are correct in that all the notes are the same. However, using the open G string gives you a different overall tone to the song than using the G note at the third fret of the E string does. The sound of both the C and G strings ringing creates more complex overtones than you would generate from using the G note on the E string.

Because both ways are correct, the choice of which tablature to play is completely up to you and your ears. There are all sorts of possibilities when it comes to where you can play your notes. Here is yet another way:

 Track 5 (0:37)

Chapter 4, Example 3.

In this example, you play the open G string the first time and then use the G note at the seventh fret of the C string when the G note appears next in the melody. The F note is also played on the C string, allowing it to continue ringing while you play the note of the open E string. Again, this is a subtle difference, but these subtle differences will become part of your personal playing style somewhere down the road.

SMOOTH STRUMMING

Knowing more about basic music theory, whether it is where your notes are on the fretboard or which notes make up any particular chord, can only enhance your skills and the music you create with your ukulele. When you practice, figure out alternative ways of playing melodies and chords.

Other Simple Melodies

Here are other simple melodies you are probably familiar with:

 Track 6

"Oats and Beans and Barley Grow"

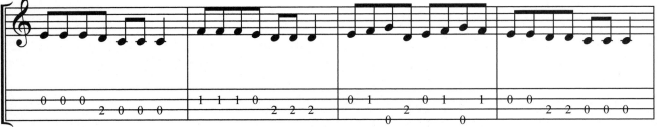

"London Bridge"

"I've Been Working on the Railroad"

"The Old Grey Mare"

Chapter 4, Example 4.

Ukulele tablature is provided for all of these examples, but you should first try to play the melodies without making use of it. Then you should try playing the melodies with notes on different places on the strings. You will probably be able to come up with many variations for "London Bridge."

Practice, Practice

Although these melodies do provide you with a way to practice note reading and finding alternate places to play notes on the fretboard, they also are meant to give you further practice in getting used to fretting with your left hand and making good, clean notes that ring out clear and true. Whenever you hear a bad note, whether it is a buzz or a clunk, or whenever you miss the string you meant to pick with your right hand, stop and assess what you have done so you can correct it. Everyone makes mistakes and you are going to make more than your fair share of them, it is all part of the learning process.

But you also should be aware of when you have made an "honest" mistake and when a mistake is turning into a habit. A simple slip of a finger happens occasionally. But if you're constantly missing the same note in the same place, then stop everything and concentrate on breaking down the problem into smaller pieces so you can correct it.

FRET LESS!

When you consistently miss a certain note or flub the same phrase of a melody you are practicing, don't go and start back at the beginning. By the time you get to the place where you are making the mistake you are bound to do it yet again! Just go over the problem area until you get it consistently right.

Start with just the measure where the mistake is happening. Get it so you can play it correctly at least six times in a row. Then start with the previous measure and play through both the problem measure and the following one, and see if you can play those three measures six times in a row without a mistake. Then add another measure on either side of the targeted measure.

Practicing in this manner—breaking down the song into smaller segments so you can practice and then put back together in a gradual way—should help you improve quickly and avoid similar playing mistakes in the future. Put thought into how you practice and you will make your practices more productive and enjoyable!

The Least You Need to Know

- Notes in standard music notation indicate both the note being played and the rhythmic value of that note.
- Standard music notation is written out on a staff of five lines. Where the notes are placed on the staff, which specific line or space, tells you what note it is.
- The rhythmic value of the note is determined by the note head (whether it is filled in or hollow) and by its stem, and whether or not the stem has dots or flags on it.
- Rests are places where you don't play any notes, and a rest's rhythmic value is determined by its shape.
- You can play many of the notes of the ukulele in multiple places along the fretboard. Your choice of where to play a note can make a song sound very different. The choice is yours to make!

Chords and Strumming Made Easy

Playing the ukulele is all about strumming chords. Strumming provides the rhythm to your songs and the chords supply the harmony. In the following chapters, you'll learn to read chord charts and how to strum in steady rhythms, in both 4/4 and 3/4 time signatures. You'll also begin to create some fancy strumming that uses both single notes and parts of chords.

You'll also learn how chords are constructed. Not only will you know how to play just about every chord, but you'll also be able to come up with variations of basic chords all up and down the neck of your ukulele.

Four Chords = Thousands of Songs

In This Chapter

- Playing your first chords
- Reading chord charts
- Learning about basic strumming
- Understanding rhythm notation
- Making smooth chord changes

Songs are made up of three essential elements: melody, harmony, and rhythm. Melody is the part a person usually sings. And, to put things in the simplest possible way, chords are harmony and strumming is rhythm. There is a bit more to it than that, obviously, but for a beginning uke player everything comes down to strumming and chords.

It is important to understand that although there are a lot of chords to learn you really don't need very many to play most songs. After you make two different chords, you can strum along with a surprising number of songs. With three chords you can play even more, including hundreds of blues, rock, pop, and country standards. For example, the song "Wild Thing" has three chords. The song "Blowing in the Wind" also has three chords.

Add a fourth chord and the number of songs you can play becomes even bigger. In fact, there is a good chance most of the songs you know have between just three to six chords. Better still, songs with five or more chords usually spend most of the time changing between just two to four of them.

Strumming chords and smoothly changing from one chord to another while playing in rhythm are the two biggest parts of playing the ukulele. Up to this point in the book, you have gotten your fingers acclimated to your uke's fretboard—from practicing the warm-up exercises and from playing some simple melodies. Now it is time to get to the heart of making music on your uke.

In this chapter, you will learn some incredibly easy chords and start playing some "strum along" style songs. More importantly, you will learn how to make chord changes smoothly and confidently and do so while keeping good rhythm.

Chords and Chord Charts

Chords are combinations of three or more different notes. To put this into perspective, when you pluck any single string of your ukulele, whether you have fretted a string or not, you are playing an individual musical note. When you strike two strings, you are playing a dyad, or a musical *interval*. Striking three or four of your uke's strings gives you a chord.

> **DEFINITION**
>
> A **chord** is three or more different notes, usually played simultaneously (or close to it, as in a strum). An **interval** is the distance from one note to another in terms of musical steps or half steps.

You might not realize it, but you can already play three different chords on your ukulele. Strum all four strings without placing any fingers on the fretboard, and you have just played a C6 chord. Now strum just the three strings closest to you, the E, C, and G strings. That is a C major chord. And if you play the three strings closest to the floor—the A, C, and E strings—that's an A minor chord.

Although it is cool to play these two chords with just three strings, their four-string counterparts are almost as easy to play. Here is a chord chart for the "full" C major chord:

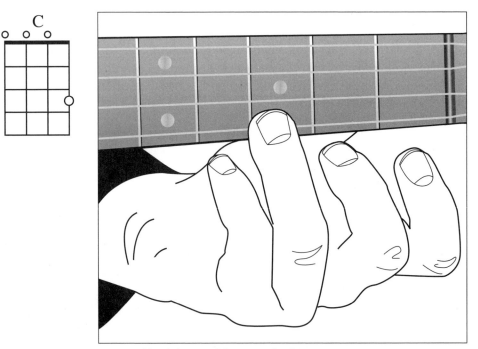

Chord chart and fingering for C major.

Reading Chord Charts

As you can see in the previous illustration, a chord chart is a visual representation of your ukulele. It shows you on which frets of which strings to position your fingers to form the desired chord.

Most chord charts are laid out in the same format, which enable you to read and understand them fairly easily. The name of the chord is usually at the top of the chart. Then there is a heavy black line, which represents the nut of your ukulele. Below the nut is a grid. The vertical lines of the grid represent your uke's strings—from left to right they are g, C, E, and A. The horizontal lines represent the frets on the neck of the ukulele.

An open circle above the nut over any string, such as the first three strings in the C major chord chart, indicates you should play the string *open*, meaning without any fingers on it. A circle within the grid indicates on which string and on which fret you should place a finger. In the example of the C major chord chart, you should place a finger (I recommend going with the ring finger) on the third fret of the A string. Strum all four strings and you have the full four-string version of the C major chord.

Some chord charts will contain a number—1, 2, 3, or 4—which will be connected to a dot in the fretboard grid. These numbers are suggestions for using certain fingers to fret a chord. 1 is your index finger, 2 is your middle finger, 3 is your ring finger, and 4 is your pinky.

FRET LESS!

You have to keep in mind finger numbering on any chord chart is merely a suggestion. It is based on how most ukulele players finger that particular chord. But one bit of information chord charts don't include is which chord immediately preceded that chord and which chord might be coming after it. Because most songs involve more than one chord, you might find it easier to play some chords in more than one way, depending on the sequence they appear in a song. Keep any suggested fingerings in mind, but don't take them as being the only way to play a chord.

The A Minor Chord

Now try making a full A minor chord, called "Am" for short (the lower case *m* stands for minor). Here is the chart:

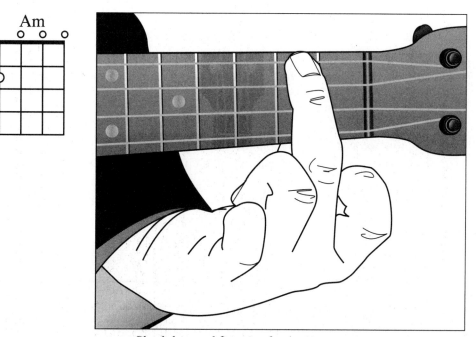

Chord chart and fingering for A minor.

To make the Am chord, you simply place a finger (the middle finger is recommended) on the second fret of the g string. Leave the C, E, and A strings open and strum all four strings. Congratulations! You can now play two chords on your ukulele.

Chords in Notation and Tablature

In both standard music notation and ukulele tablature, chords are represented by stacking the notes of that chord on top of each other. For example, strumming four quarter notes of the C chord, followed by four quarter notes of the Am chord would look like this:

 Track 7 (0:00)

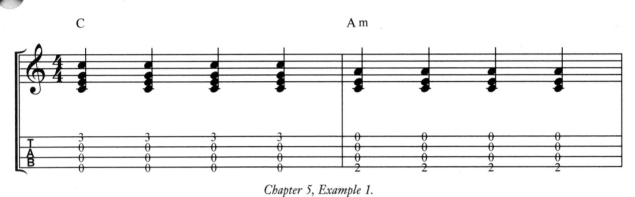

Chapter 5, Example 1.

Reading Rhythm Notation

As you can see, reading chords in either notation or tablature takes a bit of work. Fortunately, you are often spared the need to do so by the use of *rhythm notation*. Rhythm notation is kind of a "shorthand" notation, which uses only the rhythmic value of standard notation.

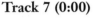 **DEFINITION**

Rhythm notation is a variation of standard notation, which uses the rhythmic shapes of notation to indicate rhythm while replacing the note head with a slash shape. Rhythm notation is primarily used to provide the rhythm for the strumming of chords for a song.

Typically, rhythm notation is used when you are simply concerned with strumming full chords. Instead of giving you the cluster of individual notes that make up the chord, you see a single slash mark in the notation where the note head would normally be. You get the rhythmic values from the shape of the notes or stems, just as you would in standard notation. Here are whole notes, half notes, quarter notes, and eighth notes written out in both standard notation and rhythm notation:

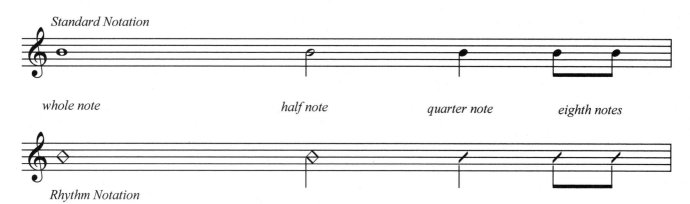

Standard notation notes and their rhythm notation counterparts.

Isn't that a lot easier to read than a whole bunch of notes or numbers bunched together? Let's take a look at what our previous example of C and Am chords (each one measure of quarter notes) would look like in rhythm notation:

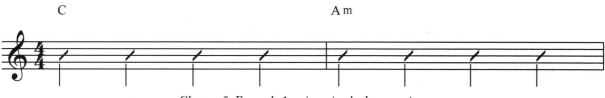

Chapter 5, Example 1 written in rhythm notation.

When playing this example, strum each chord with a downstroke—strumming the strings with a single stroke toward the floor. Be sure to count out the beats evenly. You don't want to go "one, two, three, four," for the C chord and then pause while switching to the Am and go "one, two, three, four" again. Switching from the C chord to the Am chord needs to keep in time with the quarter notes.

Remember you are always making an upstroke before every downstroke. Use the upstroke to make the switch from the C to the Am chord. Slow down the tempo if you have to, until you can play this example without any pauses in your counting. When you have accomplished this, try picking up the pace, a little at a time. You will be surprised at how quickly you'll make this chord change after you have practiced it a little.

Adding Eighth Notes to Your Strumming

If you are feeling confident about making the switch between C and Am in quarter notes, give eighth notes a try. To play eighth notes, strum down on the beat and up on the eighth note between the beats, as in the following example:

Track 7 (0:13)

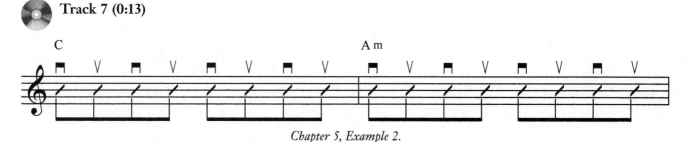

Chapter 5, Example 2.

You will notice two new symbols in this notation. Downstrokes are represented by a ⊓ and upstrokes by a ∨.

When making an upstroke, you don't necessarily need to hit all four strings. Upstrokes are more of a cocking motion, getting your fingers (or pick) in place for the next downstroke.

Again, you should practice changing these two chords in this rhythm until you feel you can handle them smoothly and cleanly.

UKE LORE

In 1976, Israel Kamakawiwo'ole, "IZ," along with his older brother Skippy and three friends, formed the band Makaha Sons of Ni'ihau. After 15 successful years of performing and touring (in the mainland United States as well as Hawaii), IZ launched his own solo career. His first album, *Ka'Ano'i*, earned him both the Hawaii Academy of Music's Male Vocalist of the Year and Contemporary Album of the Year awards. His second, *Facing Future* (containing his medley of "Somewhere Over the Rainbow" and "What a Wonderful World"), would go on to become Hawaii's first certified platinum album, eight years after IZ's death.

The Makaha Sons, currently a trio that includes Louis "Moon" Kauakahi and Jerome Koko, two of the band's original five members, are still going strong. In addition to producing their own music and concerts, they also spend a great deal of time promoting new artists of traditional Hawaiian music.

Fancying Up Your Rhythms

Obviously, strumming chords either all as quarter notes or eighth notes is fairly monotonous. It is when you start combining quarter notes and eighth notes in combination that your strumming takes on a more musical quality. Here are some examples to get you started:

Track 8

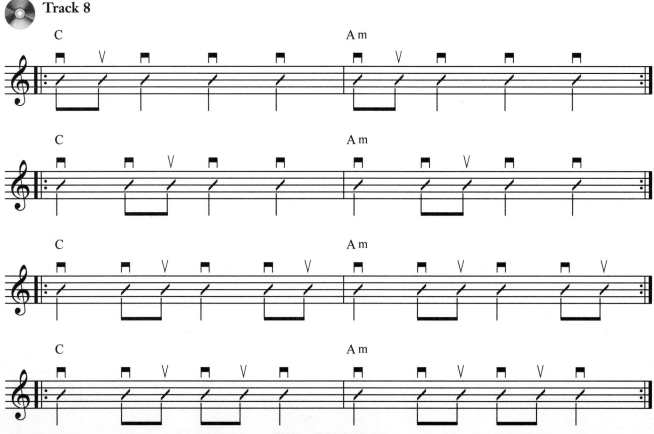

Chapter 5, Example 3.

There is nothing all that difficult here. The first line of this example uses two eighth notes for the first beat and then three quarter notes. In the second line, it is the second beat that is broken into two eighth notes. Both the second and fourth beats get eighth notes in the third line, and in the fourth line it is the second and third beats being played as eighth notes. You can probably hear that any of these strumming rhythms sound much more musical than simply strumming only quarter notes or only eighth notes.

As with both previous examples, take your time to get the rhythms right and to make the chord changes at the correct pace. You might have to initially slow down your pace, but you should be able to play these changes at a fairly quick tempo in short order.

Two More Chords

It is time to add a new chord into the mix. Here is F major:

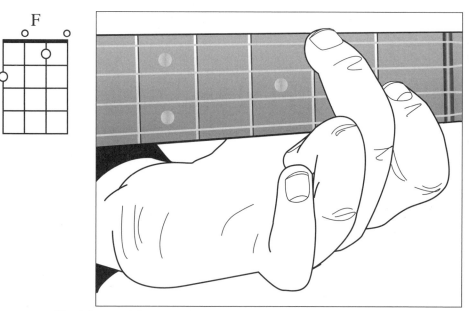

Chord chart and fingering for F major (the ring finger is not on the neck).

To make the F chord, start with your Am chord. Your middle finger is on the second fret of the g string. Then add your index finger to the first fret of the E string. Leave the C and A strings open and strum all four strings.

This might seem simple enough, but it is the first time you have tried to make a chord using more than a single finger. Be sure you are up on your fingertips with both fingers and that they are both high and arched. Play each of the four strings individually to make certain all four notes are ringing cleanly and clearly.

If you are getting muted notes, recheck your fingers. If the C string is not ringing clearly, your middle finger might not be "on point" but rather relaxed and making contact with the C string. If the A string is not sounding, make certain you are not cupping the neck in your hand. You shouldn't be feeling the lower edge of the neck along your palm.

Combining F with Am and C

When you feel comfortable and confident with the F chord, try all those previous examples, going from the Am chord to the F chord, like this:

Track 9

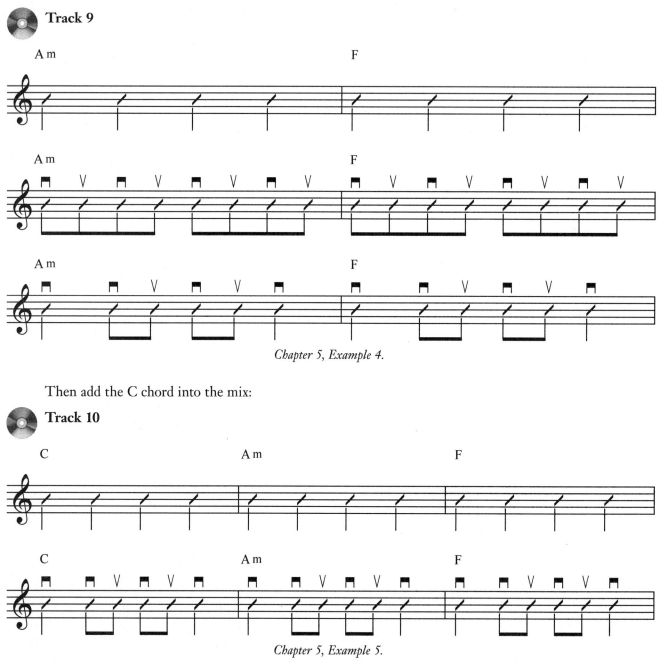

Chapter 5, Example 4.

Then add the C chord into the mix:

Track 10

Chapter 5, Example 5.

Most beginner uke players start each chord change by totally removing their fingers from the neck of their instruments. You need to avoid doing this! Chord changes come faster if your fingers don't have to travel too far.

These three chords (as well as the fourth one you are about to learn) have been chosen specifically for you at this stage of your learning. Notice the similarities between one chord and the following chord, and remember that the less you have to move, the faster you will get.

The G7 Chord

You are making great progress so far, so how about one more chord? Here is G7:

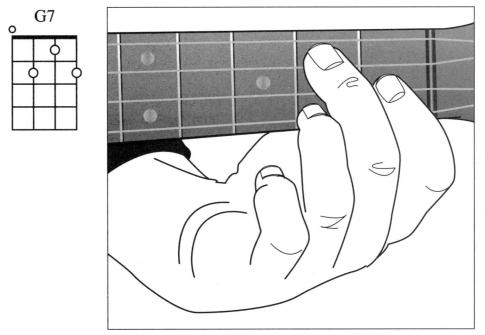

Chord chart and fingering for G7 major.

For right now, don't worry about the 7 in this chord's name. You will be learning what that is all about in the next chapter.

Instead, focus on making the G7 chord. Start with your F chord, where your middle finger is on the second fret of the g string and your index finger is on the first fret of the E string. Keep your index finger in place. Then shift your middle finger from the second fret of the g string to the second fret of the C string. This leaves the g string open. Finally, add your ring finger to the second fret of the A string. Now you can strum all four strings.

This is the most difficult chord you have tried yet, because it uses three fingers! Just as with the F chord, you need to make sure all three fretting fingers are on their fingertips and you are not inadvertently brushing against any of the other strings. Be sure to strike each string individually making certain each of the four notes is ringing true.

Exercises for All Four Chords

Just as you did with the other chords, you should do some exercises to get used to changing between each chord in proper rhythm. Here are some to get you going.

Track 11

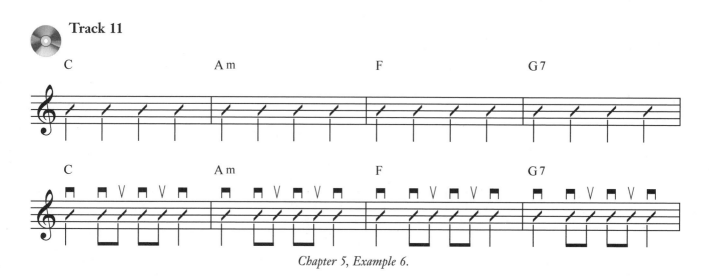

Chapter 5, Example 6.

When changing from the G7 to the C, remove your index and middle fingers from the fretboard and slide your ring finger from the second fret of the A string to the third. As with every chord change you have learned in this chapter, this will take a bit of practice, but you will get the hang of it very quickly.

Your First Strumming Song

Now it is time to put all these chords together and create a song. You might remember "It's Raining, It's Pouring" from your childhood. The following arrangement of it, on the next page, is very laidback—you can almost imagine Jack Johnson doing a version like this!

Practice, Practice

You cannot practice forming and changing chords enough. Knowing and playing chords, as well as changing from one chord to another in correct rhythm, is going to be your primary focus as a beginning ukulele player.

Each time you are presented with a new chord to learn, you need to first memorize how to finger it on your fretboard. If the chord chart has a suggested fingering, great! However, be sure to try playing the chords with different fingers to see what works best for you and to see whether there are other ways to play it (there almost always will be).

> **SMOOTH STRUMMING**
>
> You don't have to strum to practice changing chords! Just finger the chords without strumming. This means you can practice without making a lot of noise, and it also means you have all sorts of potential practice time. If you like to watch sports, you should look at each game as a way to get in two or three hours of chord practice. You'll make big advances in your playing when you get that much practice.

After you have learned a new chord, you should practice changing from that new chord to every other chord you know. Go through the step-by-step method you have used in this chapter for every new chord you learn. When you are first working on changing between two chords, don't worry about timing and keeping the beat. Just work on getting your fingers from one place to another smoothly, and then work through all the chord changes again with timing. Start out with slow quarter notes and then quicken the tempo gradually, and also change up your strumming to a combination of quarter notes and eighth notes, such as the examples earlier in this chapter.

As of right now, you should be able to play and change quickly and cleanly between the C, Am, F, and G7 chords. That is a great start and will give you confidence for what's coming next!

Track 12

Chapter 5, Example 7.

The Least You Need to Know

- Chords are combinations of three or more different notes.
- C major and A minor are two of the easiest chords to play on your ukulele.
- Rhythm notation is a way to read strumming rhythms for chords.
- Most strumming is a combination of quarter notes and eighth notes.
- Memorize as many chords as you can and practice changing between all the chords you know as often as possible.

Where All the Chords Come From

In This Chapter

- Building the major scale
- Creating the four basic chords
- Creating diatonic chords
- Practicing two sets of chord families
- Working through difficult chord changes

Chords, as you have learned, are an essential part of playing the ukulele. And it is easy to be overwhelmed by how many chords seem to be out there to learn. But before you start to worry, remember that chords are formed by grouping together three or more different notes. So there's not an infinite amount of chords to learn.

Well, that is only sort of true. If you look at the neck of your ukulele and think about the fact that the four chords you have learned to play are all fingered in the first three frets, you might wonder why the neck of the ukulele is as long as it is! The fact is that any chord you learn can be played in multiple places on your fretboard. This makes perfect sense, given that chords are just combinations of notes. It makes sense that if you know which notes make up any given chord, you could simply find them on the fretboard of your uke and play them even if you didn't have a chord chart—which is what you are about to learn in this chapter.

The other part is even more exciting. If you are playing any given song, chances are it is going to have fewer than six chords. And if you know which *key* a song is in, that is, which chord is the song's *tonal center*, you stand a good chance of knowing which chords you are going to play even before the song begins. Knowing this will certainly make your task a lot less worrisome.

DEFINITION

The **key** a song is in, also called a song's **tonal center,** is the harmonic "home" of the song. It identifies the basic major or minor chord that serves as the harmonic focal point of the song.

In this chapter, you get a quick overview of the four fundamental chords you might run into when playing the ukulele. Later, in Chapter 8, you get a rundown of more exotic chords, such as suspended chords and seventh chords. But for the sake of keeping things brief, these discussions will be fairly general. (If you're interested in studying music theory more in depth, check out *The Complete Idiot's Guide to Music Theory*.)

The 1-3-5 of Making Chords

Chords are the harmony of your songs. As harmonies, chords are usually grouped together to give a song a focus on a tonal center, which we call the key of a song. To better illustrate this, listen to these three versions of the song "Mary Had a Little Lamb" on the CD.

Track 13

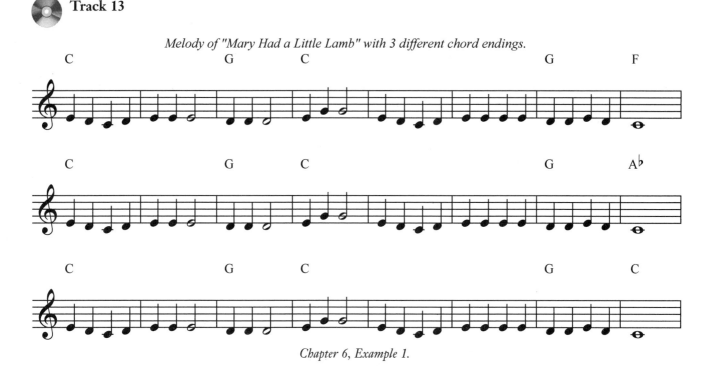

Melody of "Mary Had a Little Lamb" with 3 different chord endings.

Chapter 6, Example 1.

Which one of the three had the most satisfying ending in terms of making you think the song was definitely over? Hopefully, you think it was the third version because it ended with a C chord as opposed to the F (which ended the first version) and the A♭ (which ended the second version). In this arrangement of this song, C major is our tonal center.

The Major Scale

Before going much further, you have to be familiar with the major scale. Almost everything you will ever learn about music is defined by the major scale. So taking a few minutes to learn about this will help you with just about everything from here on out.

There are all kinds of scales. Simply speaking, a *scale* starts on any given note and then follows a specific sequence of full steps and/or half-steps until you get back to your starting note—if you remember from our discussion in Chapter 2. It wouldn't hurt to review the 12 notes you learned from Chapter 2:

C	C♯/D♭	D	D♯/E♭	E	F	F♯/G♭	G	G♯/A♭	A	A♯/B♭	B	C

You undoubtedly already know what the major scale sounds like. Do you remember "Do Re Mi" from *The Sound of Music*? That is the major scale.

DEFINITION

Scales are a specific sequence of steps and half-steps and occasionally larger intervals. Usually a scale is given a two-part name, such as the C major scale, the A melodic minor scale, or B♭ Hungarian scale. The first part of the name is a note, which serves as the scale's root and tonal center. The second part is a description (major, minor pentatonic, Mixolydian, just to name a few), which is shorthand for the specific pattern of steps and half-steps used to create that particular scale.

Here is the specific pattern of steps and half-steps you need to make a major scale; start with any note you like. We will call this starting note the *root* note. From that starting point, follow this pattern of whole steps (W) and half-steps (H) until you reach the root note again:

Root	W	W	H	W	W	W	H	W (the root note again)

Test it by starting with C. The notes of the C major scale will be:

Root	C	D	E	F	G	A	B	C (the root note again)

Verify the pattern. Starting with C, moving up one whole step brings you to D and an additional whole step takes you to E. Next you need a half-step, and F is a half-step up from E. Going one whole step up from F brings you to G, followed by A (one whole step up from G) and then B (one whole step up from A). Taking one final half-step up from B returns you to C again, completing the C major scale.

You should take a few moments and work out a few more major scales. The G major scale should look like this:

G	A	B	C	D	E	F♯	G

Notice that it is F♯ and not F, which is one whole step up from E. It is also one half-step from G, so it does indeed fit the pattern of the major scale.

Next, try working out the F major scale. It will look like this:

F	G	A	B♭	C	D	E	F

It might seem quaint and old-fashioned, but the easiest way to get the major scales into your head is to write them out. You don't have to do all of the 12 possible major scales. But it certainly couldn't hurt! You can check your answers at almost any music site online by typing "12 major scales" into your search engine. Or you could email me and I'll double-check them for you!

After you have any major scale, you should assign each note a degree (a numeric value). You will find it is a lot easier to deal with making chords by thinking of scales in a generic sense. And you should think of your starting note as your root, rather than as the "first." For instance, here is the C major scale again, this time with each note given a degree:

Root	second	third	fourth	fifth	sixth	seventh
C	D	E	F	G	A	B

Stacking Up Notes into Chords

There are four basic types of chords: major, minor, augmented, and diminished. Of those four, the major and minor chords occur most often in music and will make up the vast majority of the chords you play on your ukulele. You can add, subtract, or change notes to these four basic chords to create embellished chords, which you learn all about in Chapter 8.

> **SMOOTH STRUMMING**
>
> You should assume you are dealing with a major chord unless you see a symbol of another chord. Minor chords have a lowercase *m* following the root note, such as *Am* for A minor. An augmented chord will be indicated by either the abbreviation *aug* or a + following the root note, such as C+; diminished chords use either *dim* or a ° after the root note, such as G°.

The major chord start is made up of the root, third, and fifth notes from the major scale in question. C major, known simply as *C* is made up of C (the root note), E (the third), and G (the fifth). Using our earlier examples of the G and F, you can determine that the G chord is G, B, and D while the F chord consists of F, A, and C.

To make a minor chord, you start with the major chord and lower the third note a half-step (or flatting it, if you prefer to think of it that way). C minor, therefore, is C, E♭, and G.

Augmented chords have a regular root and third, but the fifth is raised a half-step, making it sharp. C augmented is C, E, and G♯.

Diminished chords are made by starting with the root and then flatting *both* the third and the fifth. C diminished is C, E♭, and G♭.

Here is a chart that spells out how to create each of the four primary chords:

Notes of the Four Primary Chords

Major	Root	third	fifth
Minor (m)	Root	third flat	fifth
Augmented (aug)	Root	third	fifth sharp
Diminished (dim)	Root	third flat	fifth flat

Again, you could do yourself a lot of good by taking the major scales you have written and working out the major, minor, augmented, and diminished chords for the root note of each key. If that seems like too much work, just go with the major scales of C, G, F, D, B♭, and A.

Finding Chord Families

As mentioned earlier, when you know a song has a particular tonal center, such as C major, F major, or G major, you will find certain chords seem to be used with astonishing regularity. When it comes down to it, certain chords just sound good together. Some musicians like to think of these "sounding good together" sets of chords as chord families.

Most chord families are also known as *diatonic chords*. The term *diatonic* refers to using notes taken from only one specific scale. Using the C major scale as our example means that C, D, E, F, G, A, and B would be our diatonic notes.

Diatonic Chords

To create the diatonic chords for the key of C major, begin with each note of the C major scale, C through B, using it as a root note, and then taking its third and fifth from the appropriate notes of the C major scale.

Starting with C (and taking it as your root), you would then add E (the third) and G (the fifth), giving you a C major chord. You would then move on to D and take that note as the root for your next chord. With D as your root, you add F (the third from D as you move in the C major scale) and then A (the fifth). This chord is D minor, not major. You would know this because you have already written out the D major scale earlier and you know it has an F♯ in it. So F is a flatted third, making this a minor chord.

If you go through the process of using all seven notes as root notes, you end up with the following chords:

C Major Diatonic Chords

Root	Third	Fifth	Chord
C	E	G	C major
D	F	A	D minor
E	G	B	E minor
F	A	C	F major
G	B	D	G major
A	C	E	A minor
B	D	F	B diminished

This pattern of major and minor chords, plus the diminished chord at the end, holds true for the diatonic chords of all major scales. Accordingly, it is a convention to think of diatonic chords in a generic relation to their positions in the major scale. Traditionally, Roman numerals are used with uppercase denoting major chords and lowercase denoting minors or diminished, like this:

I	ii	iii	IV	V	vi	vii
C	Dm	Em	F	G	Am	Bdim

Using these generic equivalents allows you to think of chord progressions, which can be used in any of the 12 major keys. This is the heart of learning how to transpose, which you will read about in Chapters 13 and 14.

Playing the Odds

The chords of songs are usually played in a specific pattern. For example, if the first verse of a song is four lines or phrases, with each line consisting of four beats of C, followed by four beats of Am, then four beats of F and four beats of G, each of the following verses will likely be that same pattern as well.

If you're playing in any major key, the three chords you will most likely run across are the I, IV, and V chords. That means in the key of C major, you would find yourself playing C, F, and G a lot. In the key of G, it would be G, C, and D, and in the key of F, you would find yourself playing F, B♭, and C.

FRET LESS!

Of course, songs aren't limited to using only diatonic chords! With any given song, you have the possibility of running across almost any chord. Occasionally, chords are "borrowed" from other keys either to make a stronger chord change or simply to make a chord progression more interesting. A song in the key of C, for example, could easily have an A or a D7 chord in it.

Besides those three chords, you are next most likely to find yourself playing the vi and the ii chords. The iii chord is used quite a bit as well, but usually not as much as the others. And you will rarely find yourself faced with the vii chord.

A Song with the Whole Chord Family

This arrangement of "Kum Ba Yah" manages to use six diatonic chords from the key of C major. First, you need to become familiar with all the chords used in the song. You learned four of the six in the last chapter, so that's the lion's share of the work done already!

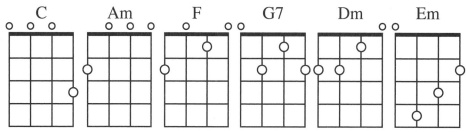

Chords for "Kum Ba Yah" in the key of C major.

There are obviously a lot of chords here, but if you take a look at the song arrangement that follows, you will see that the first and third lines use only the C and F chords. That's good news!

To prepare yourself for the other chord changes, you should go through the same steps you used to play "It's Raining, It's Pouring" in Chapter 5. Because these chord changes are a little more involved, it is a good idea to start with whole notes and then work your way to half notes before getting to the quarter notes and eventual strumming rhythm. Use the warm-up on the next page to help you get comfortable with the chord changes you will be making.

It cannot be stressed enough that you need to take your time working through these chord change warm-ups. The smoother you can make them, even at an incredibly slow tempo, the more success you'll have making the chord changes in proper timing later.

Take special care in moving from Am to Em. It is not an especially difficult change, but the Em chord will be new to you because it is the first time you have had a span of three frets to cover. You probably should use your index finger for the second fret of the A string, your middle finger for the third fret of the E string, and your ring finger for the fourth fret of the C string.

Likewise, Dm will be new. Even though it is very much like the F chord, you will probably need a bit of time to get used to having three fingers close together. Try using your index finger on the first fret of the E string, your ring finger on the second fret of the C string, and your middle finger on the second fret of the g string.

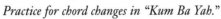

Practice for chord changes in "Kum Ba Yah."

Playing "Kum Ba Yah" in the Key of C

When you feel confident about your progress with the previous warm-up exercise for "Kum Ba Yah," give the whole song a go:

 **Track 14**

Chapter 6, Example 2.

Playing "Kum Ba Yah" in the Key of G

After you have worked your way through "Kum Ba Yah" in the key of C, how about trying it in the key of G? There are quite a few new chords here, but that's the whole point!

Here the G, Bm7, and the D7 chords will be new. Play G with your middle finger on the second fret of the A string, your ring finger on the third fret of the E, and your index finger on the second fret of the C string.

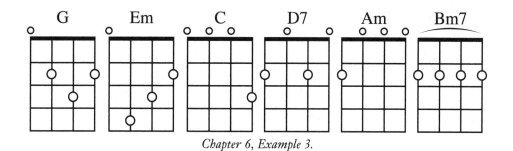

Chapter 6, Example 3.

For the Bm7, lay your index finger flat across all four strings at the second fret. This is known as barring the strings, which you will read more about in Chapter 8. For now, understand it is not about applying a lot of pressure, but rather about getting your finger to cover all four strings so the notes still ring true. Use only enough of your finger to cover all the strings. Your fingertip should just clear the edge of the fretboard closest to you as you look at it. It also helps if you can feel the edge of the fret closer to the body of the ukulele along the edge of your finger.

Just as you did in the key of C, work through each chord change first with whole notes and then half notes and quarter notes before taking on the whole song:

Track 15

Chapter 6, Example 4.

Practice, Practice

You have probably discovered that although some chord changes are fairly easy, some are moderately difficult, at least at first. Moving from Bm7 to Em to Am to D7 in the last song, for example, takes a bit of work.

But this is where not counting on fingering charts can help you. If you start with your index finger barring the strings at the second fret for your Bm7, you can then stand up your index finger at the second fret of the A string to anchor the rest of the Em chord. Then move the index finger again to the second fret of the g string for the Em chord. You will find it a snap to keep it in place and simply add your middle finger to the second fret of the E string to make the D7 chord. Plus, you will find yourself in perfect position to drop the ring finger onto the third fret of the A string when you then change from D7 to G.

Some chord changes can't help but involve a lot of finger movement. Ideally, you need your fingers to move from one chord to another as a unit. The following two simple exercises can help you get started in that direction.

First, form a chord you are working on—let's say G. When you have your fingers in place, relax them but don't lose contact with the strings. Now press your fingers hard onto the strings simultaneously, harder than you normally would to play the chord. You are likely to hear the notes of the G chord as you press the strings onto the neck of the ukulele. After you press hard, relax again but still keep contact with the strings, and don't lose the chord! Repeat this 10–12 times.

The companion exercise is pretty much the same, but you need to start by having your fingers on the strings as if you were playing the chord. Then relax and raise your fingers, as a unit, just off the strings. Keep them close enough so you can put them back on the strings at the same time.

The object of these exercises is to get your fingers acclimated to working together on the chord. Eventually, they will learn to leave one chord and arrive at another as a team.

Equally important is to practice making each chord change in rhythm. Use the various strumming rhythms from Chapter 5 as templates for each of the new chords you have played in this chapter. Take the chords from "Kum Ba Yah" and, just as you did with the four chords from Chapter 5, work your way through strumming them in succession. Give each chord eight beats to start with; then try to change chords every four beats.

If you take these basic steps to develop both your chord changing and your rhythm, you should find yourself making steady progress with your ukulele playing. You should also find that you spend less time on each successive new chord change you add to your ever-growing repertoire.

The Least You Need to Know

* Knowing the major scale is important for understanding many things about music, from creating chords to transposing.
* The four primary types of chords are major, minor, augmented, and diminished.
* Diatonic chords are created by using just the notes from a single, specific scale.
* When you know the key, or tonal center, of a song, you can have a good idea as to the chords you are likely going to play in that particular song.
* Practice working systematically through chord changes. Take your time and try to get your fingers to work together as a unit instead of individually.

Putting Some Spice in Your Strumming

In This Chapter

* Mixing single notes with chords
* The "alternate-finger-flick-all-eighth-note" strum
* Avoiding robotic strumming
* Making old songs sound new

Rhythm is the glue that holds a song together. You can often get away with playing a single wrong note or even a wrong chord, provided you get to the right note or chord quickly enough. But if you derail the rhythm of a song, almost everyone will notice.

Keeping a steady rhythm is essential to good playing. At the heart of it all, rhythm and strumming are the pulse of a song. And the surest way to maintain a steady pulse is to count. Any rhythm, any pattern of strumming, can be broken down into component parts that are usually as simple as counting to either three or four.

The basic strumming rhythms you learned in the last part of Chapter 5 are a great start. Mixing both quarter notes and eighth notes, or downstrokes and upstrokes if you prefer, makes your rhythm a lot more interesting than simply strumming all quarter notes on the down beat. In this chapter, you'll do some more creative strumming that involves playing combinations of single notes along with your chords. You'll be amazed at how a few simple changes in your rhythm will make you sound more like a seasoned ukulele player.

> **SMOOTH STRUMMING**
>
> Get into the habit of counting while working out a new rhythm and preferably counting out loud. Initially it might seem a bit childish, but counting aloud does help immensely. When counting in your head, you often will not catch yourself cheating on the rhythm here and there, but you can't help noticing when the beat isn't even when you count out loud.

Tapping your foot as you play (which you really should try to do) will also work to create an ongoing steady rhythm for you to go by. Your toe will hit the floor on any given beat and come back up again on the offbeat. Think of yourself having an imaginary string attached to your tapping toe at one end and to your strumming thumb on the other. When you count the beat, your toe hits the floor, pulling the thumb along in a downstroke. On the offbeat, your thumb does an upstroke and pulls your toe off the floor.

Hopefully you have spent a good deal of time at this point practicing your chord changing as well as your basic strumming. If so, even though you might initially think the new rhythms you learn in this chapter a bit of a challenge, you should pick them up surprisingly quickly.

Breaking Up the Beat

It is quite amazing how you can make your strumming much more musical with the simplest alterations. You have already discovered this with the combination quarter and eighth note rhythms from Chapter 5. Now it is time to take things a step further by breaking up your strum into combinations of single notes and parts of chords you already know. Don't let the *parts of chords* worry you! It simply means you will be strumming two or three strings instead of all four.

Start by strumming four quarter notes of the C chord. That is easy enough to do. After you have warmed up to doing that, you are going to play *just the C string* on the first beat while still keeping your C chord in place on the fretboard (which involves just keeping a finger on the third fret of the A string). On the second beat, strum the E and A strings (and your finger is still on the third fret of the A string, remember!) and then strum all four strings of your ukulele (still fingering the C chord) for the third and fourth beats. It will sound like this:

 Track 16 (0:00)

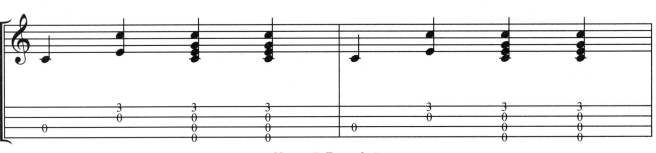

Chapter 7, Example 1.

That was pretty easy, wasn't it? Did you notice how much more musical it sounded even though it was simply strumming four quarter notes? And that's just the start of making your rhythm a lot more interesting!

The Boom-Chuck

Now try playing just the C string on the first and third beats while strumming the E and A strings (still fingering the C chord) on the second and fourth beats like this:

 Track 16 (0:12)

Chapter 7, Example 2.

This technique goes by numerous names. Guitarists often refer to it as the *boom-chuck*—the *boom* being the single note and the *chuck* being the partial chord. Some teachers call it the *bass/strum* or *root/strum* stroke. This is because the single note used for the first and third beat is usually either the root note of the chord being played or a low note in the bass range of the instrument. When you think of the ukulele, though, *bass* rarely comes to mind! Whatever you decide to call it, hopefully you are finding it an easy step up from strumming full chords for four beats.

Alternating Strings

You can make this root/strum more interesting by using an alternate note instead of the root note of the chord for the single note played on the third beat. Here is a possible way to make an alternating pattern for the C chord:

 Track 16 (0:24)

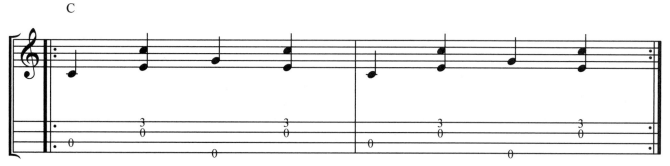

Chapter 7, Example 3.

In this example, you play the first two beats just as you did in the root/strum example previously. But here you play just the single note of the open g string on the third beat and then *skip* the C string and strum the E and A strings on the fourth beat as you did earlier.

Take your time to get the hang of this one. Laugh when you pick the C string instead of the g string, or vice versa. Everyone does it when learning so you might as well experience it, too! Although you are enjoying picking up a new strum, listen to how just one or two notes fills out the four beats just as, if not more, effectively strumming four quarter notes of the full C chord does. Letting the notes of the strings ring out over each other is a big part of the ukulele sound, and you need to incorporate it into your playing as often as you can.

A Flick of the Finger

As always, take whatever time you need to get yourself totally comfortable with this new manner of strumming rhythm before moving forward. It is important that you feel in control of what you are doing, your sense of rhythm is steady and even, and you can play this pattern at almost any tempo without worries—I say *almost* because you are probably not going to play an alternating pattern perfectly smoothly and cleanly at this stage of your learning.

When you are confident you are progressing nicely, it is time to add eighth notes into the mix. Listen to the next example while following along in the notation and tablature.

Track 17

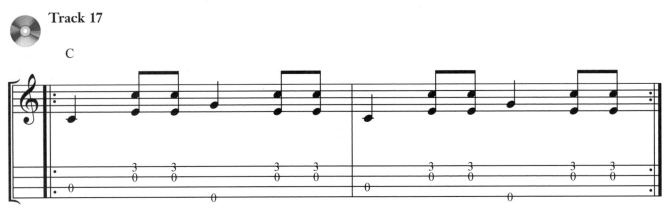

Chapter 7, Example 4.

Take this one step at a time and be sure you are fingering your C chord throughout each step. On the first beat, strike the open C string with your thumb. On the first half of the second beat, strike the E and A strings by flicking your index finger in a downstroke motion. Follow this with an upstroke of the same strings (still using the index finger) on the second half of the second beat. For the third beat, strike the open g string with your thumb. The fourth beat will be a repeat of the second, using your index finger to strike the E and A strings with a downward flick on the first half of the beat and then catching both strings again on an upstroke on the second half of the fourth beat.

You will probably find this a little tricky during your first few (or few dozen) attempts. That is normal, so don't let it discourage you. Remember to count out loud, just as you hear me doing on the CD for this example. Go as slowly as you need to get the strumming (or flicking if you prefer) as smooth and even as possible. With a bit of practice, you will get this technique down quicker than you think possible.

Picking Up Steam

After you get it smooth and even, you will pick up speed through repetition of this flick strum. It is both fascinating and scary at how quickly your fingers take to playing patterns like this.

When you are up for it, there is one more step you might be interested in trying. Give it a look and listen:

 Track 18

Chapter 7, Example 5.

Here you are adding an upstroke of a single string (the open E string) on the first half of the first and third beats. You should use your index finger for this, essentially cocking it in preparation for the downstroke flick on the second beat. Like all the examples in this chapter, this will probably take a bit of practice to get used to. But if you took your time to get comfortable with example 4, you should find you need less time adapting the additional note in this example.

Hopefully through all this, you are listening to how much you are *not* sounding like a beginning ukulele player anymore!

Polly Wolly Doodling

To help you nail down this particular strum, I included an arrangement of "Polly Wolly Doodle," a simple (and hopefully familiar) two-chord song that works nicely with all the strums you have learned in this chapter.

But because it has two chords—C and G7—it would be a wise idea to work your way through all the steps you took earlier with the C chord again using this G7 chord. Here is a condensed version:

 Track 19

G 7

Chapter 7, Example 6.

Because the root note of G7 is G, we are using the open g string on the first beat and the D note, where your index finger is sitting on the second fret of the C string for the alternate note on the third beat.

You should note that the last measure of this example involves a very quick change from C to G7. You want to practice this slowly at first, making certain you give yourself enough time to execute your chord change while practicing this alternate-finger-flicking-all-eighth-note strum (which is why it makes no sense to give a strum a name!).

You will notice the heavy double line with the two dots stacked up vertically right before it. That is a repeat sign, which means to go back to the beginning of the last line where there is a repeat sign flipped in the "forward" direction. In music notation or ukulele tablature, when you see these signs you repeat the music within these boundaries a second time.

Track 20

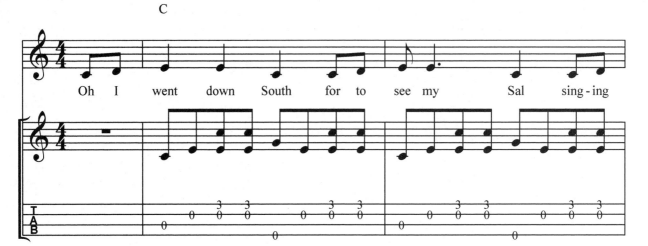

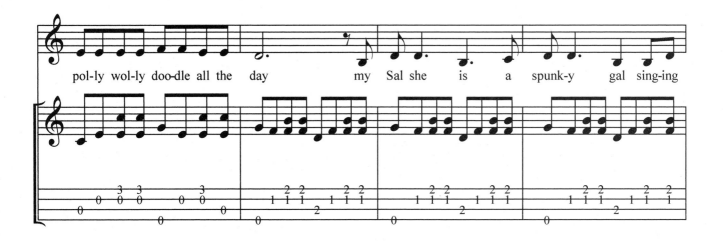

Chapter 7, Example 7.

Congratulations! That was the most difficult thing you have tried to play on the ukulele so far!

Practice, Practice

You should take a few moments to yourself. You should also be taking notes on all the steps that went into preparing yourself to play "Polly Wolly Doodle." You learned several new ways to strum and worked on being able to play those strums in rhythm and change chords as part of the strumming.

One important idea to keep in mind at this point is that you have learned a lot of different strums throughout this chapter and each one sounds fine. Ideally you should not play the same single strum throughout any one song. Doing so sounds robotic, and music is meant to be a living thing. So try to mix up your strum rhythms when you practice, like the following example shows.

Track 21

Chapter 7, Example 8.

As you can hear, these strums all sound fine when mixed together. It actually sounds like music!

Sounding like music is, of course, why you are learning to play the ukulele in the first place. Remember that everything you learned in this chapter should be just the proverbial tip of the iceberg for you. Do you want to be able to create this sort of strumming for *any* song you play? Of course, you do!

And how exactly do you go about being able to do so? By using these strums every chance you get on songs you already know how to play. Go back to "It's Raining, It's Pouring" from Chapter 5 and "Kum Ba Yah" in Chapter 6, and try these new strums. Take the time to prepare yourself by going over each chord individually and then in sequence. Both of your earlier songs had four chords so you will have more changes to make.

Just as important, you might find these new strums don't sound exactly the way you like or want them to sound. You might have to experiment with which single notes sound best with these other chords you know. Conversely, the new strums might make the songs sound even better!

Believe it or not, this is not the point. The goal is to make this new way to strum a part of your everyday ukulele vocabulary. You should be able to use these strums for any chord you know at the drop of a hat. After you have used them a million ways you might never play again, you will know exactly what they sound like and will be able to use them when any particular strum is precisely the sound you really want to have for a specific moment in a specific song you're playing. And that is really making good music.

The Least You Need to Know

* Music is an aural art. Your ear is much more important than your eyes when it comes to playing the ukulele (or any musical instrument).
* Always count out a new rhythm, and count it out loud if you truly want to learn it.
* Mixing single notes in with strummed chords gives your strumming more nuance and character.
* Try not to use a single strumming rhythm throughout an entire song.
* Use new strums you learn on your old songs to become adept at playing them.

Even More Chords and Rhythms

In This Chapter

- Discovering embellished chords
- Using chord shapes to play all over the neck
- Playing barre chords
- Strumming in 3/4 time
- Combining open chords and barre chords in a song

It should be crystal clear to you by now that learning chords and basic strumming rhythms, not to mention practicing changing between the chords you know while keeping good steady rhythm, are your top priorities as a beginning ukulele player. There are quite a number of chords, after all! As you learned in the last chapter, there are all sorts of ways to make your basic strumming sound more musical.

It is also worth pointing out that if you have been diligent about practicing what you have learned in Chapters 5, 6, and 7, you have learned most of the chords ukulele players use the majority of the time. Depending on the songs you want to play (and what musical key they happen to be in), you might be perfectly content with two or three more chords than you know right now. Most songs, as you will find out, don't have all that many chords to start out with. You will be amazed at how many songs you can play with just the C, F, G (or G7), D7, Em, Am, and Bm7 chords.

But if you decide you are okay knowing only the chords you have learned so far (even with the two or three more added in), you are missing out on an easy chance to make your playing sound really magical. At the start of Chapter 6, you read that if you know the combination of notes that makes up any chord, then you can find a way to make that chord anywhere on the neck. Well, it is actually even simpler than that! Just knowing the shapes of the basic chords—"shapes" meaning where you place your fingers on the frets to make the chords you already have learned—gives you the ability to make new chords you don't know as well. It also lets you create new voicings of the chords you do know well, all up and down the fretboard. You are just steps away from being able to figure out just about any chord you will ever come across!

Beyond the Basic Chords

As you learned in Chapter 6, the four basic chords—major, minor, augmented, and diminished—are created by using the root, third, and fifth (or altered thirds and fifths) of the root note's major scale. More complicated chords are created by simply adding more notes to your primary chords or by removing or substituting a note for the third.

These *embellished chords* are given names with numbers, which identify what has been added to the basic chord. Some numbers, such as 9, 11, and 13, might seem odd because they lie beyond what seems to be the range of the scale. But because all notes are constantly repeating one after the other, you think of the root note as the eighth degree when you are counting it. The next note would be the ninth, and it would be the same note as the second. Using the C major scale as an example, you would get these degrees:

Root	2nd	3rd	4th	5th	6th	7th	Root (8th)	9th	10th	11th	
C	D	E	F	G	A	B	C	D	E	F	etc.

Here are some embellished chords you are most likely to come across in songs:

5	Root	5th			
sus2	Root	2nd	5th		
sus4	Root	4th	5th		
6	Root	3rd	5th	6th	
7	Root	3rd	5th	♭7th	
7(♯5)	Root	3rd	♯5th	♭7th	
m7	Root	♭3rd	5th	♭7th	
m(maj7)	Root	♭3rd	5th	7th	
dim7	Root	♭3rd	♭5th	♭♭7th (same as 6th)	
m7(♭5)	Root	♭3rd	♭5th	♭7th	
add9	Root	3rd	5th	9th	
maj9	Root	3rd	5th	7th	9th
9	Root	3rd	5th	♭7th	9th

5 Chords, Suspended Chords, and Sixths

Technically speaking, 5 chords are not chords but dyads, using just two notes—the root and the 5th of the scale. The term *5 chord* has been used extensively in music written since the 1950s, especially in rock and pop songs. Guitarists call these *power chords*.

You can play 5 chords using just two strings of your ukulele, or you can use three or all four as long as you know where to find the notes. Here are some basic 5 chords:

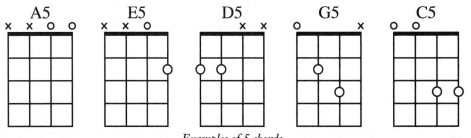

Examples of 5 chords.

Remember an *X* above a string on the chord chart means to not play that string.

In suspended chords (*sus* for short), the note of the 3rd is replaced, more often than not, with the 4th (sus4); however, sometimes it's replaced with the 2nd (sus2). Whenever you come across a chord simply labeled "sus," the convention is to use the 4th. Here are some common suspended chords:

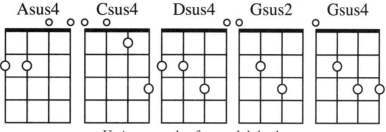

Various examples of suspended chords.

Generally, suspended chords are used either to create an ambiguous harmony or to a make a long stretch of a single chord more interesting to listen to. The suspended note (the 4th or the 2nd) generates a mild dissonance, which catches the listeners' ear and then resolves back to the harmony of the original chord, as demonstrated in the following example:

 Track 22

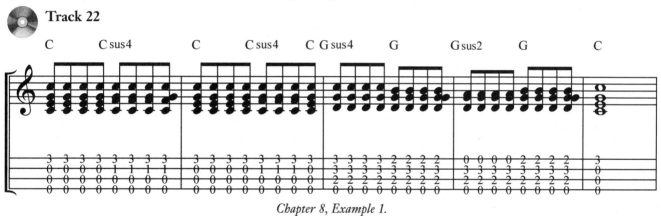

Chapter 8, Example 1.

In a 6 chord, the sixth note from the scale is added to the root, third, and fifth. As you learned in Chapter 5, C6 is made up of C, E, G, and A, which are the open strings of your ukulele.

Lucky Sevens

Unfortunately, 7th chords aren't as cut-and-dried as 6th chords. The number 7, when tacked onto a chord, directs you to add the *flatted* seventh of the scale, which is the note one full step below the octave of the root note. For example, in a C7 chord you add B♭, not B, to the C chord, giving you the notes C, E, G, and B♭. In music theory this is called the "dominant" 7th but you'll usually see it referred to simply as the 7th.

"Maj7" indicates you add the interval of the major seventh—the seventh note of the major scale—to the chord. Cmaj7 is made up of C, E, G, and B.

> **SMOOTH STRUMMING**
>
> The only time you see the word *major* used in a chord is for the major seventh. Usually you default to a major chord unless the chord name indicates otherwise, with the word minor (*m*), augmented (*aug* or a + sign), or diminished (dim or °). Seeing *maj* indicates you are dealing with the major seventh.

The lowercase *m* always stands for minor. And minor, when describing a chord, always refers to the interval of the ♭3rd. A minor 7th chord would therefore be a minor chord (m) with the flatted seventh (7) added to it: Cm7 is C, E♭, G, and B♭.

> **SMOOTH STRUMMING**
>
> As mentioned, the abbreviation *maj* always refers to adding the major seventh to a chord. The small *m* for *minor* always refers to the third of the chord. If you can keep this straight, you won't find yourself bewildered by minor major seventh chords, which add the interval of the major seventh to the basic minor chord. Cm(maj7)—for example, would be C, E♭, G, and B.

And just to make things even more interesting, there are two types of diminished seventh chords. You can have a basic diminished chord with the flatted seventh added to it, which is usually labeled as minor seventh chords with "♭5" added to it. Cm7♭5, for instance, would be C, E♭, G♭, and B♭.

A "regular" diminished seventh means flatting the seventh twice (making it the same note as the sixth) and then adding that to a regular diminished chord. Cdim7, for example, is C, E♭, G♭, and A (technically B♭♭).

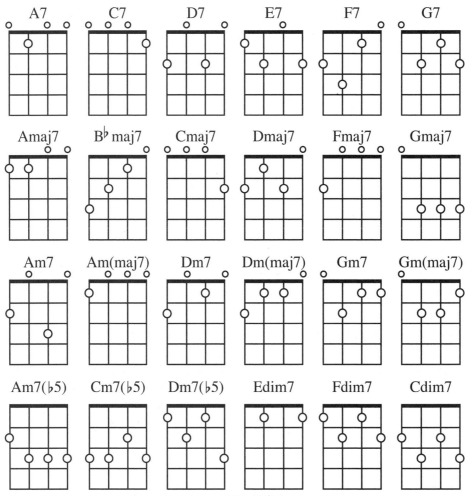

Various examples of 7th chords.

Extended Chords

Aside from the 6 chord, when only one single note is added to the basic chord, it is usually indicated with the word *add*. For example, Cadd9 is C, E, G, and D. Depending on who wrote the music, you can sometimes find chords like "C2" or "C4," but those should be thought of as "Cadd9" or "Cadd11."

> **DEFINITION**
>
> 9th, 11th, and 13th chords are called **extended chords.** They start out with the root, 3rd, 5th, and 7th and then have notes from "beyond the octave" (higher than the octave of the root note) added on. When the 9th, 11th, or 13th note of a 9th, 11th, or 13th chord is an accidental, such as E7#9, it is called an **altered chord.**

With full 9th, 11th, and 13th chords, you keep the dominant 7th note as part of the chord. C9, for instance is C, E, G, B♭, and D. Any maj9 chord uses the major 7 instead of the dominant (flatted) 7. Cmaj9 contains the notes C, E, G, B, and D. C11 is C, E, G, B♭, D, and F. Cmaj13 would be C, E, G, B, D, F, and A. That is every note of the C major scale!

You can also add accidentals to your extended chords. For example, C7(#9) is C, E, G, B♭, and D♯ or C7(♭13), which is C, E, G, B♭, and A♭.

It bears repeating that unless you go looking for songs with a lot of complicated chords in them, chances are they won't find you! But at least you know how to create them.

Turning Your Basic Chords into Any Chord You Need

Okay, here is where the basic music theory you learned combines with your chord knowledge and sets you on your way to becoming master of your ukulele. Start out with any of the open position chords you know:

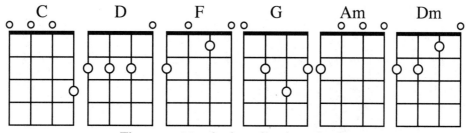

The open position chords you have learned so far.

These are called *open position chords* because they incorporate at least one or more open strings as part of the notes of the chord. Even G and G7, as you have learned them, are open position chords because you use the open g string to play them.

> **DEFINITION**
>
> Chords on the ukulele are considered to be either open or closed forms. **Open chord** forms use open strings as part of the chord. A closed chord form has each of the four strings of the ukulele covered in some manner. Many closed forms are **barre chords,** which are made when one finger (often the index finger) covers two or more strings at the same fret.

Bet you didn't realize you knew that many chords already, right? Start with C because it is the first full chord you learned. You play C with your ring finger on the A string (which, you might recall, is the note C) and leave the E, C, and g strings open.

Now suppose you wanted to play the chord C♯ (also called D♭) major for some reason. Would you panic? Absolutely not! You know that the notes that make up a C major chord are C, E, and G. You also know that the C♯ is one half-step higher than C and that one fret is the same as a half step. You can figure out the notes of C♯ major chord, either by writing out the C♯ major scale and taking the notes of the root, third, and fifth positions, or you could make the logical assumption that each note of C♯ major should be one half-step higher than its counterpart in the C major chord.

And you would be right! The notes of the C♯ major chord are C♯, E♯ (which you know is also F), and G♯. So far, so good! Now comes the fun part.

To raise up the note of C, located at the third fret of the A string, a half step, you would place a finger on the fourth fret of the A string. To raise the notes of each of your open strings, you would need to play each of those on the first fret. The note at the first fret of the E string is F (or E♯, as we call it for this particular chord), the note at the first fret of the C string is C♯, and the note at the first fret of the G string is G♯. Congratulations! You have figured out the correct fingering for the C♯ major chord. Now the question becomes how do you play it?

Raising the Barre

The simplest way, although it might not seem so at first, is to play it as a barre chord. Barre chords are created when a single finger is used to cover two or more strings at the same fret. The following C♯ major chord chart and illustration will help demonstrate:

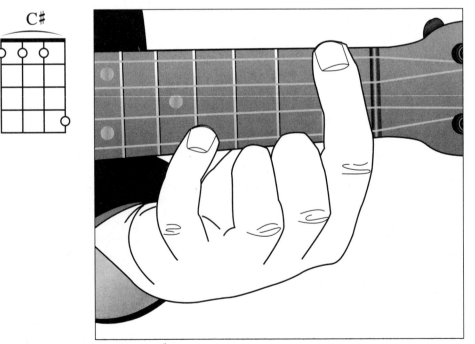

The C♯ major chord chart and fingering.

Barre chords appear hard to play, but like all the chords you have learned so far, it is just a matter of practice and repetition. Start by placing your pinky finger on the C♯ note at the fourth fret of the A string and pluck it to make sure you have a good, clean ringing note. Then place your index finger flat across all four strings of your ukulele at the first fret. The tip of your index finger should barely extend beyond the edge of the neck, as you can see in the preceding illustration.

The trick to playing barre chords is not to exert a lot of pressure with the index finger. It is about *how* your finger is placed. Try to keep the index finger parallel with the fret rather than coming at it from an angle. Also, use just enough of the index finger so its tip barely extends past the edge of the neck. Jamming your whole hand against the lower edge of the neck so the index finger extends well beyond its edge will make it difficult for you to get your other fingers involved in the chord. And you are going to need all those other fingers at some point.

FRET LESS!

Barre chords are a matter of both practice and comfort. The first thing you need to do is relax and then work toward success in stages. Place your index finger flat on any fret of the A string (it is good to start between the first and fifth) and pluck the note to be sure you have a good one. Keeping your index finger parallel to the fret, try covering both the A and E strings—it is good if you can feel the edge of the fret along the side of your finger closest to the body of the uke. Pick the notes individually to test them. Then try covering the A, E, and C strings at the same fret and finally all four. Use your middle finger to cover the index finger if it helps.

A Moveable Feast

Believe it or not, you can now play all 12 major chords! Because no open strings are involved in playing C♯ major, it is what's known as a *moveable chord*. If you slide your index finger up a fret so it barres all four strings at the second fret and then reposition your pinky at the fifth fret of the A string, you have a D major chord. Moving each finger up an additional fret gives you D♯ (or E♭ if you prefer) and if your index finger is on the fourth fret and your pinky is on the seventh fret, you are playing E major. Here are the 12 major chords you can make using this shape:

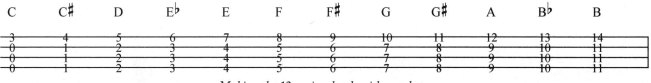

Making the 12 major chords with one shape.

Let's repeat the process for two new chords you learned in this chapter, Cmaj7 and C7:

7ᵗʰ and Maj7 barre chords using the C shape.

And how about minor chords? Use Am as your starting point and you will find you can create all 12 minor chords in the same way:

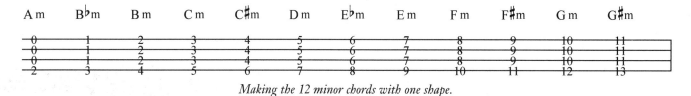

Making the 12 minor chords with one shape.

Your next task (and it is a big one) is to go through the other shapes to figure out what the closed position equivalents would be like. Sometimes, as with the F chord, you will barre only three strings with your index finger, as you can with the chart of the F♯ chord:

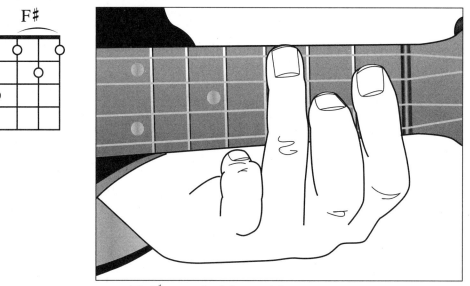

The F♯ major chord chart and fingering.

And in the case of B♭, you will be barring only two strings:

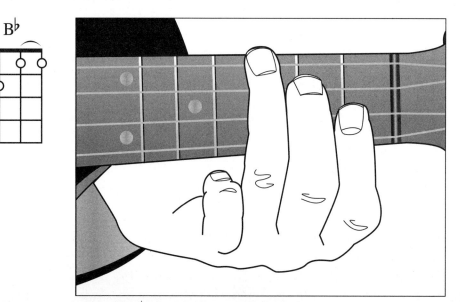

The B♭ major chord chart and fingering.

Dealing with the D Shape

The barre shape most people playing the ukulele tend to have trouble with is the D chord. The open position D chord is played like this:

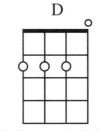

The D major chord chart.

Some people find it easiest to play this chord using the middle finger on the g string, the ring finger on the C, and the index finger on the E. Others use their index finger on the g, middle finger on the C, and ring finger on the E. And still others prefer middle finger on the g, index finger on the C, and ring finger on the E. Try them all and see what works best for you.

You are probably discovering it is tough to get any three fingers into the same fret on adjacent strings! One solution many uke players use is to play the D chord with the C shape, as you learned earlier. Another way is to use just two fingers to cover the three strings. The middle finger lies slightly flat to fret both the g and C strings and the ring finger gets to fret the E string.

Using this method also makes D-shape barre chords a little easier for many players. Here is what the E chord would be like:

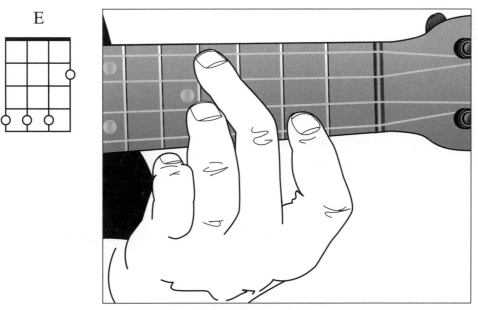

The E major chord chart and fingering.

Regardless of which way you decide to play it, to learn the D-shape chords, such as E and E♭, will require patience and practice on your part.

Three to a Measure

Because you have been learning a lot of new chords, the song at the end of this chapter, "After the Ball," contains a lot of new chords. But it has something new for you in the rhythm department, too. It has a 3/4 time signature.

You learned a bit about time signatures back in Chapter 4. In a song with 3/4 timing, each measure gets three beats instead of the four beats per measure found in all the songs you have played up to this point.

UKE LORE

3/4 timing is used for waltzes, which are ballroom dances. But you probably know quite a few songs in 3/4 timing—Billy Joel's "Piano Man," Jerry Jeff Walker's "Mr. Bojangles," and even Miley Cyrus's "When I Look at You." Of course, there are also standards like "The Tennessee Waltz."

Various 3/4 Strums

You can strum a measure of 3/4 timing in many different ways. Here is a sampling of strumming rhythms you should practice:

Track 23

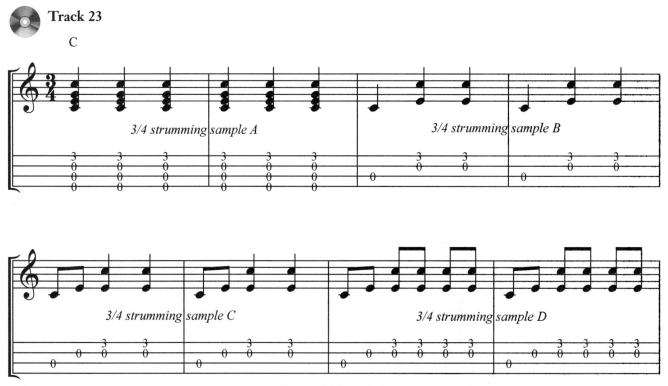

Chapter 8, Example 2.

You should practice these strums until you feel confident you can play them without thinking. Start by using one chord for the entire set of strums until you have gone through all the basic chords you know—C, Am, F, G, G7, Dm, Em, and D7 will suffice to get you going. Then take any one single strum and try to play it while changing between chords every six beats. Then try every three beats. Finally, try to string together different three-beat strums while changing chords every measure.

Going through this practice regimen will help you continue to improve with both your chord changes and rhythm skills. It will also do a great job preparing you for "After the Ball."

"After the Ball"

If you take a look at "After the Ball," you are probably thinking, "You've got to be kidding me! There are at least a dozen chords and it's in a time signature I haven't played before! And on top of that, I'll be playing both open chords and barre chords!" If so, you probably jumped to one of two conclusions—either the song will be impossible or it will be a lot of fun to try!

The reality is it is going to be a bit of both. There *are* a lot of chords, and I do mean *a lot*! Believe it or not, though, playing this song is within your capabilities. It is simply going to take work on your part, but it is work that you have spent the last three chapters learning how to do.

To get you started, here are the chord charts for each chord:

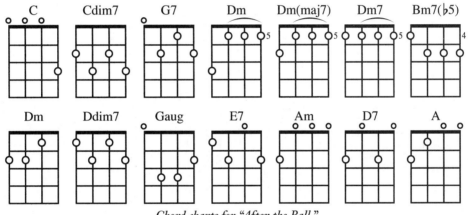

Chord charts for "After the Ball."

As with the songs you have previously worked on, take time to practice playing each chord. Go through the song's arrangement and write out in what order the chords appear to help you practice making changes. Also make note of the arrangement's rhythm, which is identical to "3/4 strumming sample C" from Example 2 (seen earlier in this chapter) in terms of its rhythm, although it uses all four strings for each chord.

Listen to the song on the CD to get a good feel for the rhythm and the strumming. You might prefer to start practicing the many chord changes by strumming just one single chord per measure or strum three quarter notes, and that is perfectly fine. After you get going, though, you probably won't be able to keep yourself from trying to spice up your strumming a bit.

Remember that you don't have to (nor should you!) play the same strum throughout the entire song, even though I do on the CD—or I tried to when I was recording it!

Okay! Take a deep breath and relax and give it a go.

Track 24

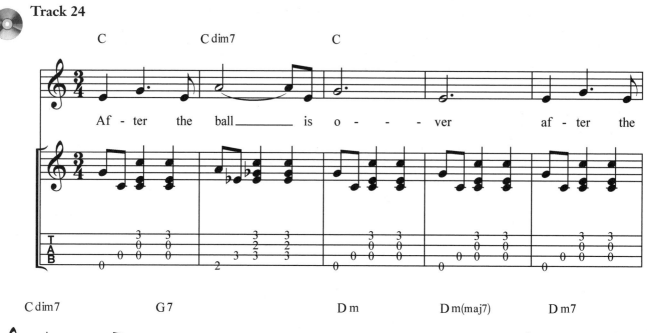

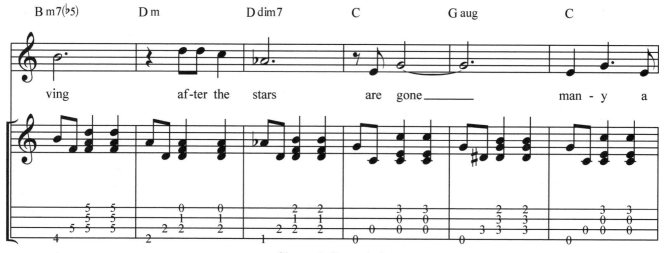

Chapter 8, Example 3.

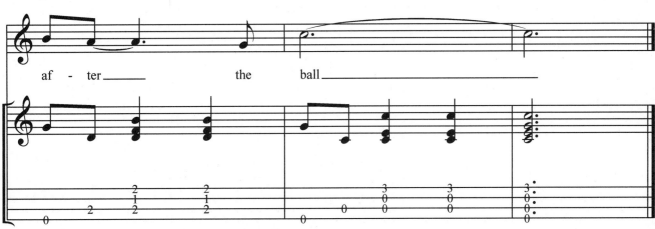

Practice, Practice

With the knowledge you have gained in this chapter, you can now figure out practically any chord you will ever come across playing the ukulele.

Notice, though, that I said *figure out* and not *play* practically any chord. Why? Because you still have to practice playing them. Simply knowing a chord form doesn't translate into playing it perfectly whenever it should pop up in a song.

The discussion at the end of Chapter 7 applies doubly so here. The best and fastest way to become adept at playing any chord is to use it as often as possible in your playing. Although this might seem silly for specific chords you rarely play, like E♭ or G♯, for instance, it is totally possible in terms of chord shapes. If you think about it, you now know two or three different fingerings of all the basic chords you have learned. Go back and play some of your two-chord songs using only closed position chords. Then try mixing it up—if the song has C and G7, for example, use an open position C to start with and then a closed position G7, then a closed position C, and then an open position G7.

I can't stress enough that you can't possibly spend enough time working on forming and changing chords. Believe it or not, at this point in your learning, you are only practice time away from sitting in with others and performing songs. You have got the basics. Everything else you learn from here on out is going to make you sound like you have been playing for a much longer time than you actually have been!

The Least You Need to Know

- 6th, 7th, and other embellished chords are made by adding notes to the root, 3rd, and 5th of any of the four basic chords.
- Open position chords use open strings. Closed position chords have each of the four strings fretted.
- Closed position chords and barre chords can be moved virtually anywhere on your ukulele's fretboard.
- A song with a 3/4 time signature has three beats per measure.
- Practice every chord you learn whenever possible, even the less frequently used ones.

Expanding Your Horizons

Congratulations! With your ability to strum and play chords (and to figure out chords you might not totally know) you can now call yourself a ukulele player. You can strum along to any song for which you can find the chords, either playing to back up your own singing or to be a part of a group. You are now ready to start working on some techniques that will help you sound like you have been playing the ukulele for a lot longer than you have!

In this part you will add texture and depth to your strumming skills with syncopation, rhythm shuffles, muted strokes, rolling arpeggios, and double stops. You will discover how to create slurs—hammer-ons, pull-offs, slides, and bends—and how to incorporate them into your rhythm playing.

Additionally, you will learn how to play your ukulele in the finger-style manner and get a taste of the world of alternative tunings—which gives you the ability to explore infinite creative musical possibilities with your instrument.

You will also get a quick and easy tutorial on transposing, which will allow you to pick up the baritone ukulele with as much ease as you now play your soprano, concert, or tenor uke. Your playing is going to improve so much over the next few chapters that you will amaze yourself as well as your friends.

Swing Time—Adding Further Depth to Strumming

Chapter 9

In This Chapter

* Adding syncopation to strumming
* Using anticipations with chord changes
* Reading and strumming triplets
* Understanding swing
* Playing the blues shuffle

Here is a little secret: quite often the big difference between a beginning ukulele player and someone who sounds like he has been playing a while is that the latter has more interesting ways to strum or change chords. The basic skill set is essentially the same, but the not-quite-beginner can do a magical technique or two, which the neophyte hasn't yet learned. Somehow it makes the player seem more naturally musical, and that is where you are headed, starting right now.

A big part of becoming more naturally musical is getting comfortable playing your ukulele. As a beginner, it is easy to get tense and tight when playing and, not surprisingly, the tension makes your music seem tentative. But with every strum or chord change you practice, you should be feeling more at ease with your instrument. Your chords will flow more smoothly into one another and your rhythm will sound more organic and less rigid.

While keeping a steady beat is an important part of playing music, it is also important that the music sounds like it has a pulse of its own. Two easy ways to get your music flowing more organically is to start strumming with a bit of syncopation and swing.

Syncopation

Up until now, all your strumming has been either in quarter notes or eighth notes. And for the moment, that is not going to change. What is also not going to change is how you keep your wrist and fingers going in a steady down-and-up motion that acts as your steady, time-keeping metronome. What is going to change is that you are going to inject a whimsical sense of play into your strumming through *syncopation*.

Simply put, syncopation is when you accent a note (or a chord) at a time other than when it is expected. When you strum, you probably tend to emphasize either the first and third beat of any given measure (assuming the song is in 4/4 time) or the second and fourth beats. Listen to this strum (which you have played before) as well as the count of the beats:

Track 25 (0:00)

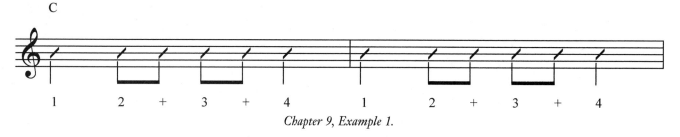

Chapter 9, Example 1.

You can hear how steady and even the beat is and how the down beats, the "one, two, three, four" of the count, are accented with the "one" and the "three" being stressed slightly harder than the "two" and the "four." Pick up your ukulele and give this strumming rhythm a try. It should seem like an old friend by now!

Skipping the Downstroke

Now let's alter this strum just a little. In the following example, you play everything just as you did last time except you are *not* going to strike the strings when you make the downstroke on the third beat. Here we go:

Track 25 (0:14)

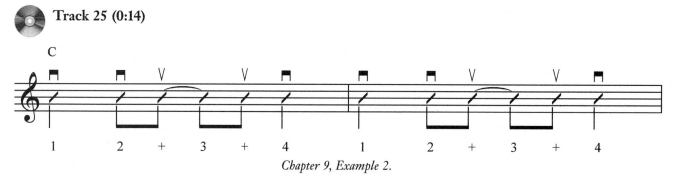

Chapter 9, Example 2.

Isn't it wild how much more musical it sounds? By taking out the downstroke on the third beat, you have shifted the accent of the strumming to both the upstroke between the second and third beats and the upstroke between the third and fourth beats. This is syncopation. It is the first step of your journey to not being a beginner ukulele player.

Getting Syncopation into Your Fingers

Like everything else you have learned, getting comfortable with strumming syncopated rhythms takes practice and repetition. Luckily for you, we have a song ready for you to practice with. Better still, to help you focus on your strumming, the song has only two chords:

 Track 26

Chapter 9, Example 3.

You need to go through the same preparatory steps here as you did for the songs in Chapters 5–8 of this book. Play each single chord in this new syncopated strumming to ensure you have the rhythm down cold. Next, try keeping the strumming going while making the chord change from C to G. When you are confident you can handle both the rhythm and making the chord change while keeping the rhythm steady, then try the song and see how it goes.

SMOOTH STRUMMING

If you have made a point of following the steps used to prepare you for the earlier songs in Part 2 of this book, you should, at this point, find it takes less time to work through each step. This is not because you have magically gotten better; it is because you are becoming a better player by having done a lot of work to get this far!

This syncopated strum you have just learned is, of course, one of many possible strums. Here are some more to try:

Track 27

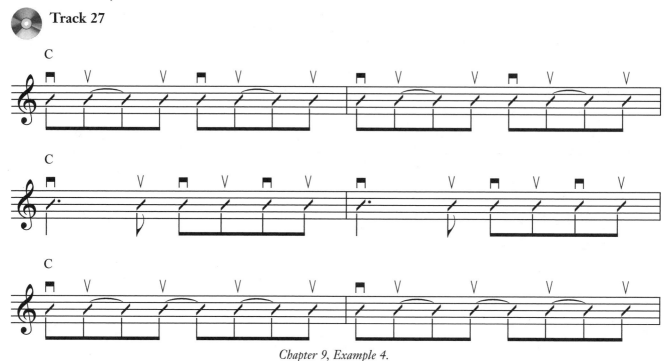

Chapter 9, Example 4.

Try the new strums with "He's Got the Whole World in His Hands" as well as some (or all) of your previous songs. Remember that none of these will work with "After the Ball" because the song is in 3/4 time.

Anticipations

Now that you have a feel for creating syncopation, you can take on anticipations. Have you ever heard Neil Young's song "Heart of Gold," in which it sounds like the chords and melody speed up even though the beat is keeping steady? Appropriately with this song, this occurs wherever he sings *gold* in the *heart of gold* phrase. (This song is not included on your CD, but try to find a copy or buy a download of it from the internet so you can hear this example of anticipation.) If you listen closely, you will hear both the word *gold* and the accompanying chord change come in a half beat ahead of where you think they should occur. This seeming hiccup in rhythm gives you the feeling the song is picking up speed when it is really still maintaining an even beat. In music, this is called *anticipation*.

Anticipation is used in songs of all styles and genres, so it is important to understand how it works and how to create it with your own strumming. Fortunately, you already have the tools at hand! Take a moment and review Example 1 in this chapter, which we will use to create a musical anticipation.

Catching Chords on the Upstroke

Using Example 1, we are going to rework it using the two chords you first learned, C and Am, playing each for two measures like this:

Track 28 (0:00)

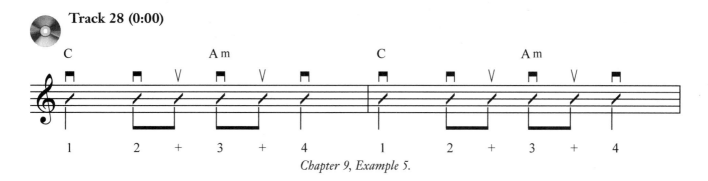

Chapter 9, Example 5.

Here you are playing the C on the first two beats and then changing to Am for the third and fourth beats. To create a musical anticipation, you need to change to the Am on the offbeat before the third beat. That is the *and* between the *2* and the *3* if you are counting out loud. It also means you are making the chord change *on the upstroke* instead of on the downstroke, as demonstrated in the following example:

Track 28 (0:16)

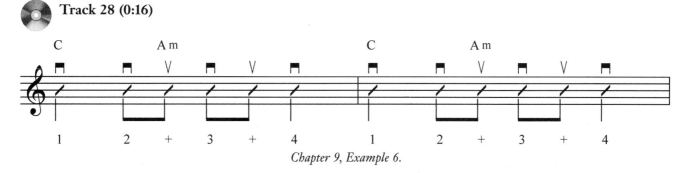

Chapter 9, Example 6.

You should play this last example slowly at first and be sure to count it out loud if you are having trouble. When you feel you have it down pretty well, take the next step and add the anticipation to a basic syncopated beat, such as the one you learned in Example 2 in this chapter:

Track 29 (0:00)

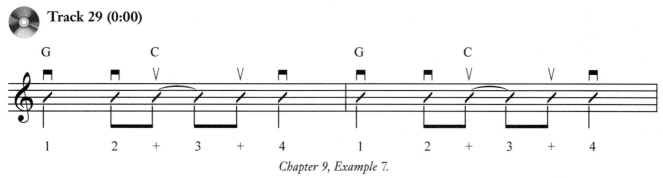

Chapter 9, Example 7.

FRET LESS!

The secret to playing anticipations smoothly is not to worry about your strumming. If you can confidently keep your down and up stroke steady, whether you are hitting the strings or not, then all you have to do is concentrate on making the chord change at a different point. This is why you should work hard at keeping your strumming strokes constant and even.

When you have the rhythm of the last example down, try changing up where the anticipation takes place or even add a second one. The following example uses a rhythm you can hear in a song like "Three Marlenas," by the Wallflowers. It also makes a clever use of the C6 chord, which is played by using all the open strings:

Track 29 (0:14)

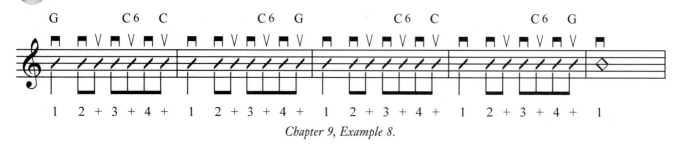

Chapter 9, Example 8.

On this example, you let the open strings of the C6 chord buy you time to make the change from G to C. On the upbeat between the second and third beat, remove your fingers from the neck and catch the open strings on an upstroke. Then get your finger ready to play the C chord on the upbeat between beats three and four. Count this out slowly at first, as you have with your other rhythm strums. After you get it into your hands, you will be pleasantly surprised at how naturally strumming this way feels and sounds.

You can use anticipations for almost every chord change you make, but you should listen to just how it affects the mood and feel of whatever song you are playing. Pay attention to how anticipation is used in the songs you know, and see whether you can pick them out in the rhythms and vocal lines. Sometimes everyone in the band participates on any single anticipation, and sometimes it is just one instrument (usually the rhythm guitar or bass) or the singer.

A New Way to Bring Back Bonnie

Remember it takes practice! Following is a very different arrangement of a familiar song to assist you.

As always, be sure to try using anticipations in the songs you have learned up to this point. It will not work in every song, so part of your practice is listening and determining when a song could involve using anticipation in its strumming rhythm.

Track 30

Chapter 9, Example 9.

continues

continued

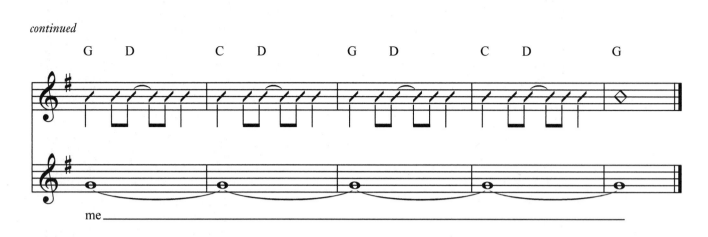

me

Triplets and Swing

It bears repeating: the ukulele is first and foremost a rhythm instrument. Being able to hear and to count out rhythms is essential to all uke players (and to all musicians, for that matter!) because even simple musical rhythms can sometimes be deceptive.

Take two Beach Boys songs—"Fun Fun Fun" and "Wouldn't It Be Nice"; both songs are in 4/4 time and are played at similar tempos, but each song has a different rhythmic feel. There is a driving beat to "Fun Fun Fun" that propels the song forward, while the rhythm of "Wouldn't It Be Nice" has a bit of a loping gait to it, even though the overall tempo of the song is fairly quick. "Wouldn't It Be Nice" almost seems to be limping or shuffling along.

The difference is what is called *swing*, and it is used across most musical genres. You should add swing rhythms to your ukulele playing. Fortunately, to play them is as easy as counting to three because swing comes from beats that are divided into thirds, called *triplets*.

You have already learned about eighth notes, which divide a beat into half. Triplets divide a beat into thirds and look exactly like eighth notes except they are bracketed together in sets of three and have a small "3" written above or below the connected flags, like this:

Triplets in standard notation

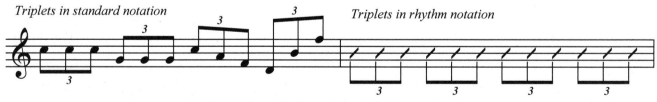

Triplets in rhythm notation

Triplets in standard notation and rhythm notation.

DEFINITION

A **triplet** divides a beat, or another unit of rhythmic time, into three even parts. There are different types of triplets; eighth note triplets are the most common ones. They divide a single beat evenly into thirds. Sixteenth note triplets divide a half beat into three even parts, and quarter note triplets divide two beats (a half note) into three evenly spaced (rhythm-wise, that is) notes.

Strumming Triplets

Triplets divide a beat into identical thirds, and strumming them takes a bit of practice. The following example demonstrates how to play and count triplets. As you will hear on the track, you should count out loud "one and ah two and ah three and ah four and ah."

 Track 31 (0:00)

Chapter 9, Example 10.

Most uke players strum triplets in one of two ways. You can go with a constant down and up strum or use a down, up, down strum for each beat in the triplet. The latter method gives the triplet a strong downstroke for each beat and can make it easier to keep track of the overall rhythm. But you also have to develop a slight hiccup in your strum because of the quick upstroke you have to make between the downstroke of any "ah" and the downstroke that starts the following beat.

Despite that little hiccup, you will find most ukulele players use this second approach. Ultimately, you should use whichever strumming method best helps you keep the rhythm smooth and even.

Making Eighth Notes Swing

Understanding triplets is essential to getting a handle on playing swing rhythms. You create a swing rhythm by playing just the first and third parts of a triplet. In other words, if you were playing while counting out loud, you would be strumming only on the beat (number) and the "ah" of any given beat, like this: "One and ah two and ah three and ah four and ah." Here is an example demonstrating the difference between straight eighth notes and eighth notes played in swing rhythm:

Track 31 (0:15)

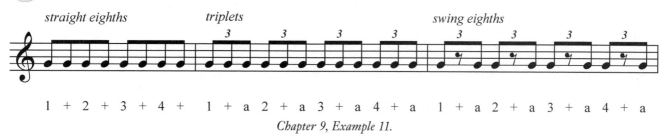

Chapter 9, Example 11.

Like triplets, you can play swing eighths in either a down and up strum or with all downstrokes. Depending on what the music calls for, you will probably find yourself using both at some point, so it is good to practice both ways.

In music notation, swing rhythms are often indicated by the following equation, which is placed at the start of a piece of music:

How swing rhythm appears in music notation.

In this example, you see two eighth notes written to one side of an equal sign (=) and a triplet on the other side. Instead of the triplet being a set of three eighth notes joined together, it has one quarter note and one eighth note. This indicates that you need to just play the first and last of the set of triplets. Some music indicates swing by posting only the notes and the equal sign, without the "Swing!", so you should be careful when you look at a piece of music to not miss it.

 FRET LESS!

Tablature (for ukulele or guitar) rarely, if ever, indicates whether a song is supposed to be played in swing eighths. It is up to you to develop your ear so you can pick out when a swing rhythm is used in a song.

Adding Swinging to Your Strumming

Because swing rhythms are used in many songs, it's good to get used to playing the various eighth note strums that you already know in swing eighths. The following example is a strum you learned in Chapter 7 done in swing. Notice the equation at the top of the example. It has two eighth notes written to one side of an equal sign (=) and a triplet on the other side. Instead of the triplet being a set of three eighth notes joined together, it has one quarter note and one eighth note. This indicates you want to play in swing eighths, that is, playing the first and last of the set of triplets.

 Track 31 (0:36)

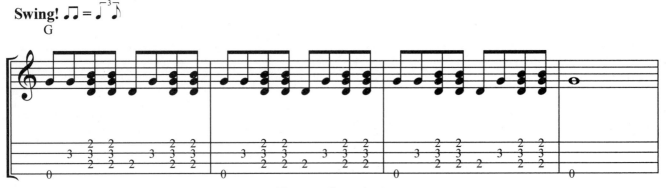

Chapter 9, Example 12.

To give you more practice with swing, not to mention using it with a variety of chords, here is an arrangement of the traditional song, "Red River Valley" to play:

Track 32

Chapter 9, Example 13.

continues

continued

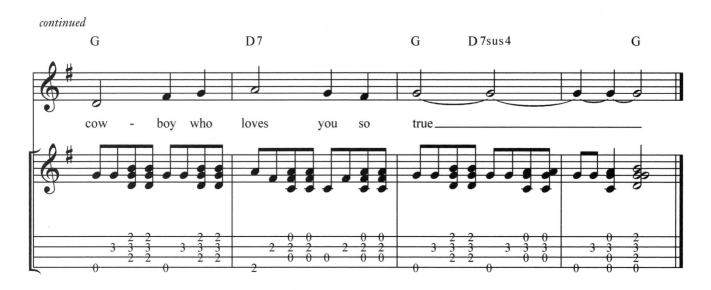

Do the Shuffle!

Swing rhythms are sometimes called "shuffle rhythms" or "blues rhythms." You can certainly imagine someone shuffling along whenever you hear that loping, uneven yet steady rhythm.

A shuffle also refers to a specific musical technique. It is a special pattern of notes used as part of that rhythm. These notes can be played singly, in pairs on adjacent strings (also called double stops), or as parts of chords. Many musicians refer to this special pattern as a "blues shuffle."

To get you started, here is a simple shuffle, played on the g and C strings:

Track 33

Chapter 9, Example 14.

Shuffles can also be played with full, four-string chords. In our next song, an arrangement of the traditional blues tune, "Alberta," you'll be using the following chords:

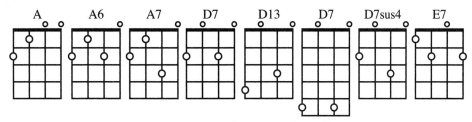

Chords to practice for chord-style shuffle.

To prep for playing "Alberta," practice shifting from A to A6 to A7 and back to A6, using one beat for each chord. When you feel comfortable with that chord progression, tackle the D7 to D13 to the fifth fret version of D7 and back to D13. The easiest way to do this is to use your middle finger for all the notes on the g string. When the accompanying note on the E string is on the same fret, play it with your ring finger. When the note on the E string is one fret away (as in the D13), use your index finger to play it.

As always, practice this slowly at first and work your way up to speed. Before you know it, you'll be playing "Alberta" along with the CD.

Chapter 9, Example 15.

Practice, Practice

If you have not caught on by now, rhythm is probably the most important part of playing ukulele. And rhythm essentially is keeping count. You have done a great job working through simple strumming and gradually getting into more complex rhythms. It is important to remember that it probably took a fair amount of practice to get to this point. As long as you can keep the count in your head, there are few rhythms you won't be able to handle with some practice.

Ideally, you should be able to call up any strum you can hear in your head, whenever you want to, and be able to do so without disrupting the beat. To do this, you need to have many strums at your beck and call, which means practicing each one to the point you can pretty much play any specific one without thinking. This way the rhythm simply flows out of you through your strumming.

There are several ways of getting to this point in your playing. Obviously, the first one (and the one on which you are currently focusing) is to play and practice various rhythms and strumming on your ukulele. But you also can make huge leaps forward by getting more involved with rhythm and strumming even when you are nowhere near your uke. You can do this by actively listening to music.

When you listen to music, make a point of paying attention to the rhythms you hear. If you are able to, use your strumming hand and tap out how you would strum along with it. Start by doing something simple, such as tapping out quarter notes (one per beat), and then add eighth notes to your tapping.

If you are doing well at keeping the rhythm steady and true, experiment with adding syncopation to your tapping. Use whichever song you are listening to as your guide. You might find it easier to "air strum" or to strum your hand lightly against your leg to mimic the up and down of actual strumming.

During the normal course of the day you can often find a lot of chances to get in some strumming practice just by listening to music and strumming along. Make the most of those opportunities, and the next time you pick up your uke you will probably find your rhythm is better than you remember it.

The Least You Need to Know

- Syncopation makes strumming sound more musical.
- Anticipations are playing the chord change on the offbeat.
- Swing rhythm is built on the use of triplets.
- Blues shuffles are played with swing rhythm.
- You can, and should, practice rhythm and strumming when you are listening to music and not playing your ukulele.

Chapter 10

Fantastic Finger Picking

In This Chapter

* Preparing to finger pick
* Learning some basic finger-picking patterns
* Making pattern variations
* Adding pinches to picking
* Creating exotic picking through open strings

Most ukulele players never use a pick to strum the strings. Yet while they might strum with their fingers, many uke players (especially beginners) tend to shy away from playing in a finger-style or finger-picking manner. In finger-style playing, you pick the individual strings, sometimes singularly and sometimes two or three in tandem, rather than strumming two, three, or four strings at a time.

But playing finger style allows you to explore more of your ukulele's potential. Instead of chunking out chords, you can provide harp-like *arpeggios*—a chord played one note at a time, usually on separate strings. This might accompany a singer or weave mesmerizing patterns of notes, which entrance your listener (not to mention yourself!). Finger picking also allows you to turn your uke into a small musical combo, playing melody and accompaniment at the same time. This is the basis of chord-melody style, which you will learn more about in Chapter 15.

 DEFINITION

Arpeggio comes from the Italian *arpeggio,* which means "to play on a harp." An arpeggio is a chord which is played one distinct note at a time, as opposed to strumming all four strings at once.

Usually arpeggios are played in a specific sequence, with the notes all ascending or descending, but the ukulele's re-entrant tuning (and the fact that it has only four strings) often creates arpeggios that change direction rather rapidly. Arpeggios on the ukulele tend to be played as individual strings picked in specific sequences.

Don't worry about finger-style playing being too complicated for a beginner to do. You probably don't know it, but you have already worked through the basics of finger picking back in Chapter 7 when you learned "Polly Wolly Doodle." Between your "alternate-finger-flicking-all-eighth-note strum" (I bet you never thought you would see that phrase again!) and the sense of syncopation you picked up in the last chapter, you have everything you need to become comfortable with finger picking except for some specific instruction for your fingers and the necessary practice. So let's get going on making your ukulele even more expressive than you imagined it could be.

Finding Your Fingers

Some uke players finger pick using only their thumb and index finger; some use their thumb, index, and middle fingers; and some manage to pick with their thumb, index, middle, and ring fingers. And then there are some who use different combinations depending on which song they are playing.

Picking single strings of the ukulele with your fingers sounds simple enough, but it might take a bit of trial-and-error to find which fingers, on which strings, will be most comfortable for you. The small size of the instrument as well as the relatively small spacing between the strings makes finger picking seem a bit daunting at first, especially if you have big fingers.

Shake out your strumming hand and get as relaxed and comfortable as possible. Then place your uke face up on your right leg if you are sitting (on your left leg if you play left-handed) or even on a table or flat surface. Gently place your strumming hand on the surface with the pad of your thumb against the outer edge of the g string and the pad of your ring finger curled against the outer edge of the A string. You should be able to place the tip of your index finger between the C and E strings and the tip of your middle finger between the E and A strings. Try to keep your fingers in place as you grab the neck with your fretting hand, then reposition the ukulele, as you would normally play it.

When you have done this, you should find your strumming thumb is both parallel and in contact with the g string. You need to keep the thumb extended, allowing the fingers to pick inward toward your palm so your thumb and fingers aren't colliding together when you are finger picking.

SMOOTH STRUMMING

Some players place their pinky finger on the face of their ukuleles, just below the A string, to serve as an anchor, which gives them a sense of placement security in terms of where their fingers are in relation to the strings. It is a personal choice, although it is good to be able to play without an anchor should you need to. There will probably be times when you need to combine strumming and picking, and being anchored could hinder strumming movement.

Many ukulele players feel picking the uke's strings with one's nails provides the best possible sound, while others use the pads of their fingers to play. Both methods produce great sounds; it is purely a personal choice.

FRET LESS!

If you are finger picking the ukulele with your nails, they need to be just long enough to catch and pick the string. If they are too long, they are likely to snag on the string and eventually break (the nail, that is, but also possibly the string). If nails are your thing, be prepared to devote some time to trimming, filing, and shaping them for playing.

"Outside-In" Picking

You have only four fingers and a thumb, and you will probably never use your pinky to finger pick, but there are still all sorts of possible combinations when it comes to choosing which fingers to use. Because you have some experience involving your thumb and index finger as part of your strumming, start by reviewing the alternating bass strum for C from Chapter 7, but this time use your thumb on every beat and strum the rest of the chord on the offbeat:

Track 35 (0:00)

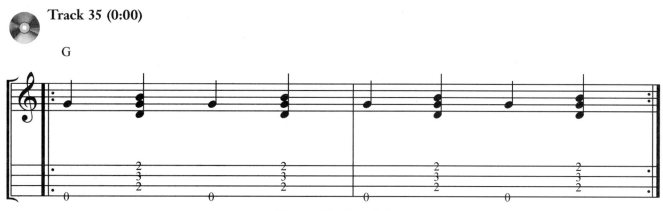

Chapter 10, Example 1.

Then take out the strumming of the chord. You will be using your thumb to pick four quarter notes, like this:

Track 35 (0:20)

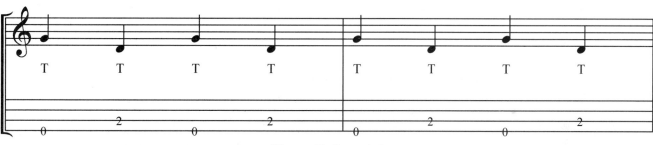

Chapter 10, Example 2.

So far, so good! All you are doing at this point is simply counting out the beat with your thumb (which is labeled *T* in the tablature). Now it is time to add your fingers to the mix. In the following example, you will play the A string (where your finger is fretting the third string) on the offbeat between the first and second beat with your middle finger (labeled *m* on the tablature) and the open E string with your index finger (labeled *i*) on the offbeat between the second and third beats. Then you will repeat the whole process for the third and fourth beats:

Track 35 (0:32)

Chapter 10, Example 3.

That was fun, wasn't it? And it sounds great, so congratulations on becoming a finger picker! Some people think of this as the *outside-in* picking pattern because you play the outer strings first and then the inner ones. But please don't get too hung up on naming various picking patterns. You will soon see naming them isn't as important as playing them!

SMOOTH STRUMMING

Limiting all finger movement to a minimum is essential to good finger picking. Keep your fingers close to the strings even when they are not being used to play.

Of course, picking a pattern such as this is just the first step. You also need to be able to change chords while picking. After you have played the last example smoothly and evenly and feel like you can do it on autopilot, give this next example a try:

Track 36

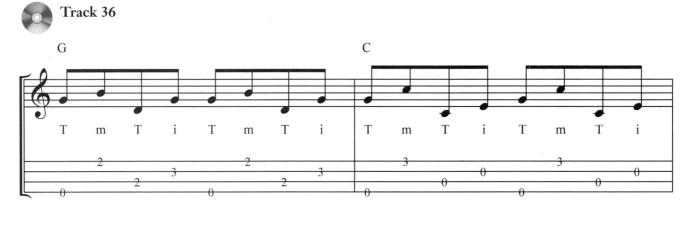

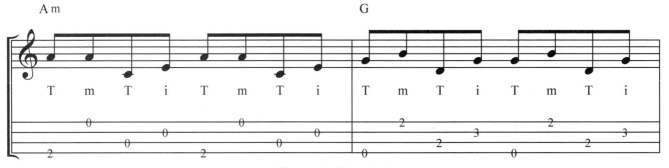

Chapter 10, Example 4.

This is the same picking, but now you are adding chord changes to the mix. Just as when you were adding chord changes to your strumming, you should play at as slow a tempo as necessary to make the chord changes on the correct beat. Because of all the practice you have already had at this, you will probably find yourself making quick progress. But if not, don't worry—you will get it soon enough as long as you keep practicing.

More Picking with More Fingers

Here is a slight variation on the last example. Your thumb plays the exact same strings on the same beats, but you reverse the order of the strings played by your fingers:

Track 37 (0:00)

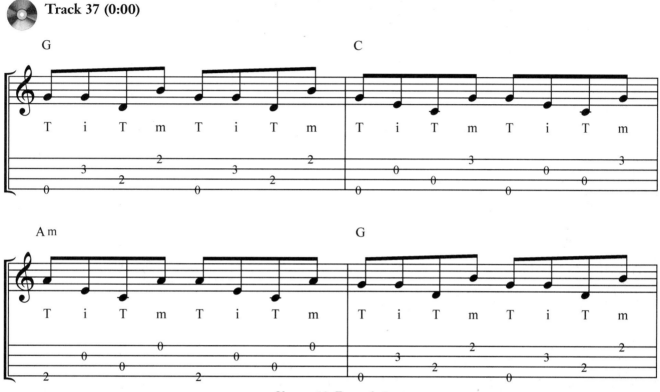

Chapter 10, Example 5.

Although this last example uses the same G — C — Am — G chord progression as the previous one, you might find it best to work through the picking one chord at a time until you feel you have your picking pretty solid.

FRET LESS!

As soon as possible, do your best not to watch your fingers pick the strings. Initially you won't be able to help yourself, but the sooner you can go without looking at either hand, the sooner you will start to develop the feel and awareness of your uke's strings that is needed to become a confident performer.

When you feel good about the last example, try both of the following picking patterns. These add the ring finger (labeled "r" in the tablature) to the mix:

Track 37 (0:16)

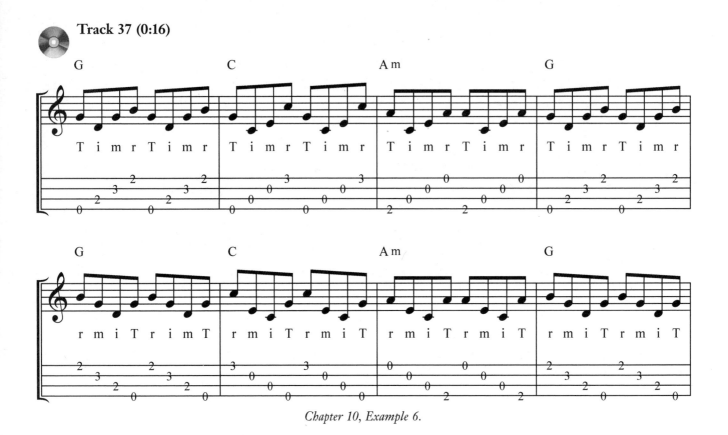

Chapter 10, Example 6.

These might prove a little tricky, especially if you have large fingers. Don't be shy about trying other options, such as using your thumb for the first three notes and then the index finger (or the middle finger) for the fourth in Pattern A. Treat the finger suggestions as serious suggestions, but feel free to experiment.

The Trap of Picking

It is actually a little frightening how quickly one's fingers can adapt to finger-style playing without much practice. Forgive the pun, but it takes surprisingly little time for most fingers to pick up a pattern.

This seeming gift, however, is also a big stumbling block when it comes to playing. Just as you shouldn't strum a rhythm the same exact way repeatedly throughout a song, you shouldn't have your picking sound robotic and invariable either. Also, in some ways, it is harder to get into the habit of adding a bit of variety to your finger picking than it is to your strumming.

You will be getting some big time tips on this in Chapter 11, but in the meantime here are some helpful tips you can get started with immediately.

Varying Rhythms

Just like your earliest attempts at strumming, you are initially bound to think of finger-picking patterns solely in terms of eighth notes. But don't mistake having a lot of notes for being musical. Playing a continuous stream of even eighth notes is boring for both you and your audience.

Making variations in the rhythmic value of notes, such as adding quarter notes and even the occasional half note to a pattern, can give your picking some breathing space, as you can hear in the following examples:

Track 38

Chapter 10, Example 7.

Changing On-the-Fly

As you learn more and more picking patterns, you need to get into the habit of changing from one pattern you have learned to others you have already learned. Being able to shift from one pattern to a rhythmic variation of that pattern to a totally different pattern makes your music much more interesting.

In the following example, three different picking patterns are used:

 Track 39

Chapter 10, Example 8.

The first two patterns (Pattern 1 in the first measure and Pattern 2 in the second) are fairly similar, but alternating them makes the piece seem more of a song than an exercise. And you can hear that even though Pattern 3 (which begins in the fifth measure) is radically different, it still feels like part of the whole piece and not something that was simply added on.

Play this example slowly enough to transition smoothly from one pattern to the other, particularly the shift from Pattern 1 to Pattern 3. It will take some practice (and you are going to flub up), but after you get the picking into your fingers you will be able to switch between the patterns without thinking, which is the goal.

The Pinch and the Pedal

This next finger-picking technique is called a pinch. Instead of playing a single note at a time, you are going to play pairs of notes, using one finger (or your thumb) to play each individual note.

Take a look at this exercise:

🔘 **Track 40**

Chapter 10, Example 9.

The first pair of notes are the F note (first fret of the E string) and the A note found at the second fret of the g string. You are going to play both notes simultaneously by picking the A note (on the g string) with your thumb using a downward motion while, at the same time, picking the F note (on the E string) with your middle finger, using an upward motion. Be careful not to hit the open C string with either your thumb or your middle finger. That is because you will play the open C string next, using your index finger. Keep your fingers fretting the strings on their tips so all the notes, the pinched pair as well as the open C string, ring out as long as possible.

> **FRET LESS!**
>
> Whenever possible, you need the fingers of your fretting hand to keep close to constant contact with the strings. In other words, don't move a finger from the note it's on until you absolutely have to. This will help keep the note ringing and allow you to cut down on unwanted string noise from unintentionally picked strings.

In addition to the pinch, this exercise introduces you to the concept of a *pedal point*, which is also called a *pedal note* or a *pedal tone*. A pedal tone is a repeated note that stays constant while other single notes, pairs of notes, or even chords are changing around it. It is usually played every other note when it occurs, serving as a tonal anchor for the notes or pairs of notes which play against it.

> **DEFINITION**
>
> A **pedal point** or **pedal tone** is a note that is played steadily over a period of time (usually a measure or more), alternating with other single notes and chords. It serves as a focal point for the other notes and chords, often creating interesting harmonies.

This pinch-and-pedal technique is an excellent way to bring a new voice to your ukulele. With it, you can create accompaniments that remind the listener of a piano or keyboard and works exceptionally well with chord-melody-style playing, which you will read about in Chapter 15.

The Real Beauty of Finger Style

Finger-style playing takes on new dimensions when you combine finger picking with the unique tuning of the ukulele and your knowledge of embellished chords to create truly striking and memorable picking patterns. Sometimes you can create exciting picking by removing a single finger from your chord to take advantage of the note of the open string or by adding one extra note to the chord.

Here is an example of how you can really spice up your finger picking:

Track 41

Chapter 10, Example 10.

This is essentially the first chord change you learned—C to Am—with the D note (the second fret of the C string) added to both chords. If you were to set your fingers in place and strum these two embellished chords, the result would sound very muddy and dissonant. But when played finger style, you get an exotic feel from the chords.

The next example is an arrangement of "What Child Is This," which you may recognize as the melody of the traditional ballad "Greensleeves." It incorporates a number of chord alterations as part of the picking pattern.

You should first work through it measure by measure and then line by line, making sure you are comfortable with all the picking before moving on. As always, start at a reasonable pace to ensure you make the fretting changes smoothly.

Track 42

Chapter 10, Example 11.

Track 42

Chapter 10, Example 11.

continues

continued

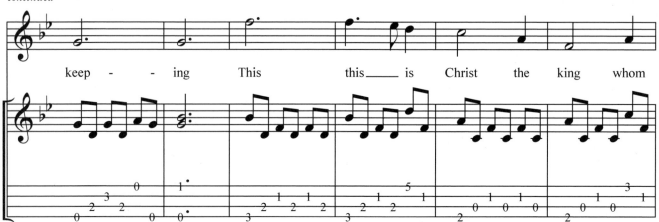

keep - - ing   This   this ____ is   Christ   the   king   whom

shep - herds   guard ____ and   an - gels   sing   haste   haste ____ to

bring   him   laud   the   babe ____ the   son ____ of   Mar - - y

Practice, Practice

When practicing finger picking, first focus on the pattern your right-hand fingers will play to get the picking itself on autopilot. Start with a single chord and just pick and pick until you have your fingers doing exactly what you want. Only then should you start mixing in the chord changes.

Your long-term goal with finger picking is the same one you have for strumming—to have so many picking options contained in your fingers that you are able to change patterns almost without thinking as you play a song. Doing this requires that you learn whatever patterns you can, but you must also work at varying your picking patterns. It is all too easy to get hooked on one and never change from it, so you have to make a point of keeping your fingers on their toes, so to speak.

UKE LORE

The key to ukulele virtuoso Jake Shimabukuro's playing lies with his fingers and his belief that it's possible to come up with arrangements for any song on a ukulele. Whether he's playing a Beatles' classic like "While My Guitar Gently Weeps," a bit of Paganini, or his own iconic arrangement of Queen's "Bohemian Rhapsody," Jake is always demonstrating how fun and how versatile the ukulele can be.

You should do a lot of experimenting and embellishing on your own to create your own finger style. With the basic knowledge of finger picking you gained in this chapter, coupled with the slur techniques you will learn in the next chapter, you will find you have whole worlds of finger picking to explore and have fun with.

The Least You Need to Know

- Finger style adds even more possibilities to the music you can make with your ukulele.
- There are different styles and techniques of finger picking—there is no one singular way to do it.
- Good uke players often change finger-picking patterns, styles, and techniques seamlessly in the course of playing a single song.
- Pinching two notes at once creates instant harmony.
- Combining finger picking with open strings can create striking and memorable patterns.

Super Slurs

In This Chapter

- Using hammer-ons and pull-offs
- Adding slurs to strumming and finger-style rhythms
- The art of the slide
- Using your ear to perform string bends
- How to practice your slurs

So far, your fretting hand and strumming hand have been working as a team to produce any single note. Your left hand frets the note on the fretboard, while your right hand picks the string. Each hand has its respective task and things go nice and smoothly. Notes played this way are called *articulated* notes.

Of course, as you might have guessed, there are other ways to create notes on your ukulele, too. The most common non-articulated notes are called *slurs*. On the uke, slurred notes are made by one of four special techniques—hammer-ons, pull-offs, slides, and bends. These are manufactured by the left hand on the fingerboard without the assistance of picking by the right hand.

DEFINITION

For the ukulele player, **slurs** are notes produced by a means other than picking the string, usually by the use of the fretting hand to create the note on the fretboard of the uke. The four basic types of slurs are hammer-ons, pull-offs, slides, and bends.

Because slurs usually involve individual notes rather than chords, you won't find any slurs in rhythm notation. Or you shouldn't! In ukulele tablature and standard notation, slurs are indicated by the same arc used to tie notes together (see Chapter 4). They are easily differentiated in that notes linked together in a tie are the same note (sharing the same line or space on the staff) whereas those linked together in a slur are different notes.

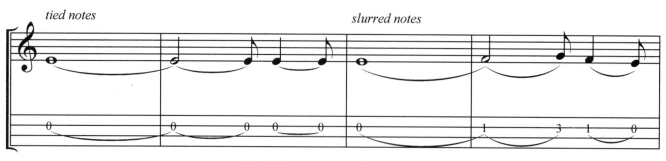

The difference between ties and slurs.

Hammer-Ons and Pull-Offs

Playing each of the four ukulele slurs is simply a matter of following the instructions of the name of the slur. To play a hammer-on, you "hammer" a finger of your left hand "on" to a specific fret of a specific string *after* you have already picked that string with your right hand.

In the following example, you first pick the open A string and then hammer a finger (use your ring finger to start with) onto the third fret of the A string.

Track 43 (0:00)

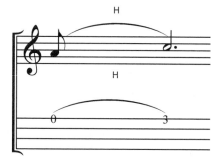

Chapter 11, Example 1.

Start by placing your ring finger on the third fret of the A string, as you would when playing the C chord. Then raise it slightly off the string, between a quarter-inch and a half-inch.

Now pick the A string; then hammer the tip of your ring finger back onto the third fret. Make good contact and keep contact with the fretboard after you've hit the string. The "hammer," the contact of the finger with the string, creates the second note (C at the second fret of the A string) that you hear without you having to pick the string a second time.

Initially your hammer-ons may not sound as strong and clear as those on the CD. That's to be expected because you've not used your fingers in this manner before. Remember that even though you need enough finger strength to sound the hammered note cleanly and clearly, you still need to keep your fingers fairly close to the strings. This will be difficult at first—your tendency will be to pull your fingers back to seemingly strengthen the hammer. But as you gain both finger strength and confidence, it will get easier to keep your finger close to the string. You also want to keep your finger on the fret of the neck where you've hammered. Don't just pull your finger off after making the strike on the string, keeping in contact makes the note ring out.

A Sack of Hammers

As you gain experience and confidence in your ability to hammer, you will be able to perform the technique fret-to-fret, or multiple hammers, as done in the following example:

 Track 43 (0:05)

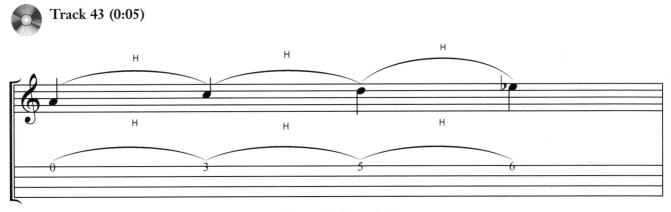

Chapter 11, Example 2.

The simple trick to playing multiple hammers is to keep the finger fretting the first note on the string when hammering with the next finger and then keeping that finger in place while doing a third hammer. In this last example, use your index finger for the first hammer-on, keeping it in place while using your ring finger for the second hammer-on and then your pinky for the third.

Pull-Offs

If we were talking physics, the pull-off might be the equal and opposite reaction to the hammer-on. A pull-off is fretting a note with a finger on your left hand and then, after picking the string with your right hand, pulling your left-hand finger off the string, sounding the note of the open string.

 Track 43 (0:11)

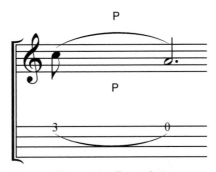

Chapter 11, Example 3.

How you take your finger off the string is essential to this technique. It's called a *pull-off* and not a *lift-off* for a reason! Merely lifting the finger from the string will not result in much sound. You need to *pull* your finger off the string, using a slight sideways tug and release on the string as the finger lifts off. Your fingertip pulls the string and then releases it, essentially picking the string again for you. This "pick from the pull" makes the second note sound without your right hand having to pick the string a second time.

Multiple Pull-Offs and Trills

Just as with hammer-ons, you can string pull-offs together to make multiple pull-offs. You can also combine hammer-ons and pull-offs together for spectacular results:

Track 43 (0:18)

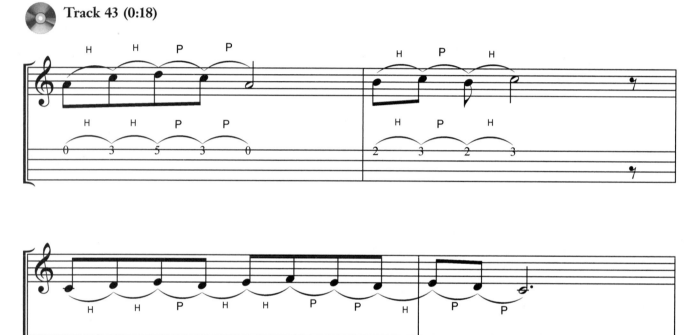

Chapter 11, Example 4.

A quick, repeated combination of hammer-ons and pull-offs between two notes is called a *trill*. In notation, a trill is indicated with a thick wavy line accompanied by the letters *tr*. You'll run into trills in one of the soloing track samples in Chapter 17.

Grace Notes and Timing

The trill brings up a very important point—all slurred notes have timing values, just as regular notes do. In all the examples so far in this chapter, each note, whether articulated or hammer-on or pull-off, was an eighth note and should have received one-half beat.

Slurs are essential to becoming a speedy ukulele player, but just because you can hammer-on or pull-off from one note to the next lightning-quick doesn't mean that you're supposed to. Be sure to read the rhythm values of slurs and play them with the appropriate timing.

Sometimes, though, slurs *are* played very quickly. It's almost like a uke player picked a note by accident and thought "oops" and used the slur to get to the right note as soon as humanly possible. These "oops" notes, which are really supposed to be there, are called *grace notes*, and they are indicated in both music notation and tablature as tiny notes right before the slurred note. Listen to the following example and pay close attention to the difference in the timing of the eighth notes and the grace notes:

Track 44

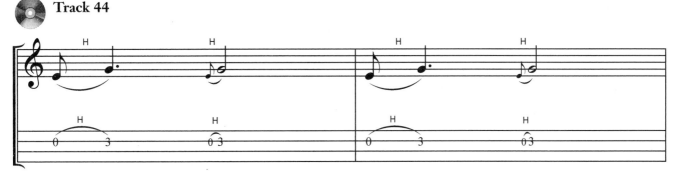

Chapter 11, Example 5.

Because we've spent so much time discussing rhythm, you can certainly understand how important it is to make sure you understand the desired timing of all notes, whether articulated or slurred. The last thing you want to do is to speed through a series of slurs when you're meant to string them along to a specific, even rhythm. This is another example of why knowing a little bit about reading music notation is incredibly useful to you as both a ukulele player and a musician.

Slurring Your Strums

One of the most common misconceptions for new players is that slurs and slur techniques are strictly soloing techniques. Nothing could be further from the truth! Using hammer-ons, pull-offs, and other bends (to be discussed in a moment) adds so much more depth to simple strumming playing that you might find yourself wondering why everyone doesn't use them when strumming.

In the following examples, first notice the chord being played and set your fingers accordingly. Then note in the tablature any differences in fingering. For instance, the first chord is D minor but on the first strum the E string is played open instead of having a finger on the first fret as you would normally do when playing the Dm chord. That's because you're going to add that note as a hammer-on *after* you've strummed the full chord:

Track 45

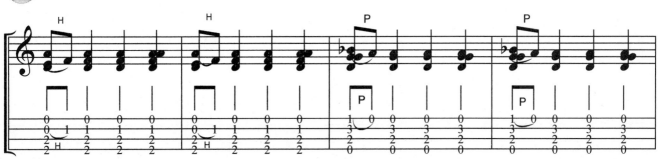

Chapter 11, Example 6.

Likewise, the Gm chord that follows starts out normally with all fingers in their proper places. But after you strum it, you then perform a pull-off with your index finger, taking it from the first fret of the A string to sound the note of the open A string.

There are a lot of ideas for you to explore and examine in these examples, so don't worry about taking them all in at once. Go through them one at a time, and then be sure to experiment with them by plugging hammer-ons and pull-offs into some of the songs you've learned already. You might come up with ideas like this one, using the strum from "Polly Wolly Doodle" back in Chapter 7:

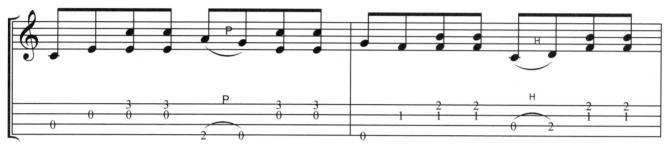

Suggestions for adding slurs to old songs.

The more you play hammer-ons and pull-offs, the more finger strength and confidence you will gain. You will soon discover that you can hammer-on notes on two or more strings at once—even whole chords at the same time—as in this example, which can be used as a variation of "My Bonnie Lies Over the Ocean" from Chapter 9:

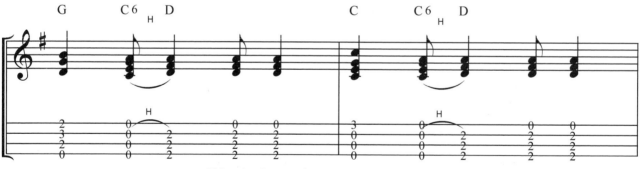

Using simultaneous hammer-ons and pull-offs.

It's a very short step up from adding hammer-ons and pull-offs to your strumming to adding them to your finger picking. Look how simple it would be in "What Child Is This?" from Chapter 10:

Adding hammer-ons and pull-offs to finger picking.

You've learned only two of the four ukulele slurs so far, but hopefully you've gained a clear sense that using slurs simply as a soloing technique limits your potential as an all-around ukulele player. Use them any chance you get! Even the simplest use of hammer-ons and pull-offs adds an incredible amount of texture to the most basic of strumming, so be sure to explore ways to add slurs to your playing.

UKE LORE

Vaudeville performer Roy Smeck was known as "The Wizard of the Strings" because of his mastery of the guitar, banjo, mandolin, and especially, the ukulele. Roy brought the instrument to the silver screen in one of the earliest sound films and he would later take his uke and other instruments on tour all around the world. "The Wizard of the Strings" made hundreds of recordings and authored some of the earliest ukulele tutorial books.

Slides and Bends

The remaining slurs you'll learn are slides and bends. They can seem easier than hammer-ons and pull-offs, but they do require a bit of patience on your part to develop and ultimately use. Each of these techniques contributes its own unique variation and depth to the ukulele.

Sliding In to Notes

Slides are probably the most deceptive of slurs. They sound impressive and look easy enough to do, but performing them requires more practice than you think.

The essence of a *slide* is simple enough—you place a finger on a fret and pick the string to sound that note. Then you slide your fretting finger over the frets to a second note somewhere along the same string, as you can hear in the following examples:

Track 46

Chapter 11, Example 7.

For the first slide in this example (shown in the first measure), place a finger (try the ring finger here) on the G note located at the third fret of the E string. After you pick that note, slide your ring finger up two frets so that it sits at the fifth fret of the E string. That will be the same note as the open A string. Now try it again on your own, this time pinching the open E string at the same time you make the initial pick of the D note on the C string. These two notes will clash until you finish the slide and have both notes the same, albeit on different strings. This will sound a little like the very beginning of Jimi Hendrix's version of "Hey Joe."

A good sense of touch is the secret to successful slides. You should initially fret the first note as you normally do. As soon as you start your slide (after picking the first note), you need to ease up slightly on the pressure exerted with your fretting finger so that it glides over the frets smoothly en route to the target note. Too much pressure and your sliding finger will catch on the frets and you won't be sliding at all! Too little pressure results in not getting any sound out of your slide. Additionally, you will need to increase the pressure of the fretting finger again after you reach your desired note. If you don't, your second note won't sound at all.

All of this is a lot to remember at first, so don't get discouraged if it takes a little time to get good at slides. As I showed in the other previous examples, slides can go up or down the neck and can be done on more than a single string at a time.

Bending Strings

One of the reasons for taking so much care fretting notes with your fingertips—pressing the strings directly onto the fretboard—is because when you don't, you're usually pushing the string along the fretboard to one side or the other. This causes the fretted note to be sharp and can cause the other notes in your chord to sound out of tune, even if they are perfectly fine. Pushing a string one way or the other, closer to either of its adjacent strings as you fret, instead of pressing it directly downward onto the fretboard is called *bending* the string. Bending increases the string tension, which leads to getting a higher pitch. Depending on how much you bend the string, you can change a fretted note anywhere up to a step and a half higher than the note you meant to play.

However, bending strings can be used intentionally as a slur technique. It doesn't require strong fingers as much as it does good ears. To do it right, you have to be more concerned with hearing your target note than with how much you're bending. With the small size of the ukulele and the nylon strings, it doesn't take a lot to slur from one note to another, provided your target note isn't all that far away from your starting note.

 Track 47

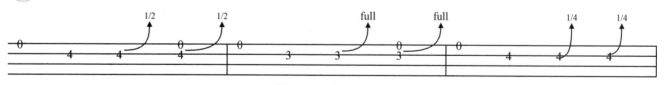

Chapter 11, Example 8.

For the first two measures of this example, play the open A string. Then place your ring finger on the fourth fret of the E string and play that note, which is A♭, by the way. Then pick the E string again (with your finger still on the fourth fret), and after the initial note sounds, push the string toward the center of the fretboard. You need to push and not press, so your finger shifts slightly to get alongside the string as opposed to on top of it.

> **FRET LESS!**
>
> Ukulele players don't usually do a lot of bending. Bending can wear out nylon strings faster than the steel strings of a guitar. Nylon strings also require a lot more bend to achieve a change of pitch than steel strings. On the ukulele, full bends and half-bends tend to be avoided. Quarter-bends, though, can be used to good effect and especially sound good when playing blues, Celtic, rock, and bluegrass music.

You're going to push the E string until the note sounds like the A note of the open string. It won't take that much bending, and you should focus on making the bend from the wrist as opposed to the finger. Rotate your wrist using a motion similar to turning the key in the ignition of a car, and you'll find that your ring finger will push the string along the fretboard toward the center of the neck with no trouble at all. This is called a *half-bend* because you've raised your original note a half-step in tone.

For the last part of this example, you play both the E string (still with the ring finger on the fourth fret) and the A string simultaneously in a pinch and then bend the E string until it hits the A note. This is called a *unison bend*; you've no doubt heard it used in lots of songs, such as the closing notes of the guitar solo in Led Zeppelin's "Stairway to Heaven."

You can hear and play a full bend in the second measure of the example. This means that the note achieved by the bend will be one full step higher than the starting note. Because it's convenient to have the open A string as your target note again, your note from which to start the bend will be the G note at the third fret of the E string. Simply repeat the previous steps you took a moment ago to bend the G note up to A. It should take a bit more effort than the half-bend did.

Occasionally you will run into quarter-bends, shown in the last measure of the example. Quarter-bends are tricky because, technically, your target note doesn't exist! It's kind of halfway between A♭ and A. A little nudge should be all it takes to push your initial note slightly (but not overly so) sharp. Quarter-bends are used a lot in blues and Celtic music and give your ukulele an almost voice-like quality. They cause it to be slightly out of tune for a brief moment before righting itself, much like a singer or an unfretted instrument, such as a violin. The effect is both haunting and arresting when done well.

Practice, Practice

For slurs to become second nature to you, you have to put in time practicing them individually as well as in combinations. Chapter 18 has a great "song"—"Old Time Mountain Uke"— written specifically as a slur exercise for the ukulele. If you practice what you learned in this chapter, you should find it within your current capabilities to play it, or it certainly will be with a little practice.

FRET LESS!

It's incredibly important to take the time to practice your slurs correctly right from the start. Many players learn or develop incorrect and often difficult ways to make slurs on their ukuleles and then have to both "unlearn" their bad habits as well as re-learn the correct methods. "Unlearning" often takes a lot more time and energy than learning correctly in the first place!

One great way to practice both hammer-ons and pull-offs is to revisit your "one finger one fret" exercises from Chapter 3 and play each note first as a hammer-on and then as a pull-off. You can come up with all sorts of combinations to make practicing these two slurs fun.

When practicing slides, be sure to give yourself three specific tasks. First and foremost, work on the physical mechanics of the slide—in other words, make certain that your finger slides smoothly and evenly over the string with just the right amount of pressure to keep the sound of the slide going (but not so much that your finger gets caught up on the frets and can't slide). Second, practice the accuracy of your slides—you need to land on the correct note, after all! And finally, but no less important, concentrate on having the notes at both ends of the slide sound clear and clean.

Practicing bending, even if you don't do a lot of it, does help you develop both your mechanical technique and, more importantly, your ear. Being able to discern the intervals between notes is a great skill to have and one you can practice and develop through bending. When you practice bending, try singing the target note to which you want to bend the original note. If you're working on a half-bend, see if you can sing and match the note at the next fret (if you're working on full bends, then match the note two frets away). When you can hear the note you want before you even make the bend, you're off to a great start with your ear training.

The Least You Need to Know

- Hammer-ons, pull-offs, slides, and bends are the four basic slurs you can perform on the ukulele.
- All slurs, but especially hammer-ons and pull-offs, should be considered an important part of rhythm and strumming. Slurs are not used just for soloing.
- Be careful of the timing of slurs. Every slur has a rhythmic value, so be sure to give each note its due time.
- Good slides start with a light touch on the fretboard.
- As a ukulele player, you probably should use bends sparingly, but bending is great practice for ear training.

Chapter 12

A Different Strummer

In This Chapter

- Discovering percussive playing styles
- Palm muting, string muting, and percussive strokes
- Playing sixteenth notes
- Strumming island rhythms
- Developing strumming finesse

Most dictionaries define *rhythm* along the lines of "patterns of pulses" or "patterns formed by notes of varying lengths and accents."

Did you notice that there was no mention of chords or strumming?

Chances are when you see the words *musical instruments* and *rhythm* in the same sentence, you picture drums, congas, bongos, tambourines, or any number of percussion instruments. You might also think of the bass guitar or guitars in general, but probably not ukuleles. Hopefully by now that has changed!

But if it hasn't, it soon will. In this chapter you explore the percussive side of the ukulele and discover that it has a lot more to offer than just musical notes and chords and finger-picking patterns. Who'd have thought that, on top of everything else, there's a whole percussion section wrapped up in this little instrument?

In the Palm of Your Hand (Sort of)

Most percussive-style strumming techniques involve a slight adjustment in how you approach striking the strings of your ukulele. Instead of using only the fingers of your strumming hand to pick or strike the strings, you'll be getting the palm of your hand involved in your strumming.

Saying *palm* is a little misleading. It's more of the palm side of the heel—the edge along the far side of your hand from your wrist up along your pinky. If you gave a table a karate chop at a 45° angle with your palm facing down, it would be the part of your hand that made contact with the wood.

Pick up your ukulele and hold it as if you're going to do a finger-style pinch of the C and E strings (the thumb picking down on the C string while the index finger picks upward on the E string). Now relax your hand and let the heel set down on the strings by the saddle.

Palm Muting

Raise your hand back into the pinch position and perform a pinch on the C and E strings. The two open strings ring clean and clear. Now lower the heel of your right hand again so that it just barely makes contact with the strings (some players like to have the heel rest just along the edge of the ukulele's saddle) and perform the pinch again. You can still hear the notes of the open C and E strings, but they have a sharply muted and percussive tone to them. This technique is called *palm muting*.

> **DEFINITION**
>
> **Palm muting** is the technique of strumming or picking the ukulele's strings while simultaneously muting them slightly with the fleshy edge of the palm's heel, producing a distinct percussive tone to the notes.

The note-to-percussive-sound ratio in palm muting is determined by how much pressure and contact your heel makes with the strings, as well as how far from the bridge the heel contacts the strings. The lightest contact gives you the sound closest to the pure ringing notes of the open strings. More pressure brings about more of a muted percussive quality.

Palm Reading

Palm muting is a great percussive effect to use on both single note lines and double stops. It also can provide a change in rhythmic dynamics when used as a temporary substitute for full chord strumming, as you'll hear in the following example:

 Track 48 (0:00)

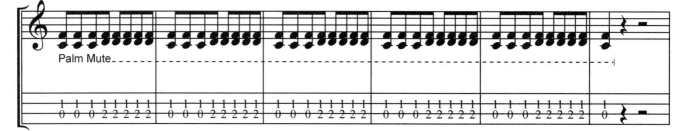

Chapter 12, Example 1.

From Palm to Mute to Chop

Sometimes you want more percussive noise than notes. And sometimes you *only* want to hear the percussive hits on your ukulele. That means you have to totally deaden the strings or do so enough that whatever "note" sound is produced is drowned out by the percussive noise.

The easiest way to do that is to use your fretting hand to mute all four strings. This is called *string muting*. Simply place your left hand (one finger will do, but you can use all four) across all four strings firmly enough to keep the strings from ringing out but not so firmly that you're creating actual notes that are sounded when you strike the strings.

String muting is indicated in music notation, tablature, and rhythm notation by an *x* that takes the place of either the number (in tablature) or note head (in music and rhythm notation), as you will see shortly.

Sixteenth Notes

The next example introduces you to sixteenth notes, which have a rhythmic value of a quarter of a beat. That means that there are four sixteenth notes to the quarter note and there are two sixteenth notes to an eighth note. Sixteenth notes are a great way to bring a bit of flash to your strumming rhythms.

Most musicians tend to count out sixteenth notes aloud in the following manner:

One ee **and** ah **two** ee **and** ah **three** ee **and** ah **four** ee **and** ah

When strumming with sixteenth notes, you need to double up the down and up of your normal strumming. Instead of strumming down every beat (in bold and underlined) and coming up on the offbeat (in bold but not underlined), you'll be strumming down for every eighth note—that's on the beat *and* on the offbeat—and strumming up on the sixteenth notes that come between. In other words, you will strum down on all the bold counts and strum up in between.

If you think about it a moment, it's really not a change in how you strum, but rather a change in how you count. And to help you count and also to give you some practice with string muting, here is an exercise to work with:

Track 48 (0:15)

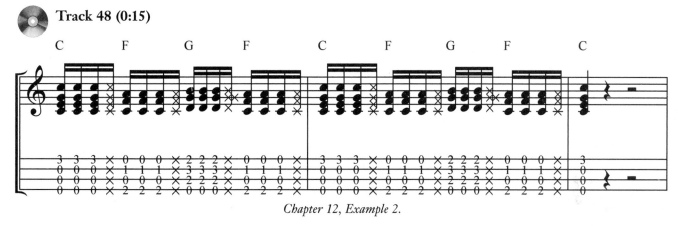

Chapter 12, Example 2.

Smooth Chunkiness

You can also create a very different sort of percussive string mute by using a slightly altered strumming stroke with your right hand. Instead of strumming straight down across the strings, strum the strings so that the heel of your palm connects with them at a 45° angle between the saddle and the sound hole. It's like giving the strings an oblique karate chop while strumming with your thumb and fingers at the same time. It sounds like this:

Track 48 (0:29)

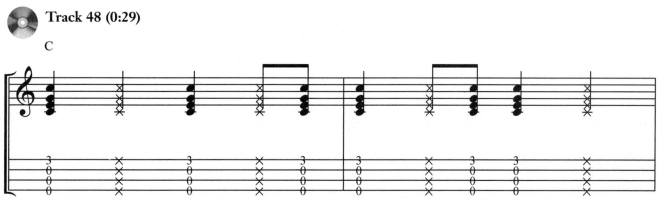

Chapter 12, Example 3.

This particular technique goes by many names, from *string muting* (which is confusing when you realize that it doesn't differentiate itself from the string muting done with the fretting hand) to *chunk* or *chnk* (which are silly). For the sake of our discussion, we'll call it a *percussive stroke*.

Percussive strokes, like palm muting, can vary in tone depending on when, where, and how lightly or firmly you connect with the ukulele's strings. It's often difficult to get two back-to-back percussive strokes to sound exactly the same, but that's part of what makes them work so well—they give some dynamic punctuation to your strumming.

Here is an arrangement of the traditional spiritual "Sometimes I Feel Like a Motherless Child" that demonstrates how you can incorporate the percussive strum into your playing. Be sure to note that this arrangement is in swing time and uses triplets as part of its rhythm.

Track 49

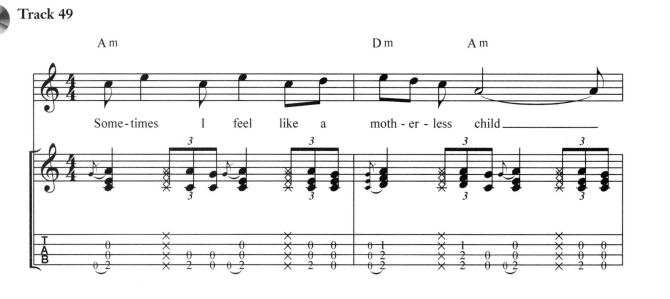

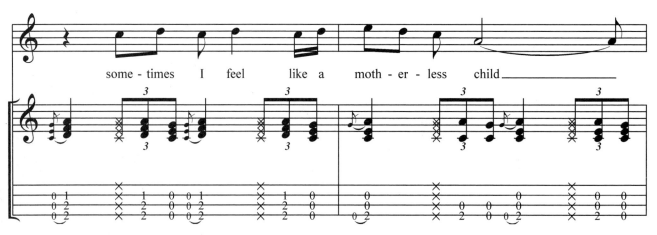

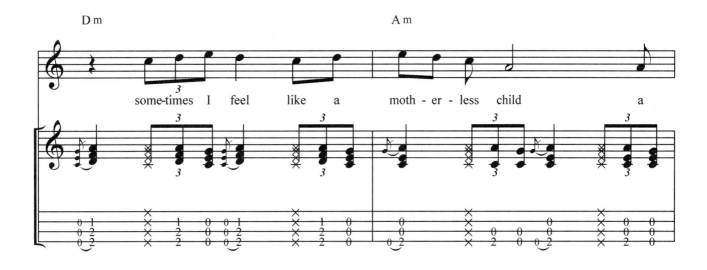

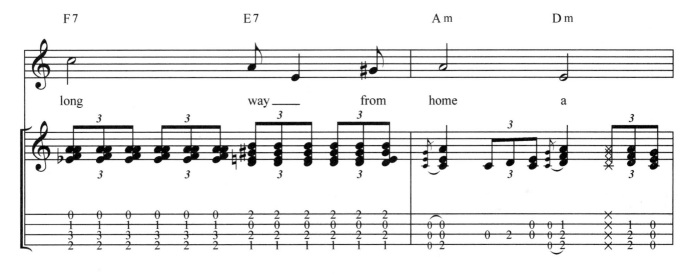

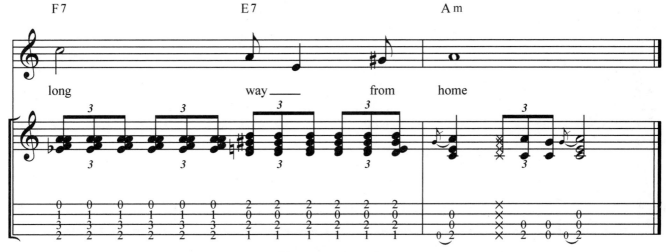

Chapter 12, Example 4.

Giving Rhythm an Accent

Many times rhythms are defined more by nuance than by how many beats a song has and whether you strum quarter notes, eighth notes, or sixteenth notes. Consider this: If you were to ask five different people to play the same song for you, even a simple, two-chord song, you would most likely hear five different versions. Even if you asked each player to strum strictly in eighth notes, you'd still hear five different strums. For example, one might stress the first and third beats while another stressed only the second beat. Yet another would accent every offbeat and another might give the offbeat between the second and third beat a heavy upstroke.

UKE LORE

Australia's Old Spice Boys is a trio consisting of Azo Bell on ukulele, Billy Milroy on a one-string bass made from a tea chest, and Tim Reeves on a single snare drum (sometimes with a cymbal). They manage to create a huge swing sound in no small part to Bell's ability to coax a great deal of music out of his ukulele through his intense strumming style.

You have all sorts of options when it comes to *how* you strum any beat. Obviously there is the downstroke or upstroke choice, but there is also how hard or how lightly you hit a stroke and, as you'll soon read, you also have the choice as to how many strings you strike in a strum. All these choices can be thought of as accents or stresses in strumming, and accents can help define the pulse of a rhythm.

You often subconsciously create stresses when you strum out the chords of a song, but it's a good idea to consciously work on creating specific stresses as part of rhythm practice. Here are a few exercises to help. In music and rhythm notation, accent marks are indicated by a greater than sign (>) placed over a note or rhythm slash, as shown here:

Track 50

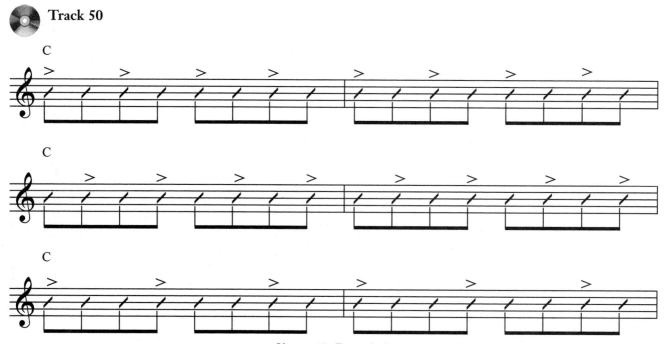

Chapter 12, Example 5.

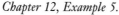

Island Hopping

With the addition of sixteenth notes and percussive strokes to your growing strumming skills, you can now play just about any rhythm imaginable. For example, in reggae and ska (which are two genres of Jamaican music), songs have their rhythmic stress on the offbeat, like this:

Track 51 (0:00)

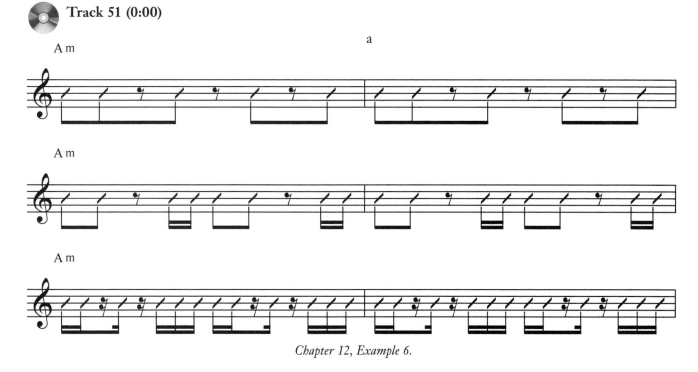

Chapter 12, Example 6.

With rhythms such as the one in the second line, you can play the pairs of sixteenth notes with two quick upstrokes to give the offbeat a harder accent.

The Rolling Arpeggio Strum

Another dramatic yet simple way to give your strums a decidedly tropical feel is to roll out the first beat and a half. This roll shouldn't be confused with the *rasgueado*, which is the term for a flamenco guitar technique (which you'll be learning about in Chapter 17). It's actually a simple use of strumming with a combination of eighth notes and sixteenth notes, like this:

Track 51 (0:29)

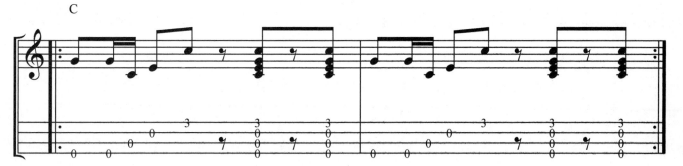

Chapter 12, Example 7.

In the first part of this example, you strike the g string with your thumb on the first beat. On the second half of the beat, you strike it again and quickly roll your strum through the g, C, and E strings. The E string is played as another eighth note, so it gives your strum a bit of a breather before catching the full chord on upstrokes on each remaining offbeat.

What you're doing musically is creating a pulsing arpeggio. This versatile strum can be used in a variety of songs and works well in combination with percussive strokes (used in the first beat in the second line of the last example) or with finger picking (used in the last line). To give you more practice with the roll, here's an arrangement of "Sloop John B," a song you've undoubtedly heard before:

Track 52

Chapter 12, Example 8.

Playing with Finesse

Playing and mastering any musical instrument depends on being in touch with it. Despite what you might see in videos or at a concert, playing the ukulele well also involves finesse. After you have gotten comfortable and confident with your ability to strum and change chords (as hopefully you have by this point), your attention should turn toward learning the subtleties of playing.

Pick up your ukulele and strum across all four open strings. That shouldn't be all that big a deal; you already know that this is a C6 chord. Now, just as you did way back in Chapter 5, strum just the g, C, and E strings, which are the notes of a C major chord. Then just strum the open C, E, and A strings, which gives you the Am chord. Now, can you strum four consecutive beats and alternate hitting just the three strings you want? This is finesse.

It's easy to develop heavy-handedness on any instrument, and perhaps more so with the ukulele. Your playing will improve by leaps and bounds when you discover when to bang out a chord and when to coax it out of your uke. The lighter touch you have, the easier you'll find playing difficult passages of music.

To help you work on your finesse, and also to demonstrate how it can work with your strumming and rhythm, here are a few ideas for you to try:

 Track 53

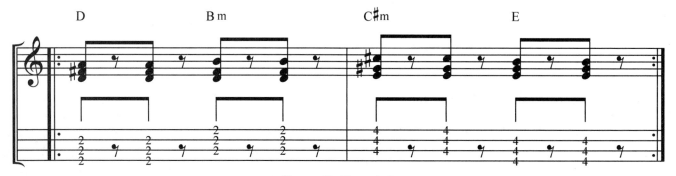

Chapter 12, Example 9.

Choke Hold

The last line of the previous example demonstrates a quick change between four chords—D, Bm, C#m, and E—that also involves string muting. This is accomplished through a technique often called *choking*, which is another fretting-hand-muting technique that's very useful to learn. Basically it involves raising the fingers of your fretting hand off the strings just enough to deaden the notes they would be playing if you fretted the chord normally.

DEFINITION

Choking is a percussive strumming technique in which the fretting hand lightly mutes the strings while still maintaining its position for fretting a chord.

In this particular example, when you play the D chord, your index finger barring all four strings at the second fret. After you strum down through the chord on the beat, lift your index finger off the strings just enough to keep contact with them while not pressing them into the fretboard. This mutes those three strings and also allows you to shift your strumming from the E, C, and g strings to the A, E, and C strings.

The Percussive Strum's Connected to the Upstroke …

Here is an arrangement of "Dry Bones" to give you more practice with the choking technique as well as with developing your strumming sense of touch.

You'll be using the choke technique to switch between all the chords. In the first two measures, when you play the A chord, your index finger is on the first fret of the C string and your middle finger is on the second fret of the g string. After you strum down through the chord on the beat, lift your two fingers off the strings just enough to keep contact with them while not pressing them into the fretboard. This mutes those two strings.

Switching from the A chord to the D chord, after a little practice, should be fast and easy because you're trying to *not* hit the A string. So all you need to do to change the A to a D is to lay your middle finger down on the second fret across all four strings. You then raise it slightly to create the second choke.

Also, just to give you a taste of some of the things you'll be learning in Chapter 16, there's a very cool riff tossed in to finish the song:

Track 54

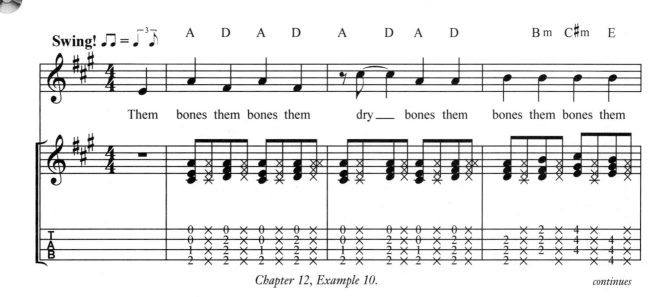

Chapter 12, Example 10.   *continues*

continued

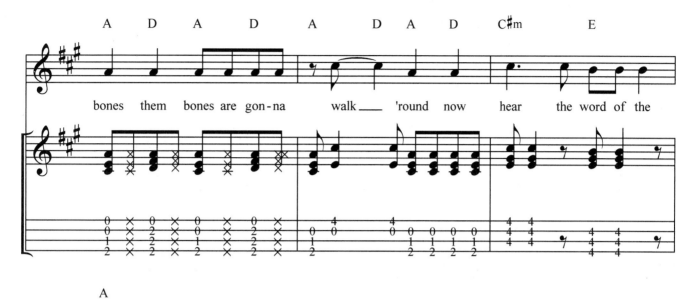

Practice, Practice

After going through the teachings and examples in this chapter, you should now have an incredibly varied rhythm vocabulary. You should be able to use this vocabulary when and wherever you see fit, so keep practicing it.

All the practice hints you've read so far in this book, especially those in Chapter 9, apply to the material in this chapter. Remember that listening to music and to all the rhythm and strumming ideas of other ukulele players and musicians is just as important as practicing strumming and rhythm with your ukulele in hand.

Strumming may be a matter of keeping the beat, but it's about an individual's personality as well. Whether you realize it or not, you're taking the knowledge you have gained and you're molding it— along with your own musical ideas—into your personal unique ukulele playing style. This style will, hopefully, continue to grow and evolve with every new bit of music you hear and every new technique you learn and get into your fingers.

The Least You Need to Know

- The ukulele offers many percussive techniques that can liven up your strumming rhythms.
- Palm muting and percussive strokes are right-hand techniques; string muting is done with the left hand.
- Sixteenth notes have a rhythmic value of one-quarter of a beat.
- Some rhythms, such as reggae and ska, rely on accenting the offbeat rather than the beat.
- Playing with finesse comes when you develop the ability to strum only the strings you want to because sometimes playing just two or three strings can be less muddy and more powerful than strumming all four.

Turning Tunings
on Their Heads

In This Chapter

- Exploring tunings beyond standard tuning
- Tuning with a low G string
- Raising your ukulele to aDF#B tuning
- Learning the skill of transposing
- Using alternative tunings to create new picking patterns

Discovering the percussive capabilities of the ukulele is only one way to begin enjoying how much your uke has to offer. You can also explore the seemingly limitless possibilities that *alternative tuning* presents.

Back in Chapter 2 you learned how to tune your ukulele to the standard tuning of gCEA. You also got a hint that, because there's such a thing as "standard tuning," there are other ways to tune the four strings of your instrument. That's a bit of an understatement! You can tune each of your uke's strings to any note you'd like, provided it's not so high as to make the string snap as you tighten it or so low that the string flops around and doesn't give you an audible note.

In this chapter, you visit a few of the many ways to tune your ukulele and take in some of the sounds you can create with alternative tuning. You also learn the simple skill of transposing, which you'll find very useful in both this and the following chapter (not to mention in your future musical adventures).

Additionally, you will put much of your knowledge of basic music theory to practical use, learning how to work out chords in any alternative tuning you might come up with. If you're concerned that you've just spent all sorts of time and effort learning your ukulele and now you have to relearn everything from scratch, don't be! Going through the easy steps of mapping out your fretboard and finding new ways to play old chords will actually encourage you to explore your ukulele even more when you go back to standard tuning.

The Lowdown on Low G

One alternative tuning, called *low G tuning*, involves no worries at all in terms of "relearning" the fretboard, but it does require an adjustment to your ukulele itself. In low G tuning, the note of the G string is one octave lower than the G note of standard tuning, which puts the note lower than the C (third) string.

To set up your ukulele in low G tuning, you have to take off the G string already on your uke and replace it with one that can play that octave-lower G note. Your standard G string won't do much more than flop around should you attempt to tune it that low. You will need a thicker string that can play that note when tuned up to proper tension. See Chapter 22 to learn all about changing strings.

DEFINITION

Alternative tuning is any tuning arrangement other than standard tuning, such as low G. Most alternative tunings do not have specific names the way low G tuning or D tuning do. Instead they are identified by listing their note names in order, left to right, from the fourth string to the first. For example, because standard tuning is gCEA, if you were to tune the first string, A, down a full step, this new alternative tuning would be gCEG.

Low G strings tend to be wound strings—meaning they have a core composed of fine nylon threads that are wrapped in bronze wire or silver-plated copper wire. Recently, some ukulele string manufacturers have created a new synthetic material called Nylgut that is less subject to wear and climate changes than traditional wound low G strings.

The big reason for using low G tuning is to give yourself a few more bass notes—five, to be exact. That might not seem like a lot, but it does change the overall tone of the ukulele. For some uke players, playing a G chord with an open low G or an Am chord with an A note an octave lower than the A string sounds deeper and fuller than it does when playing with the standard g string.

Also, some uke players, especially those who play (or played) a lot of guitar, occasionally find the re-entrant tuning a little disconcerting.

FRET LESS!

Typically, the low G string of a ukulele tends to be the string that breaks most often. The nature of its wound construction makes it vulnerable to drastic changes in humidity as well as to general wear and tear.

When you go into a music store and ask for a set of ukulele strings, the odds are that you'll be given a traditional set with the high re-entrant G string. If you want the low G string, be sure to ask for it. And don't be surprised if they have to order it for you; think ahead and ask for at least two sets. Or see if the store has single low G strings that they can sell you so you can have spares.

The low G string also gives you the option of playing different alternative tunings that need the lower notes, such as GCEg, which uses a low G string for the fourth string and also involves tuning the A string (first string) down one full musical step (the equivalent of two frets) to g. This is an ideal tuning for chord melodies, and many ukulele arrangements of traditional Hawaiian songs have been written for this tuning.

SMOOTH STRUMMING

With two single low G strings, you can create what I call "Tahitian tuning." Use the first low G string to replace the g and the second low G string to replace the A string. Now both your G and A strings will be an octave lower than standard tuning while the C and E strings remain the same. Since the notes of the strings are still the same, you can use all the chord fingerings that you've learned and get a very different sound as both the C and E strings will now be the higher strings in terms of pitch.

A Step Up

Speaking of Hawaii, when the ukulele was hitting the big time in the 1920s and 1930s and Tin Pan Alley couldn't write enough songs about the fiftieth state, the ukulele's standard tuning wasn't what we now call standard. Back then, pretty much everyone tuned each string of their ukes one full step higher to aDF♯B. This is often called *D tuning*.

To the ears of many ukulele players, the D tuning gives the instrument a sweeter sound, particularly on the concert- and soprano-size ukuleles.

UKE LORE

A legacy of the D tuning's popularity still exists today in the fact that many sets of ukulele strings still are labeled as D tuning. There is little difference between a string that is labeled to be an A and one that is meant to be a B, so if you happen to buy a set, you should have no qualms whatsoever about using them for standard tuning.

D tuning's biggest advantage is that it allows you to play along on songs in keys such as D, A, or E, which are favorites of guitar players. This can make jamming along with other musicians a lot easier, although there is (of course) one slight catch—you sort of have to learn new chords.

Transposing

If you just got into a bit of a panic, relax! *Sort of* is your clue that this isn't going to be at all hard. What you need to do is to learn the simple trick of *transposing*.

If you've tuned each of the strings of your ukulele up one whole step so that you're now playing in D tuning (aDF♯B) instead of standard (gCEA), what do you think is going to happen when you put a finger on the third fret of the first string and play what you think is a C chord? Because each string has been raised a whole step, your C chord is also raised a whole step; therefore, now when you place your fingers on the neck to play C, you're actually playing D.

Because you have raised every string up a whole step, you have also raised every chord you know how to play up a whole step. The shapes and fingerings you have learned are still chords. That has not changed, but now every note of each chord is a full step higher. In other words, you don't need to learn how to play new chord shapes—you just need to learn the new names of the chords you already know. This is what transposing is—the conversion of the chords of one key into the chords of another. It's one of the most useful musical tools you can have, and it's one of the easiest to learn.

DEFINITION

Transposing is changing the notes (and chords) of a song from one key to another.

D Tuning Conversions

The easiest way to learn how to transpose is to make a chart writing out all 12 notes (which you learned in Chapter 2), in ascending order, in a single line. Because we're discussing the C chord, start your list with the note C to make things easier. You might also find it helpful to write out the numbers 1–12 over each note, like this:

1	2	3	4	5	6	7	8	9	10	11	12
C	C♯	D	E♭	E	F	F♯	G	G♯	A	B♭	B

Notice here that each of the accidentals (the sharp or flat notes) is identified by a single name rather than both. This is just to have fewer note names on the sheet. You can use all flats or all sharps or whatever makes you most comfortable.

Next, write out all 12 notes again in ascending order, but this time start on the D note. Why? Because to put your ukulele in D tuning, you have to tune your C string up one full step to D. Each note of the second line should be a full step up from the corresponding note in the first line. Your chart should look like this when you are done:

1	2	3	4	5	6	7	8	9	10	11	12
C	C♯	D	E♭	E	F	F♯	G	G♯	A	B♭	B
D	E♭	E	F	F♯	G	G♯	A	B♭	B	C	C♯

You now have a "standard tuning to D tuning" conversion chart. Find the root note of any chord you already know in the first line, and when you play that chord in D tuning, you'll actually be playing the corresponding chord in the second line. The only thing to remember is that any other part of the particular chord name—minor, diminished, 6, maj7, and so on—is also part of the new chord. So an Am chord in standard tuning, played by placing a finger on the second fret of the g string, becomes a Bm chord in D tuning. G7 becomes A7, and so on. For example, if you want to play a song that has the chords Bm, A, and E, change to D tuning and you can play what used to be Am, G, and D chords in standard tuning.

For a handy "D tuning chord conversion chart," check out the Quick Guide, "Chord Conversions Made Easy" at idiotsguides.com/ukulele.

You might see that playing in D tuning is pretty handy for songs that are in the key of E or A. Later in Chapter 20, you'll get a demonstration on why it's a good idea to keep D tuning in mind when playing with others, especially if quite a few guitar players are involved.

SMOOTH STRUMMING

If you find yourself constantly changing from standard tuning to D tuning, you might seriously consider getting yourself a second ukulele! That way, you'll always have one ready to go in each tuning.

The Wide Open Spaces

It gets more interesting when your investigations of alternative tunings involve changing just a single string. Start with standard tuning (gCEA), and tune just the A string down a full step. You're now in gCEG tuning, which is often called *open C* because when you strum all four strings, you get a C major chord.

FRET LESS!

Open tunings is a guitar term that refers to any alternative tuning in which the open strings, when strummed, create a recognizable chord. Because most combinations of four different notes can make up all sorts of chords, you could easily argue that any ukulele tuning is an open tuning. Standard tuning, for example, could be called "C6 open tuning" or D tuning could be called "D6 open tuning." In the long run, it's better to name your tunings by the notes of the individual strings, listed from fourth to first.

Your A string is now a whole step lower, so you have to adjust the chords you already know by placing any of their notes on the A string up two frets. Thus, the very first four chords you learned—C, Am, F, and G7—would be fingered like this on the fretboard:

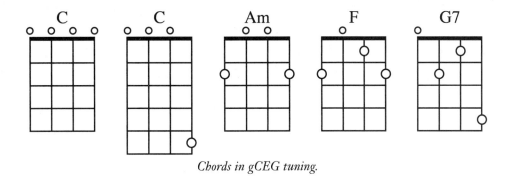

Chords in gCEG tuning.

Mapping Your Explorations

To get a fuller understanding of what an alternative tuning can offer you, it's a great idea to draw a map. You can do it on your own or find free printable copies of blank ukulele fretboard templates online. Just fill in the notes like this:

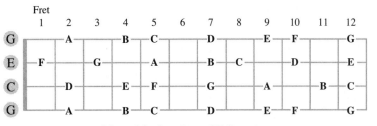

Map of fretboard in gCEG tuning.

Now think of what you already know about chords. You probably noticed right off the bat that if you lay a finger across all four strings at any given fret, you have a major chord whose root note is on the C string at that particular fret. Place your finger across the second fret, and you're playing a D major chord. Barring the fourth fret gives you an E chord.

Using your knowledge of how chords are constructed, you can easily create charts.

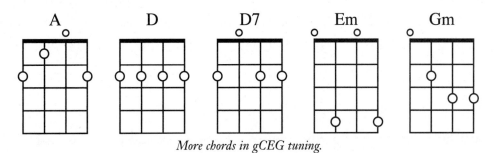

More chords in gCEG tuning.

Making the Most of a New Tuning

The real fun of alternative tunings comes when you start exploring beyond the standard major and minor chords. You will find that almost every alternative has something to offer—a bit of personality that you can use in your own music.

This is particularly true when you start adding the notes of open strings into the mix. For example, try playing your normal standard-tuning F chord while still tuned in gCEG. Because of the open G at the first string, you now have an Fadd9 chord. And when you switch between the open strings of the C chord and this Fadd9, you can make your ukulele sound like the cool rhythms that Keith Richards of the Rolling Stones uses:

Track 55

ukulele tuned as follows:
1st string - G   2nd string - E
3rd string - C   4th string - g

Chapter 13, Example 1.

Notice that you can play this shape up and down the fretboard by using your index finger to barre across any given fret and then playing the F shape with your middle and ring fingers.

Another Tuning to Try

With your ukulele tuned to gCEG, it's not that big of a stretch to lower the C string down a half-step to B and the E string down a full step to D. Your uke will then be tuned gBDG, which gives you a G chord when you strum across all four open strings.

Having both the outer strings tuned to the same note gives you a lot of interesting possibilities when it comes to finger picking your ukulele. You can use either g string as a pedal point and play chords (both major and minor) on the other three strings. Add a bit of hammer-ons, and it's easy to come up with something like this:

Track 56 (0:00)

Ukulele tuned as follows:
1st string - G   2nd string - D
3rd string - B   4th string - g

Chapter 13, Example 2.

Making Complex Picking a Snap

Alternative tunings can help you create mesmerizing and intricate finger-picking patterns. Choosing a tuning that has two or three notes musically close to each other gives you the opportunity to come up with arpeggios that share notes while the basic chord changes.

As an example, start in standard tuning and then lower the g (fourth) string down a whole step to f. Your ukulele will be in fCEA tuning, which you might recognize as the notes of the Fmaj7 chord. Because the E and F notes are a half-step from each other, you can create a cascading effect with your picking, like this:

Track 56 (0:21)

ukulele tuned as follows:
1st string - A   2nd string - E
3rd string - C   4th string - f

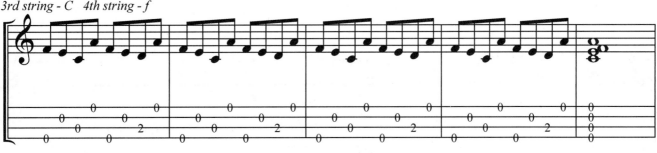

Chapter 13, Example 3.

Replacing the note of the open C string with the D note at the second fret also sounds wonderful. The following arrangement of "Swing Low Sweet Chariot" uses this fCEA tuning to great effect, giving the song a lullaby-like mood:

 Track 57

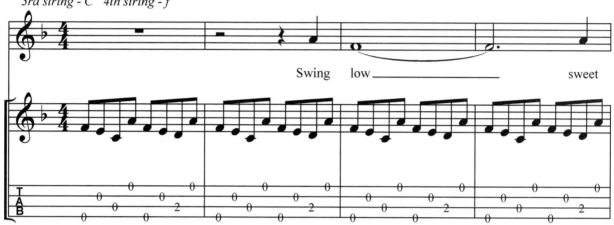

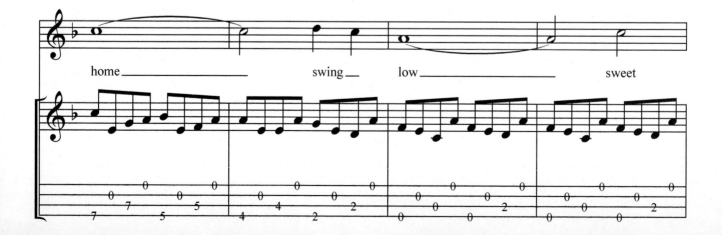

Chapter 13, Example 4.

The important point to recognize with this last example is that the arrangement is made possible by the use of this particular tuning. Having the open E and A strings ring throughout the song gives it its mood and its charm.

Practice, Practice

Because you can tune each of your ukulele's four strings to practically any note of your choosing, there is a huge number of possible alternative tunings for you to explore. That alone makes the idea of alternative tunings both exciting and a little daunting.

Initially keep your explorations limited to a single open tuning, preferably one that's not too different from standard. Be sure to take notes and make a map, so that next time you play in the new tuning you don't have to rework all your chords and finger-picking patterns from scratch.

As you get comfortable with any alternative tuning, try to find several songs to use it with and practice those. This way, you don't have to change to a different tuning with each subsequent song you're practicing! These can be different arrangements of songs you normally play as well as songs specifically played in the new tuning. Alternative tunings can be interesting musically and help you create and play songs in arrangements uniquely yours. But it's good to realize that alternative tunings are also excellent tools for learning and exploring your creativity. You'll find new finger-picking patterns and chord voicings and you'll give your knowledge of chords a constant reinforcement.

Using different tunings on your ukulele will always remind you of how exciting it is to play music. Every new musical discovery makes playing your uke that much more of a joy.

The Least You Need to Know

- There is more than one way to tune your ukulele.
- You need a different G string to tune the fourth string to the G note an octave lower than standard, which is low G tuning.
- When you tune your ukulele to aDF♯B, each note is raised one full step. Each chord is a whole step higher as well.
- Transposing is a useful skill to know, and it's easy to learn.
- Alternative tunings can help create interesting picking patterns that would be impossible to play in standard tuning.

The Big Baritone

In This Chapter

- Transferring your skills to the baritone ukulele
- Baritone ukulele tuning
- A handy chord chart for the baritone uke
- A sample of the baritone sound
- Accompanying other uke players

The origin of the baritone ukulele is open to debate. Some say it was created by John Favilla of Favilla Instruments (whose best instruments rivaled those of Martin back in the 1950s) at the request of his son Herk. Herk taught guitar and envisioned the baritone ukulele as a way for teaching the fundamentals of the guitar to students either too young or too small to handle the full size and six strings of the guitar. The first Favilla ukuleles were made in the very late 1940s. Herk Favilla wrote and published what most people consider the first baritone ukulele method book in 1950.

Others believe the instrument was invented by Eddie Connors, a popular banjo player of the 1920s. Connors was asked by none other than Arthur Godfrey to design a baritone ukulele for him, which he did in the early 1950s. If you look up the 1953 portrait of Godfrey by Jon Whitcomb, you'll see the legendary television star playing a baritone ukulele.

Regardless of who was the moving force behind the baritone ukulele's creation (perhaps it was all of them), Godfrey's popularity and endorsement of it made the baritone ukulele (and all things ukulele, really) a hot item during the early 1950s.

UKE LORE

Arthur Godfrey served as a radio operator in the Navy as well as with the Coast Guard and used that knowledge, as well as his musical talent, to become a household name through his radio and television broadcasts. Seeing and hearing him play his ukulele, which he learned to play during his Naval days, gave the instrument a huge resurgent boom in popularity during the 1950s.

What is more mysterious than who invented the instrument is why practically every ukulele book or tutorial you may find is either a "regular ukulele" tutorial method, meaning it works for the soprano, concert, or tenor ukes, or a "baritone ukulele" method. This is rather puzzling because if you can play one, you can easily play the other. All the techniques you've learned so far in this book are transferable to playing the baritone uke. In fact, you got the last piece of the puzzle in the very last chapter.

Louder and Lower

The first thing you probably notice about a baritone ukulele is its size. It's closer to being a three-quarter-size student guitar than it is to being a tenor ukulele. Its size also makes it louder.

When you hear its louder sound, you're also hopefully hearing two other identifying characteristics. The sound produced by the baritone ukulele is decidedly lower than that of other ukuleles. Because of its longer neck, the strings have to be both longer and thicker than regular ukulele strings. And when you examine the strings you'll find that the fourth string is lower than the third. The baritone ukulele does not, as a rule, use re-entrant tuning.

Your observation of the baritone ukulele being like a small guitar is important because the baritone uke is tuned to the same notes as the high four strings of the typical guitar in standard guitar tuning. From the fourth string to the first, the baritone ukulele is tuned DGBE. The E string is the same note as the E string of the regular ukulele.

Baritone Conversions

Take another look at the DGBE tuning of the baritone ukulele and compare it to the standard gCEA tuning of other ukuleles. But instead of comparing note names or which note is higher or lower, pay attention to the intervals of the notes in relationship to each other. You will find that all the intervals of the adjacent strings are the same in both instruments. From D to G is a fourth, just as the interval from g to C is. Both G to B and C to E are intervals of a major third (two full steps), and both remaining intervals (B to E and E to A) are fourths.

This means that you can think of the baritone ukulele as a regular uke with each string tuned down three-and-a-half musical steps. And that means we can use transposing to learn how to play any chord on the baritone ukulele. All the chord shapes are going to be the same as the ones you've learned. Just as with learning to play in aDF#B tuning, it's just the chord names you have to relearn.

So this means that all you've got to do to start playing the baritone ukulele is work out what to call the chords. You can do that by writing out all 12 notes in two lines, as you did in the last chapter. The first line should still start with C, but the second line will now begin with G, which is the string of the baritone ukulele that corresponds with the C string of the regular ukulele:

1	2	3	4	5	6	7	8	9	10	11	12
C	C#	D	E♭	E	F	F#	G	G#	A	B♭	B
G	G#	A	B♭	B	C	C#	D	E♭	E	F	F#

After you've done this, you can then work out your basic chords for playing the baritone. Remember that all the "extra" parts of a chord name, such as minor or 7 or augmented, are still part of the new chord. For a handy "Baritone Ukulele Chord Conversion Chart," check out the Quick Guide, "Chord Conversions Made Easy" at idiotsguides.com/ukulele.

Baritone Uke Chord Chart

With practice, you can learn to transpose on the spot in your head. But that will take time and patience on your part. In the meantime, though, it doesn't hurt to have handy a set of chord charts specifically for the baritone ukulele:

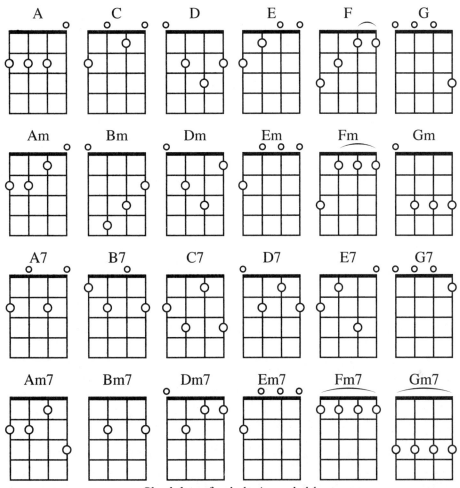

Chord charts for the baritone ukulele.

When you know your new baritone ukulele chords, you will find that you can play just about anything on the baritone that you can on a regular ukulele. It will definitely sound different, but you'll soon get used to its thicker strings, greater fret spacing and wider fingerboard, and its low D string will even start to grow on you.

SMOOTH STRUMMING

Because of the resonance of its bigger body, you might find that your hammer-ons, pull-offs, and other slur techniques sound clearer on the baritone uke than on the smaller ukes. After you practice those same slurs on the baritone, you'll soon find that you're even better at them on the regular uke than you were before.

Likewise, if a particular chord is giving you fits on the regular ukes, try the same shape on the baritone to give your fingers the confidence that they can perform the task. You'll often find the chord comes more easily after a little practice on a baritone.

A Bit o' Baritone Brogue

To give you a bit of the flavor of the baritone ukulele, here is an arrangement of the traditional Irish song "The Star of the County Down" that features the use of the baritone uke's lower strings. It uses a similar finger-flicking strum as "Polly Wolly Doodle" from Chapter 7:

Track 58

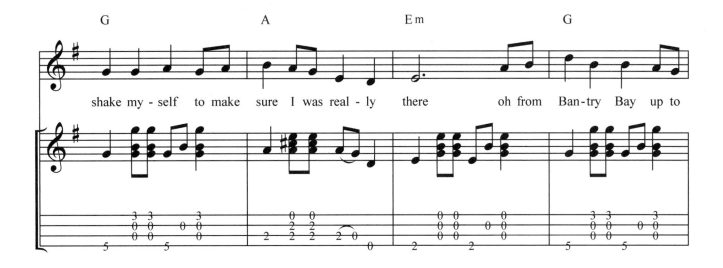

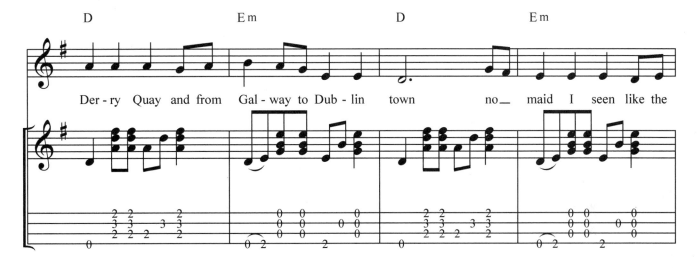

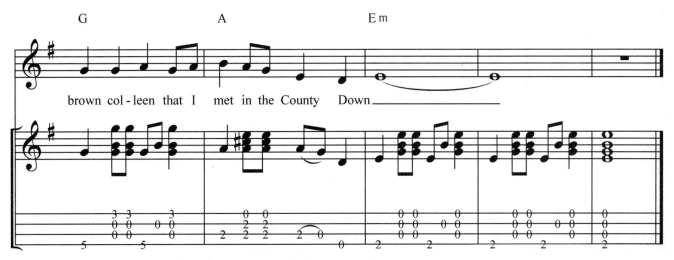

Chapter 14, Example 1.

Back on the Sloop John B

Typically when two uke players get together and one of them has a baritone ukulele, the bigger instrument takes on the role of a bass player. Suppose, for example, you wanted to play "Sloop John B" from Chapter 12 on the baritone as a duet with someone playing a soprano, concert, or tenor uke. You choose something like this arrangement, which combines picking and alternative bass notes:

 Track 59

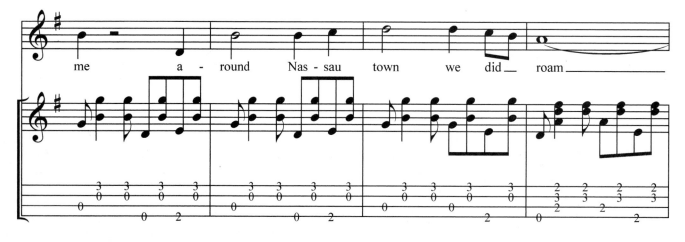

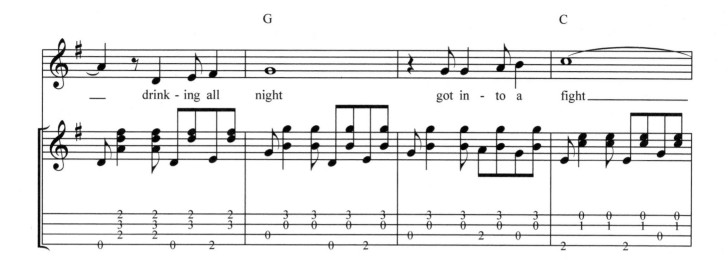

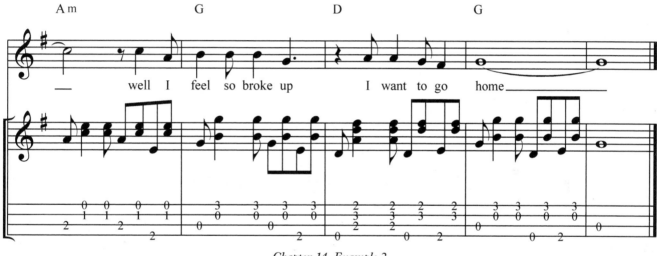

Chapter 14, Example 2.

On Track 59 of the CD, you can hear just the baritone ukulele part, done with the vocals. The following cut, Track 60, has both the baritone and the tenor ukulele playing together.

 Track 60

The baritone ukulele is also a great soloing instrument as well as one for the solo player, so be sure to try out all the techniques and ideas covered in Parts 4 and 5 on your baritone, too.

Practice, Practice

Now, it's one thing to realize that you can play the baritone ukulele using the skills you've learned so far from this book. It's quite another to do it without some practice!

It should go without saying that you're going to want to go through all the steps you've taken in the first three parts of this book if you choose to take up the baritone ukulele. But do so with the chord chart in this chapter in hand. The good news is that, with all the work you've already done, you should find that you pick things up a little (and perhaps even a lot) more quickly than you did the first time.

The not-so-good news is that you're more than likely going to mix up your baritone chords and your regular uke chords from time to time. This is perfectly normal, and you have to be patient with yourself. Getting frustrated with simple mistakes that happen to everyone is a waste of time, so spend that time getting over them instead.

If you have the capacity to record your playing, you might try making a recording of yourself playing a song on a regular ukulele (be sure to start the recording with a count so that you know when to come in) and then practice playing along with the recording on the baritone ukulele. It's a great way to come up with a second part to a song.

The Least You Need to Know

- The baritone ukulele is larger than the soprano, concert, and tenor ukuleles. It also has longer strings and does not use re-entrant tuning.
- The strings of the baritone ukulele are tuned to DGBE. These are the same notes as the four highest strings of a guitar.
- You can use the same chord shapes of the chords you already know for regular ukes on the baritone ukulele. You will have to learn them by their new names, though.
- The baritone ukulele can be a solo instrument and can also be played as part of a group.
- All the techniques used to play a regular ukulele can be easily transferred to the baritone. If you can play one kind of uke, you can play them all!

Going Solo

The ukulele might be small and only have four strings, but it can be a whole band if you want it to be! In this part you will discover the art of playing chord-melody style—arrangements where the ukulele takes on the melody and bass parts of a song as well as the accompanying chords.

You will also learn how to create fills, the tasty little musical flourishes that can add even more excitement and depth to your playing. Using the basics of chord melody and fills, you will find you can create solos to play when you are jamming with others. You'll even get some backing tracks you can use to practice your soloing skills.

Chord Melodies

In This Chapter

- Creating a simple, basic chord melody
- Using finger picking to enhance chord melodies
- Arranging melodies using entrant tuning
- Adding slur techniques to spice up melodies
- Planning and practicing chord melodies

Pretty much up to now you've concentrated on playing the ukulele to provide the accompaniment, or background if you will, to someone else singing a song. Songs, as a rule, are made up of three essential parts: melody, harmony, and rhythm. A song's melody, simply put, is the part of the song that is sung (or hummed or even whistled). Any song's melody is a line of single notes, each note with a specific rhythmic timing.

The chords that accompany the melody are the *harmony* of a song. On the ukulele, these can be strummed or picked as individual notes in finger-picking patterns or arpeggios. As you might remember from the "Mary Had a Little Lamb" example in Chapter 6, harmony helps define a song's tonal center. Quite often the harmonies of a song are taken from the diatonic chords of the key in which the song is played.

Rhythm, again in the simplest terms, is the pattern of pulses given to a song. The strumming or the finger picking you use to play the ukulele, including the various percussive strumming techniques you learned in Chapter 12, constitute the rhythm of a song.

Now, some of you might not sing. Not everyone does, or perhaps it would be better to say not everyone feels comfortable doing so. Simply strumming or finger picking chords can be fun for a while, but you might find yourself wanting to play something that is identifiable as a specific song. And that's where *chord melody* playing comes in.

Your First Chord Melody Arrangement(s)

Chord melody is playing a song on your ukulele so that the melody is clearly heard and identified, just as it was when you practiced familiar melodies in Chapter 4. But while you are playing the melody on your uke, you can also accompany that melody just as you would accompany a singer—by providing the chords or parts of chords that make up the song's harmony.

DEFINITION

Chord melodies are instrumental song arrangements for a single ukulele in which the melody of the song is usually played while, simultaneously, accompanied by chords that can be either strummed or played as arpeggios. Chord melody is most often associated with jazz, but you can create chord melodies of songs from almost any musical genre.

Some chord melodies are very simple, using just one or two notes to bring harmony to the melody line, while others use different chord voicings all over the fingerboard to best follow the melody line. Some involve using alternative tunings, such as low G tuning to incorporate lower notes into the arrangement, or perhaps gCEG to take advantage of easier fingerings of open position chords.

Melody Making

All you need to create a chord melody arrangement is a song's melody and its basic chord structure. Because this will be your first attempt at chord melody, let's use a melody that's both simple and very familiar, like this:

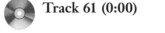 **Track 61 (0:00)**

Chapter 15, Example 1.

If you didn't immediately recognize this melody as "Twinkle, Twinkle, Little Star," that's understandable because it's in a different key than the melody you played in Chapter 4. The first note of the melody in Chapter 4 was C (the open C string); here it's G, which can be played on the open G string or the third fret of the E string.

The reason for playing it this way is to make creating this particular chord melody easier and to make it work. Because the C note that began the Chapter 4 version of "Twinkle" is the lowest note possible on the ukulele (unless you use a low G string or have changed the tuning), the melody note won't stand out on its own unless it's played all by itself. That doesn't mean this C note can't be used when playing chord melodies because it can, and you will learn how shortly.

Take a moment or two to practice playing the "Twinkle" melody example, using these specific notes on these specific strings for the time being.

Putting the Chords into Chord Melody

Now that you have a melody, here are the chords you'll be using:

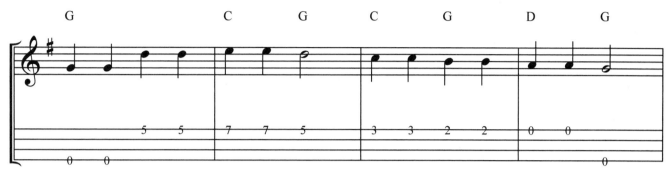

Chords for chord melody of "Twinkle, Twinkle, Little Star."

Now, here is how you'll play your very first ukulele chord melody arrangement:

Track 61 (0:14)

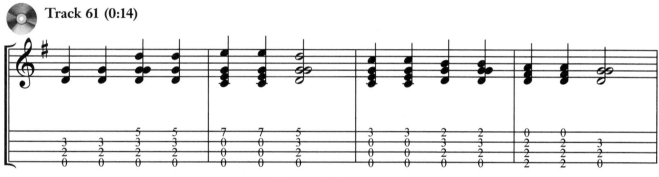

Chapter 15, Example 2.

The first thing you need to do is to get all your fingers in position on their respective strings. Your index finger is on the second fret of the C string. Your middle finger is on the third fret of the E string, and your pinky is on the fifth fret of the A string.

After your fingers are in position, play the first two beats by strumming *only* the g, C, and E strings. On the third and fourth beats, strum all four strings. You should hear the melody notes clearly over the accompanying chords.

Slide your pinky up to the seventh fret of the A string to start the second measure. You can also remove your index and middle fingers from the strings (giving you the C chord for the accompaniment), but don't let them go too far! You'll have to put them all back to their original positions for the third note of this measure.

SMOOTH STRUMMING

Strumming chord melodies requires you to be very accurate as to which strings to strum. One way to ensure this is to use a modified *pinch* or *sweep* strum. This is done by striking downward with your thumb while plucking upward on the string with the melody note with a finger. You can either hit just the one string with the melody note or make a short sweep of the adjacent strings with your finger as you play the melody note. When you make the sweep, the melody note should ring loudest even though you also catch a few notes of the accompanying chord as well.

Congratulations! You've just played your first—but certainly not last—chord melody arrangement!

Getting Fancier

When you feel comfortable enough with this idea, kick things up a notch by adding some slightly more involved finger picking, such as this:

 Track 61 (0:35)

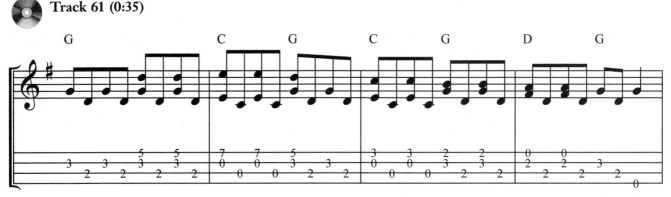

Chapter 15, Example 3.

This new arrangement is built around the same chord shapes you learned in the first chord melody example of "Twinkle, Twinkle." If you go through this new chord melody arrangement very slowly at first, and move your fretting fingers in the same manner as before, you should find that you can play it without a great deal of problems. Remember to keep the rhythm steady and even.

This second chord melody arrangement of "Twinkle, Twinkle" should also demonstrate that you can imply a whole chord while picking one or two notes of it at a time. The idea of "implied harmony," the use of one or two (and occasionally three) notes of a chord to give the impression of a fuller chord, is essential to playing chord melody style arrangements on your uke. Because you have only four strings on your ukulele, sometimes you'll have to make do with playing only one or two of them; the longer you can let the strings ring out over each other, the more the harmony will linger in the air.

> **FRET LESS!**
>
> Implied harmony, especially when used in a chord melody arrangement, is important to understand because any two notes can be a part of many different chords. The notes of the open C and E strings, for instance, are part of the C chord, but they are also part of Am, Fmaj7, and D9, just to name a few.

Getting Creative

One of the intriguing aspects of playing chord melodies on the ukulele is that its re-entrant tuning gives you some interesting choices when it comes to where to play the melody. Take this snippet of Beethoven's "Ode to Joy," from his *Ninth Symphony*, as an example:

Track 62 (0:00)

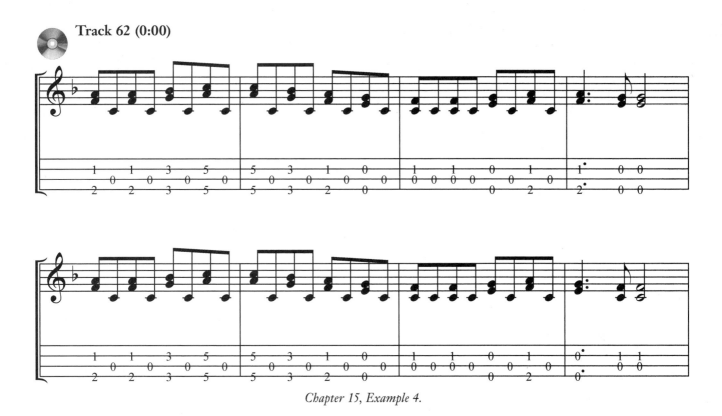

Chapter 15, Example 4.

Here the melody, with the exception of the F note whenever it occurs, is played on the G string. Doing so allows you to play a pinch-and-pedal finger style that works well with this arrangement.

The ukulele's limited range of low notes also means that you occasionally might have to take liberties with a melody to make it work. The second part of "Ode to Joy" could be played in either of these manners:

Track 62 (0:32)

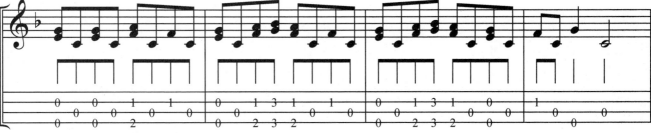

variation on second part of "Ode to Joy"

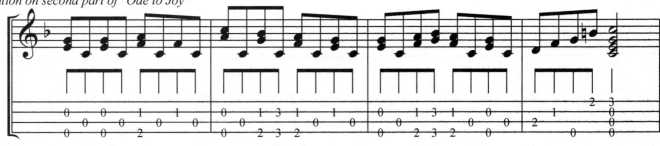

Chapter 15, Example 5.

The first line is the actual melody, which ends on the note of the open C string.

In the second version, a short ascending arpeggio at the start of the fourth measure replaces where the melody line would normally go down to the note of the open C string. As you can hear, both versions work fine.

You'll get another great example of this melodic sleight of hand with the chord melody arrangement of "Aloha Oe," which you'll find at the end of Chapter 18.

It's Amazing What You Can Do!

Because chord melody is all about making your ukulele sing the melody, you can—and should—use all the various slur techniques and knowledge you learned in Chapter 11 when putting together your own chord melody arrangements.

This final example using "Amazing Grace" takes advantage of a good number of hammer-ons and pull-offs to give it a very Celtic atmosphere.

Using hammer-ons and pull-offs in this manner, your uke essentially imitates a human voice bobbing from one note to the next. Also, because it's rare to perform any hammer-on or pull-off with the exact same dynamic, you are giving a very singular interpretation of this piece each time you play it.

UKE LORE

Ernest Ka'ai, who is often referred to as "Hawaii's greatest ukulele player," is also said to have been the first ukulele player to combine chords and melody in his musical arrangements. His 1906 tutorial book, *The Ukulele, A Hawaiian Guitar and How to Play It*, which not only covers the basics but also explores exotic chords and complex strumming techniques, paints the ukulele as an instrument for the serious musician.

Track 63

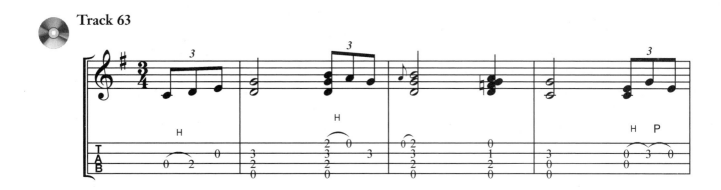

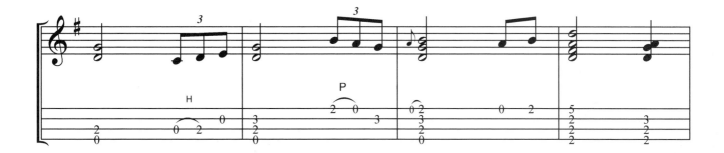

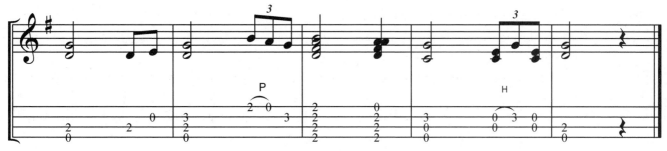

Chapter 15, Example 6.

Practice, Practice

Chord melody requires as much planning as it does practice. You need to learn the melody of a song and then possibly transpose it to a key more suitable to the voice of your ukulele. Some melodies are very simple, using a maximum of six or seven different notes. Other melodies can span a dozen or more notes at numerous places all up and down your fretboard, which means your arrangement will involve finding chord voicings all over the fretboard, too.

Using the information about chords you learned in Chapter 8 will certainly be helpful with chord melodies because knowing the notes of each chord will help you find the best possible voicings to accommodate your song's melody. Try to use chord voicings that are reasonably close to each other in terms of fret position so that you can make easy chord changes while playing.

> **SMOOTH STRUMMING**
>
> Finding the raw material for making chord melody arrangements is as easy as picking up a book. Any song book will have the melody of the songs written out for you, and most will have the chords as well.

Also, make use of your ukulele's re-entrant tuning. Sometimes you'll find that playing the melody note on the g string is a lot easier than doing so on the A string for some chords. Don't forget that all the notes of your open strings can be used for both melody notes and chords as well.

Although you can create both simple and very involved chord melody arrangements, it's a good idea to remember that the song and the setting in which it's played should dictate the interpretation you choose. Playing a lullaby should be soothing and put someone to sleep. Unless, of course, it's your intent to keep that person wide awake to hear your dazzling speed and fancy fretwork.

Chord melody arrangements are a great way to practice just about all the techniques and musical ideas you've learned so far in this book. They are also a lot of fun to play! If you're just singing a song and strumming a basic accompaniment, being able to create simple chord melodies on the spot will give you an instant solo for that song. That's a great ace to have up your sleeve!

The Least You Need to Know

- Songs are made up of three basic parts: melody, harmony, and rhythm.
- When playing chord melody arrangements, your ukulele handles both the melody and chord accompaniment at the same time.
- Chord melodies can use simple strumming or complex finger picking—remember that you're the arranger!
- Remember that the re-entrant tuning of your ukulele opens up a lot of possible ways to play song melodies.
- Incorporating slurs like hammer-ons and pull-offs into your chord melody arrangements can give the melodies voice-like qualities.

Adding Fills to the Rhythm

In This Chapter

- Playing around with chords to create fills
- Learning the major and minor pentatonic scales
- Discovering blue notes
- Using fills to spice up chord changes
- Developing a fill vocabulary

In Chapter 9, you learned one of the differences between a beginning ukulele player and a seasoned one is that the one who has been playing a while has more interesting ways to strum or to change chords. Another difference to add to the list is a seasoned ukulele player can strum a single chord over a long period of time and it never gets boring.

In fact, if you watch good ukulele players, you will see that their fretting hand rarely sits in one place. Even when they are playing a single chord, their fingers are constantly darting about. Some fingers stay in the chord shape while others grab for nearby notes and then return to the original chord position. They fill the spaces in the strumming with runs of single notes and then jump right back into strumming again. It is almost as if they are soloing and playing rhythm at the same time.

Adding *fills*, which are short musical passages that are usually runs of single notes, to your playing creates a break from potentially monotonous strumming, providing both you and your listeners some variety and interest. You will find fills a big help if you are a uke player who primarily uses a single ukulele to accompany a vocalist (even if the vocalist in question is yourself).

Your First Fill

Creating fills can be as simple as playing around with some of the chords you already know. You are already playing chords as part of the rhythm, either through strumming or picking. You have also played around with chords a bit through the various slur techniques you learned, such as the hammer-on and pull-off examples you played in Chapter 11. Now, take any chord you know (it is best to start with the first chords you learned, such as C, Am, F, and G) and play around with it. Play the F chord, for example, strumming it and then pulling off your index finger from the first fret of the E string and then hammering back on. Simple fills can be created from something as basic as this.

DEFINITION

Fills are short musical phrases—generally runs of single notes that embellish and add a bit of a musical flourish to the basic strumming of a song.

Next, think about playing "Sloop John B" from Chapter 12. You go through six measures of G before changing chords, which can seem like an eternity! You could create an easy, simple fill around the G chord like this:

Track 64

Chapter 16, Example 1.

Keeping your G chord in place, you add your pinky to the third fret of the A string and then pick only the A string with your strumming hand; then you pull off your pinky, sounding the B note at the second fret of the A string. Follow up with picking both the E and C strings—and there you have it, an instant fill!

Creating Fills with Scales

Every chord you know has untapped potential for creating fills, but not every fill you come by playing around with a chord will necessarily sound good in the context of a song. For instance, the G chord fill you just learned in the previous example might not sound good in certain circumstances. If the song you are playing is in a major key, knowing the major scale of that key can help.

Take a look at the notes of the C major scale:

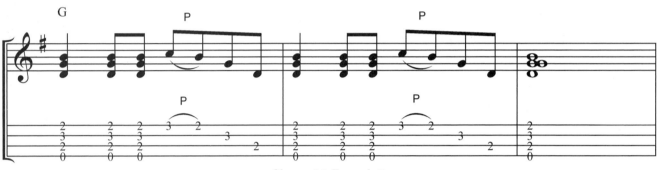

The C major scale.

Most of the notes of a chord's major scale are easily accessible from the chord's shape on the neck of your ukulele, making them ideal for fills. Look and listen to this simple arrangement for "Sloop John B" in the key of C major, using notes of the C major scale to fill in some of the spaces in the strumming:

Track 65

Chapter 16, Example 2.

continues

continued

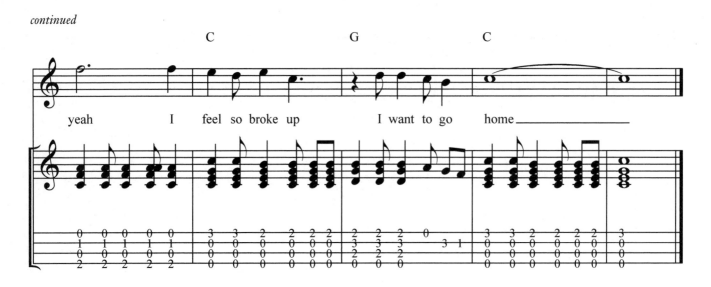

yeah   I   feel so broke up   I want to go   home_____

You can hear that simply taking the notes of the C major scale in descending order gives the song's accompaniment a bit more nuance than it would have if it were simply strummed. And that is the purpose of using fills—to make a song more interesting than it would otherwise be.

When a song uses only the diatonic chords of its key (assuming it is a major song), the notes of its major scale are often a good choice for creating fills. The key word there is *often*, as you will discover after you learn about major and minor pentatonic scales next.

Scaling Down a Scale

Some ukulele players, especially those who play guitar, find major scales a little unwieldy. Instead, they prefer to use *pentatonic scales*, which have five notes instead of seven. To create a major pentatonic scale, you start with the root and then add the second, third, fifth, and sixth positions of the standard major scale. The C major pentatonic scale, for example, is made up of the notes C, D, E, G, and A.

DEFINITION

Pentatonic scales have five different notes, as opposed to the seven notes of the major scale. There are major pentatonic and minor pentatonic scales, which are created using the following notes of the major scale:

Major:	Root	2nd	3rd	5th	6th
Minor:	Root	♭3rd	4th	5th	♭7th

There are also minor pentatonic scales. To make one, you start out with the root and then add the minor third, the fourth, the fifth, and the flat seventh notes. The C minor pentatonic scale has the notes C, E♭, F, G, and B♭.

Playing the Blues

Sometimes a fill (or, as you will read in Chapter 17, a solo) needs more of a blues or rock feel. One of the best ways to accomplish this is to use notes of the minor pentatonic scale, even when the song you are playing is in a major key. The blues vibe you get from blues songs comes from the tension created by the use of blue notes.

In musical terms, *blue notes* are the minor third, flat fifth, and flat seventh of the major scale. In the key of C major, the blue notes would be E♭, G♭, and B♭. You might recognize the E♭ and B♭ as being part of the C minor pentatonic scale.

When these blue notes are played over the C major chord, you create musical tension, which later gets resolved when you play the regular third or fifth of the major scale.

Try playing the following two examples. In the first example, let the strings ring out. In the second example, lay your index finger across the third fret to get the notes on that fret of both the C and A strings, and use your middle finger to hammer-on to the note of the fourth fret of the C string:

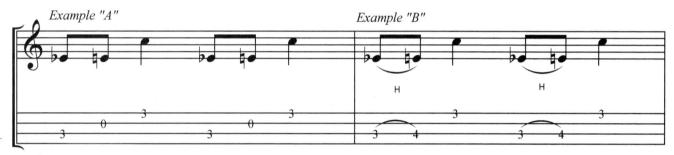

Tension and resolution in the blues.

You can hear and feel the tension clearly in the first example, especially when you let the strings ring out and get the clashing of the E (the open E string) and the E♭ notes (third fret of the C string) ringing together. In the second example, the E♭ gets replaced by the E note at the fourth fret of the C string and a sense of resolution or harmony is being achieved.

UKE LORE

Lyle Ritz worked as a salesman at the Southern California Music Company while in college. Because Arthur Godfrey was hot at the time, he often found himself showing and playing ukuleles for potential customers. Jazz guitar legend Barney Kessel heard him play and signed him to Verve Records, where Ritz's two jazz albums, *How About Uke?* and *50th State Jazz* became legendary in Hawaii.

You can also use blue notes in this way to create fills with a distinct blues-like feel. The following song, "Man of Constant Sorrow," is in the key of F major. The F minor pentatonic scale has the notes F, A♭, B♭, C, and E♭. This arrangement uses the two blue notes of the F minor pentatonic—A♭ (the minor third) and E♭ (the flat seventh)—which are combined with the strumming to create a rhythm fill that is played as part of the strumming of the F chord. It gives the song a strong blues-style mood.

Listen to how the first few measures of this song set up its mood and emotion. Strumming just the F major chord, without adding either of the blue notes, is certainly fine but nowhere near as interesting.

Track 66

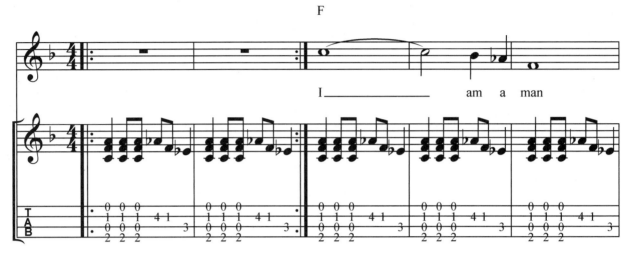

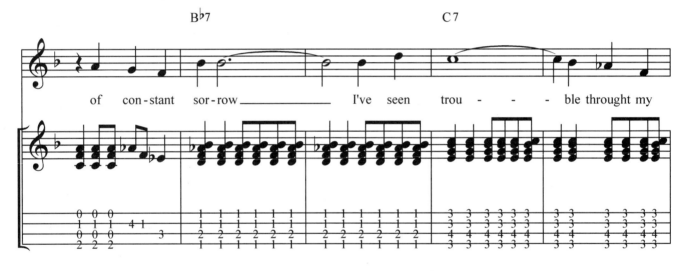

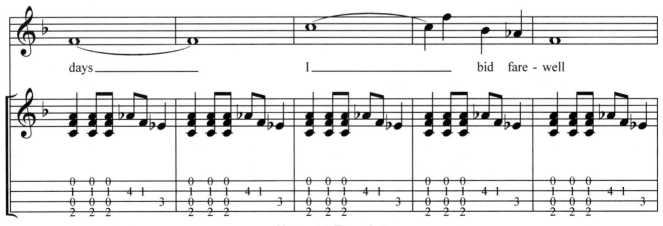

Chapter 16, Example 3.

Combo Platter

You can create an even stronger blues vibe by using notes from both the major scale and the minor pentatonic scale in your musical fills. You actually got an early introduction to this type of fill at the end of Chapter 11 in the song "Dry Bones." In the last few measures of the song (between the final A chord and the closing A9 chord), there is a run of single notes on the A, E, and C strings:

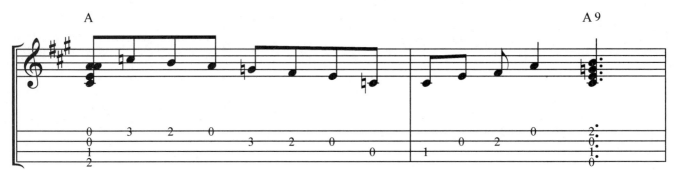

Combining the major scale and minor pentatonic in a fill.

Here, the use of the C and G set up the blues feel of the ending that gets resolved when the C note of the open C string becomes C♯ (the first fret of the C string) at the start of the second measure.

An Assortment of Fills

When creating and playing fills, your biggest concern should be the ease with which you can switch from strumming full chords to picking individual notes or double stops to emphasize the fill. You can easily come up with fills based on all the chords you have learned after you get into the habit of exploring which notes are easily reached while fingering a particular chord.

The G chord is a particularly good place to start because it gives you a lot of notes to work with by simply hammering-on to notes of the chord or performing pull-offs with them. Here is a sample fill based on the G chord that uses both hammer-ons and pull-offs:

 Track 67 (0:00)

Chapter 16, Example 4.

Fills as Chord Changes

Fills are essentially flourishes that make typical strumming or picking more interesting for you as the ukulele player and for your listeners. Besides spicing up the rhythm and strumming of a single chord, fills can make simple chord changes much more exciting. Here is a simple fill used to make the transition from G to C:

Track 67 (0:12)

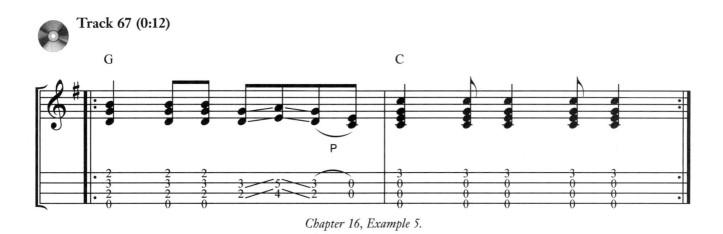

Chapter 16, Example 5.

This fill takes advantage of where you place your fingers to play the G chord. After playing the G chord, raise your middle finger off the A string. Then using your index and ring fingers, slide them from their place on the G chord (index finger is on the second fret of the C string and the middle finger is on the third fret of the E string) up the neck two frets; then slide them back to their original positions before pulling off both strings to sound the open notes. The pull-off frees up your fingers so they are ready to play the upcoming C chord.

Here is an example of a C to F fill:

Track 67 (0:27)

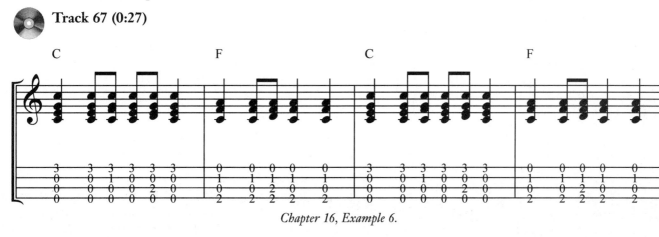

Chapter 16, Example 6.

This last fill takes advantage of your fingering of the F chord, using your index fingers to play the E string and then your middle finger to play the C string before settling in at the second fret of the g string to play the F chord.

Chord Changes as Fills

Just as you can use fills to liven up your chord changes, your chord changes can inspire the creation of fills. Going from C to G7 to C probably seems like old hat to you at this point, and you might not think it is even possible to make this progression sound at all interesting. Give this next example a listen and see whether you are willing to change your mind:

Track 68

Chapter 16, Example 7.

This seemingly complicated bit of picking, usually referred to as a *banjo roll* because it is the sort of flurry of notes a banjo player would come up with, is the result of combining chord voicings of C and G7 further up the neck and then leaving the A string open while picking. With a bit of imagination (and more than a bit of practice), you can come up with all sorts of fills for practically every chord progression you have heard.

Customizing a Fill

It is important to remember that fills are made up of notes, which means you can play around with various elements of each fill you learn or create. For example, suppose you really liked the following fill, which works nicely as a jazzy transition between the F and B♭ chords:

Track 69

Chapter 16, Example 8.

It definitely sounds cool, but you might not find yourself playing a lot of songs that have an F to B♭ progression. You are more likely to play songs with G to C, so why not transpose each note up one full musical step, like this?

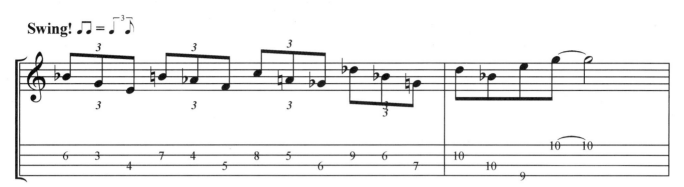

Chapter 16, Example 8—fill transposed up one full step.

If you have a fill you especially like, do yourself a favor and transpose and learn it in as many keys as you see fit. This is how you build your fill vocabulary.

Likewise, you should make a point of playing around with the individual notes and their timing. Making small variations to your fills allows you to use them over and over without wearing them out.

Practice, Practice

As you evolve as a ukulele player, your fretting hand will be almost as busy as your picking hand, sometimes perhaps even more! Go over each chord you have learned and figure out which notes you can reach easily with a free finger while still maintaining the chord. Take notice of which strings and notes allow you to readily make a hammer-on or pull-off to create a fill for the chord you are playing.

Besides experimentation, listen to other ukulele players—not to mention guitarists and other musicians—for ideas for fills. If you have a book with the guitar parts of songs written out, you can easily translate those fills to the ukulele.

Start slowly and simply. Be more concerned about keeping close to your chord shapes so you don't lose the rhythm. Any fill that is so complicated you can't maintain the beat of a song is a fill you need to practice first at as slow a tempo as possible.

Be certain to work on transposing fills into different keys as well as playing around with the timing of the notes. Transposing will help you keep up your knowledge of the fretboard, and being able to come up with numerous timing possibilities for your fills will ensure each fill you add to your fill vocabulary can become a dozen or more different fills! Plus, you will be developing your sense of phrasing, which will become important if you decide to make a go of improvising and soloing.

The Least You Need to Know

- Fills are short musical phrases used to liven up basic rhythms and strumming.
- Many fills come from playing around with the notes and fingering of basic chords and chord shapes.
- The major and minor pentatonic scales each have five notes.
- Playing a minor (or minor pentatonic) scale over major chords can create a blues-style feel.
- Try to transpose all the fills you learn into different keys, and play around with the timing of the individual notes to create variations.

Soloing

In This Chapter

- Learning basic soloing guidelines
- Adding the rasgueado to your bag of tricks
- Tapping and tremolo picking
- Three backing tracks for soloing practice

When you go to any major art museum, you are likely to see art students making sketches of various masterpieces. They learn about form, composition, and perspective by copying the great works of other artists and then using what they learn to create their own original pieces.

Musicians often learn to solo in the same way. Ages ago (or at least before CDs and the internet) musicians copied solos by ear, listening over and over (and over) again to songs they knew and wanted to learn. One great advantage to this now seemingly quaint and old-fashioned method was (and still is) that it developed their musical ear and listening skills quite rapidly, which helped the players learn a lot about music in regard to song structures, chord progressions, and playing in various keys and styles.

Nowadays ukulele players, like guitarists, learn primarily through tablature, with a few also using music notation to help. Doing so obviously doesn't rely on or build up one's listening skills. Additionally, many players who use tablature don't seem to make the connection that the little fills and runs they learn in one solo are transferable to other solos and can help them develop their improvisational skills.

Ukulele players also learn to solo through noodling around—playing with the notes of scales and chords, much as you did when learning to create fills. Many solos are, in fact, created by stringing a bunch of fills in a row.

You might not realize it, but you already have the tools to create a good solo on your ukulele. You can play slurs such as hammer-ons, pull-offs, slides, and bends. You also have the ability to find scales and chords of different voicings all over the neck. You have some practice with using melodies from your study of chord melody from Chapter 15, and you now have the ability to come up with short fills. Now you can just put all these skills together to create your own solos.

A Few Guidelines

Solos can be as simple or complicated, as short or long as you see fit. You can play one or two notes repeatedly over a song's chord progression, or you can hit every note on your ukulele's fretboard with lightning-quick fingers. Whatever choice you make, keep in mind a good solo is one that adds to the depth and enjoyment of a song. It should be a part of the song and not stand apart from it. You should match and enhance the style and mood of whatever particular song you are playing.

As you begin exploring the art of soloing, start by keeping things short, simple, and slow. Concentrate on getting your notes clean and clear and on using good picking, strumming, and fretting techniques. Speed comes with repetition so if you can play a phrase cleanly, you will eventually be able to get it up to speed.

FRET LESS!

For whatever reason, ukulele players often divide solos into two classes: technical (which usually implies the solo is filled with a million or more notes played at a speed that makes you wonder if the uke player is being paid by the note) and emotional (where the melody of the solo is given center stage). Both styles are valid and both have their place in songs when soloing. Neither is better than the other, and your best solos often incorporate a bit of both melody and speed.

It helps to think of solos as little songs within the songs. Good solos usually have memorable melodies, quite often derived from the melody of the song being played (playing the song's melody is a time-honored soloing technique). And like a song, a good solo will have a distinct beginning, middle, and end. Think of the solos you like best, and it is likely (regardless of what instrument they are played on) they are the ones you find yourself singing along with.

Serious Finger Flicking

However, a solo can also be purely rhythmic, something as simple as a few chords played in a highly stylized manner. One way to add some distinctive kick to your strumming is with the *rasgueado*, a fla-menco guitar technique ukulele players often refer to as the *roll strum* or *roll stroke*.

Performing a rasgueado seems simple on paper—you flick out your fingers, starting with your little finger, one at a time in rapid succession across all four strings, as shown in the figure on the next page.

Like many of the techniques you have learned, this one requires more than a bit of practice. Start at a slow speed to make certain you are getting all your fingers in play and the flicking motion for each is relatively even.

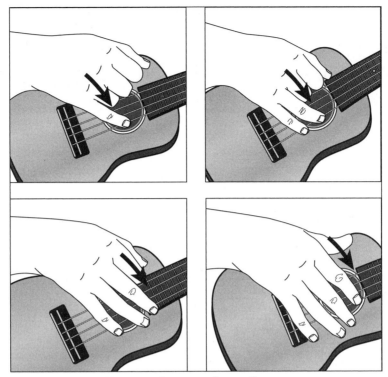

Executing the rasgueado or roll strum.

Because you control both the speed and evenness of the flicking, not to mention the number of fingers used (some players occasionally opt for using just three fingers), the rasgueado can add a lot of flair to simple strumming, elevating a rhythm to the same highlights as a flashy solo, like this:

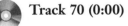

Track 70 (0:00)

Chapter 17, Example 1.

Good players can perform rasgueados in both directions, downward and upward. Check out on YouTube the video of "Let's Dance" by Jake Shimabukuro if you would like a lofty goal to strive for!

Cramming in More Notes

Another way of adding a bit of flash and speed to your playing is to put your hammer-on and pull-off skills to good use in combination with your finger picking, as in the following example:

 Track 70 (0:17)

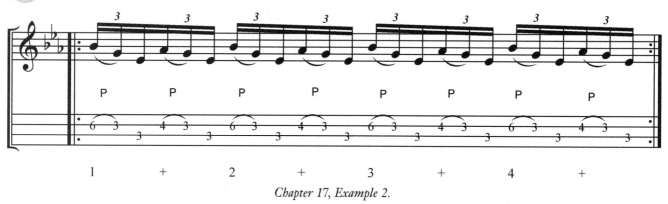

Chapter 17, Example 2.

Here you see a series of sixteenth note triplets, which means each set of triplets is played in the space of a half a beat. Using your index finger to barre all four strings at the third fret, use your pinky, ring, or middle finger to play the note at the sixth fret of the E string. Pick the string with an upstroke of a finger of your right hand and then perform a pull-off with the fretting finger. Finish the triplet with a downstroke of your thumb on the C string. Then keeping your index finger right where it is, place your middle finger on the fourth fret of the E string and repeat the process.

Notice on the CD, this last example is played slowly and with counting to ensure you make each triplet evenly. This should help you keep all the notes even as you speed up, as you can hear in the second half of the audio on this example.

Tapping

Being proficient at both hammer-ons and pull-offs definitely can add to your playing speed, even more so when your strumming hand gets involved in the proceedings. That is precisely what happens with "tapping," which is basically supercharged hammering-on and pulling-off. Your right hand is used to hammer, or tap, a note on the fretboard while the left hand both hammers and sets up the other notes played in sequence.

The following illustration demonstrates what will happen in the next example on the CD. Your left hand is positioned with the index finger (labeled 3) on the third fret of the E string and the ring finger (2) positioned above the fifth fret of the same string:

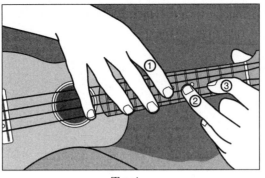

Tapping.

The index finger of the right hand (labeled 1) starts things out by hammering-on to the seventh fret of the E string. When the note is played, the right-hand finger lifts up as the left-hand ring finger (2) performs a hammer-on at the fifth fret and then executes a pull-off, sounding the note at the third fret where the left-hand index finger is placed. It will sound like this:

Track 70 (0:48)

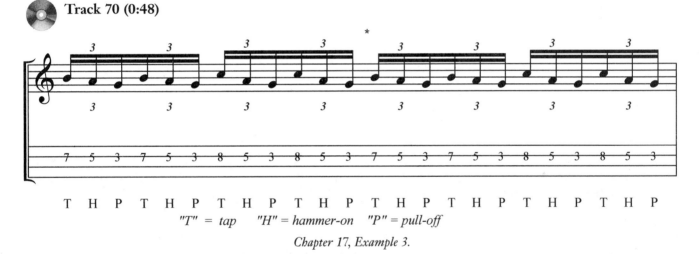

T H P T H P T H P T H P T H P T H P T H P T H P

"T" = tap   "H" = hammer-on   "P" = pull-off

Chapter 17, Example 3.

Tapping is definitely impressive, but because of the ukulele's nylon strings you are not going to get the clarity you might experience when tapping on an electric guitar. You are bound to experience excessive string noise (more like a ping, really) on the initial tap, and the pull-offs have to be clean to ensure clear notes are produced. When used judiciously, tapping will certainly add more than a bit of flash to your solos.

Tremolo Strumming

Sometimes speed is used to produce long-sounding single notes or chords. Tremolo strumming (also called *tremolo picking*) uses a very rapid strumming motion of your right hand to produce a striking quavering quality to the notes you play, making your ukulele sound much like a mandolin or balalaika.

Some ukulele players prefer to use a pick for tremolo strumming, but you can achieve a more interesting tone by performing this technique with your fingers—one or several of them, as demonstrated in the following example:

Track 71

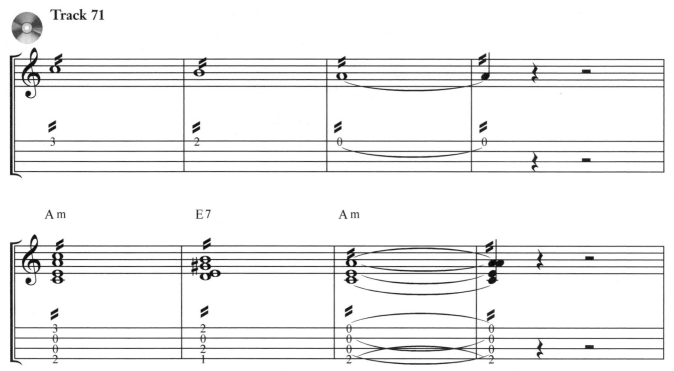

Chapter 17, Example 4.

In the first three measures of this example, single notes on the A string are given the tremolo strumming treatment. Place a finger on the third fret of the A string. Then position your right hand's index finger so it runs parallel to the string and so that the pad of the finger is making light contact with the string. Keeping both your finger and your wrist fairly stiff, continuously vibrate your hand in a down and up motion across the A string, keeping the pad of the index finger in light contact with the string.

You can use multiple fingers for tremolo strumming, playing whole chords, as shown in the last three measures of the previous example. A good way to get a feel for this is to lightly lay the first three fingers of your right hand so the middle of the pad of each finger rests in the space between the strings. Again, keeping all of your right-hand fingers and your wrist as stiff as comfortably possible, vibrate your strumming hand lightly down and up across all four strings.

Each of these new techniques gives your ukulele a new voice you can incorporate into your soloing as well as (in the case of both the rasgueado and tremolo strumming) your rhythm. Be sure to experiment with them and work them into the songs you already play.

Tracks to Solo Along With

To help you get started on creating solos, here is the first of three backing tracks you can play while you noodle and experiment. This one is in 4/4 time and in the key of F, using the following chord progression.

Track 72

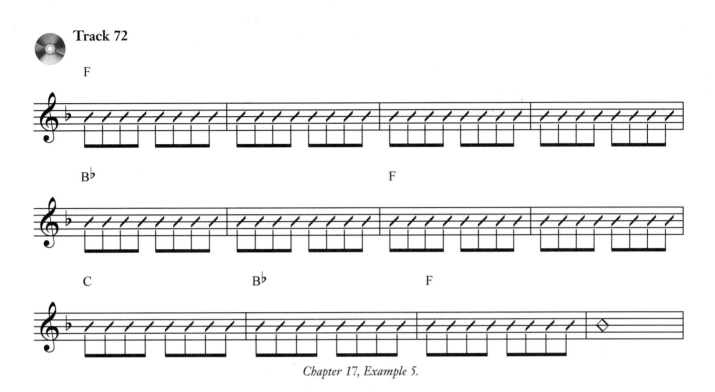

Chapter 17, Example 5.

You can use either the F major scale or the F major pentatonic (F, G, A, C, and D) to solo over this progression. Also, as you learned in Chapter 16, using the F minor pentatonic (F, A♭, B♭, C, and E♭) over the chords will help give you a nice blues feel when you solo. Combining notes from both the major and the minor pentatonic also works nicely.

F Major Pentatonic Scale

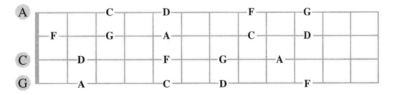

F Minor Pentatonic Scale

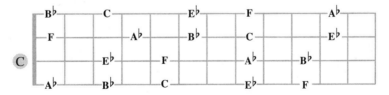

Notes of the F major and F minor pentatonic scale.

Creating Phrasing

Play the first backing track and get a feel for the music. Then choose just one, two, or three notes from the F minor pentatonic scale and try to come up with some nice rhythmic phrasing. The object is to get comfortable playing a few notes and to establish a sense of phrasing.

Thinking about how solos are like melodies in that they can be sung will help. Melodies tend to be sung in phrases, with each phrase having a long note or rest at the end to give the singer a chance to catch her breath. Here is an example of how you can use the notes from both the F major and F minor pentatonic scale and—with the help of techniques you already know—come up with some melodic phrases that fit this first backing track nicely:

Track 73

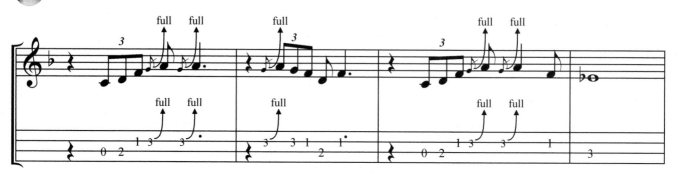

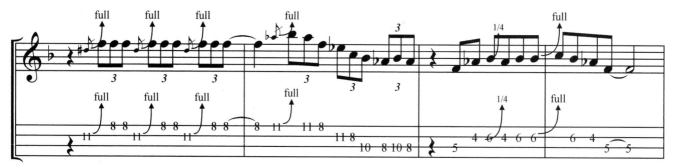

Chapter 17, Example 6.

Try playing, and playing around with, each phrase in this last example. Study where the notes of each phrase can be found on the fretboard. Also check out how bends are used to give the solo even more of a blues-style vibe.

Then cue up the backing track again and have another go at making your own solo. Don't try to copy the last example, but use it instead as a template for your own ideas in terms of both notes and timing.

Back Along the Watchtower

Blues-based songs are probably the most user friendly on which to practice soloing. When you feel that you have made some progress on this first backing track, try your hand at the second one. Here is a track to help you:

Track 74

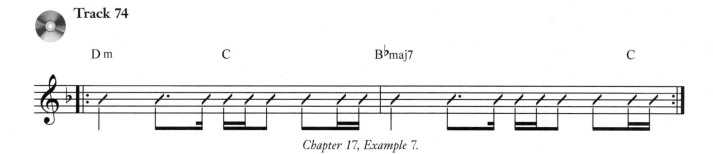

Chapter 17, Example 7.

This backing track is in the key of D minor and uses three chords: Dm, C, and B♭maj7. It is the same generic chord progression as "All Along the Watchtower," albeit in a different key.

You can use either the D minor pentatonic scale or the notes of the full F major scale for soloing, as the F major scale and the D minor scales share the same notes (you can find out more about that in the online Quick Guide page for this chapter). Here are some musical ideas that might help get you started:

Track 75

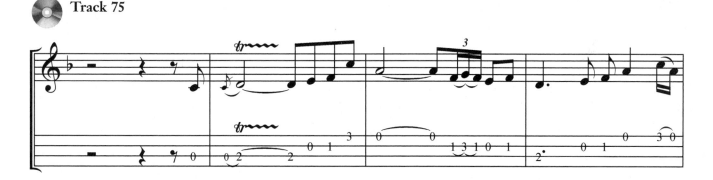

Chapter 17, Example 8.

All on Your Own

Now that you have taken your initial steps at soloing, it is time to give you a backing track of your own. This one is slightly more complicated in that the song has two separate parts:

 **Track 76**

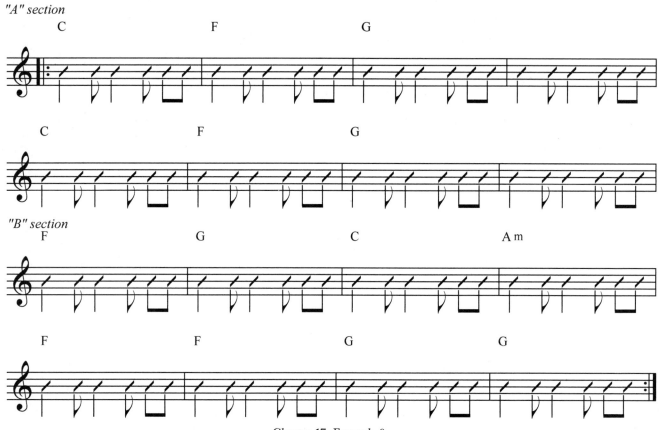

Chapter 17, Example 9.

The "A" section of the backing track uses the chords C, F, and G, while the "B" section tosses in an Am chord as well. Each of the two sections is structurally different.

For either section, the C major or the C major pentatonic scales should serve you well in your soloing explorations.

Practice, Practice

There is a huge difference between most solos and improvisation. Most of the solos you hear on recordings, whether played on a ukulele or another instrument, are *not* improvised but have been created and arranged for the particular song of which they are a part. These solos often start out as improvisations, which generate various musical ideas that serve as the foundation of the finished solo you hear.

Improvising is an important part of soloing, just as learning to copy a solo note-for-note is. Both will develop your sense of timing and phrasing, as well as give you experience in making your solos fit the song at hand.

Do yourself a favor, though, and don't expect to magically remember every note you improvise! When you come up with a phrase that blows you away, take the time to write it down for future reference. Writing out your solos, or at least the outlines of them, can keep you from repeating the same ideas in all your soloing. The more ideas you have in your head, the bigger your improvising vocabulary becomes and the more interesting solos you will be able to come up with.

UKE LORE

There have been many great ukulele soloists throughout history, some of whom you've read about throughout this book. Two contemporary ukulele masters worth checking out are Herb Ohta, Jr. (whose father Herb Ohta, who also went by "Ohta-San," was one of those historical players of legend) and Daniel Ho. Search for them on YouTube and/or iTunes.

Remember that the song itself should be the ultimate factor when putting together a solo. You can either match its mood and style or deliberately play against it to create a striking contrast.

Soloing is all about making an emotional statement, but you still need all your technique to shape it into powerful music.

The Least You Need to Know

- The rasgueado is a flamenco guitar technique that works well with the ukulele and solos.
- Getting proficient at slurs such as hammer-ons and pull-offs will help you develop speed for those times you want to use them in your soloing.
- Tapping requires both your left and right hands to work together on the fretboard performing hammer-ons and pull-offs.
- Solos should add to and enhance the mood and essence of each individual song.
- Use improvisation to help you create solos, and be sure to practice playing full solos as well.

All Together Now!

For most people, the true joy of making music comes from playing it and sharing it with others. It is time to take your ukulele (and all the skills and knowledge you have learned in this book) and put it together to play whatever you would like in almost every musical style and genre you can think of.

In the following chapters, you will get a sampling of various musical styles to study and play. More importantly, you will learn *how* to play music with others. There is no reason you can't take part in musical jams with other musicians, no matter what instrument they may play. You will get practical tips on playing as part of a band as well as with a ukulele ensemble. After all, you are going to enjoy playing your uke so much you will want to play every chance you get!

Sampling the World

In This Chapter

- Playing solo blues or backup jazz
- Going classical or old-world folk
- Rocking out on your uke
- A traditional Hawaiian song
- Finding time and purpose for practicing

A song is a song. There is no such thing as a "piano song" or a "guitar song" or a "violin song" or even a "ukulele song." You can play any song you like on any instrument you care to play. What you have to keep in mind is the character of a song is likely to change depending on which instrument you choose to play it on. Just because you can play the notes of the first movement of Beethoven's "Fifth Symphony" (think "da-da-da-dum …") on your ukulele doesn't mean your interpretation will win over a lot of listeners.

But the ukulele is an incredibly versatile instrument when it comes to playing songs in many musical styles and genres. Your uke can sound like a classical guitar or even a harpsichord or a balalaika if you want it to. All the techniques and ideas you learned in Parts 3 and 4 of this book, from strumming syncopated rhythms to pinch finger picking to adding hammer-ons and percussive strokes to using chord melody and fills to create solos, are meant to help you turn your ukulele into your personal musical voice.

To help you develop your uke's voice, this chapter presents seven songs of different musical styles. Five of them are solo ukulele pieces; the other two are sung with the uke being the accompanying instrument. Each song incorporates several of the ideas and techniques you have learned and should give you a great sampling of what you and your ukulele are now capable of.

UKE LORE

Getting a ukulele for Christmas led to a lifelong passion for May Singhi Breen. She taught ukulele, and not only wrote tutorial books but also was the first to record a ukulele lesson on a 78 rpm record. She also wrote ukulele arrangements for many of the popular songs of her day.

You will also find detailed, step-by-step instructions on how to play each song in the "Book Extras" section on *The Complete Idiot's Guide* website, www.idiotsguides.com.

"Blue Uke"

The early blues players created a legacy of music that became the foundation for country, jazz, and rock and roll. This piece, written specially for this book, uses a combination of finger-picking patterns and fills based on chord shapes to give your uke some great blues sounds.

 Track 77

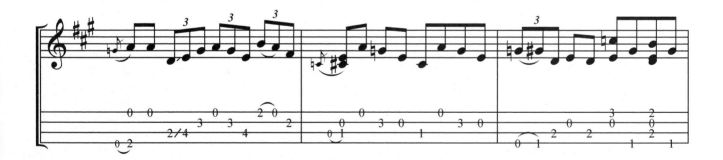

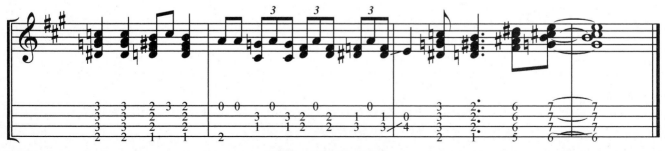

Chapter 18, Example 1.

"Brahms' Lullaby"

Your ukulele, combined with a light picking hand, makes this classical favorite a delight to play.

Track 78

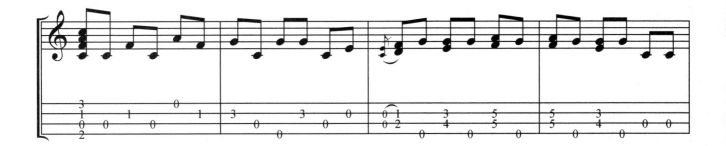

Chapter 18, Example 2.

"Old Time Mountain Uke"

Another original piece written for this book, "Old Time Mountain Uke," uses every slur you know—hammer-ons, pull-offs, slides, and bends—and combines them with the notes from both the C major and the C blues scale (C, E♭, F, G♭, G, and B♭) to create a bluegrass instrumental.

You will hear this piece first played very slowly and then played again at a more appropriate bluegrass tempo. You, of course, should feel free to play it even faster!

Track 79

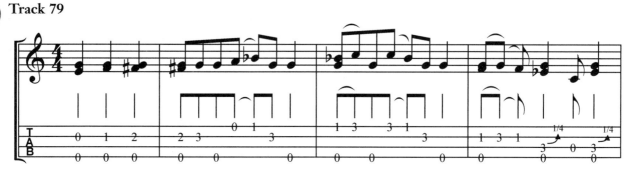

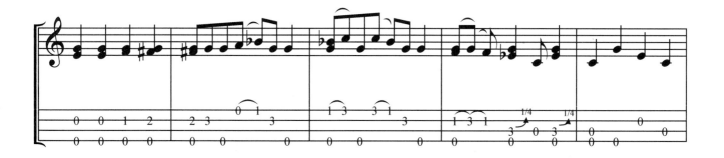

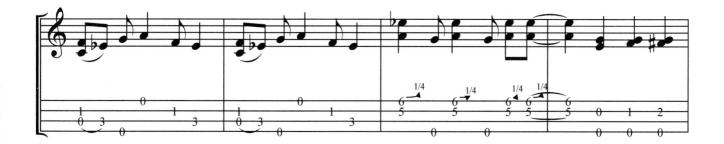

Chapter 18, Example 3.

"Shine On, Harvest Moon"

This song from the early 1900s has become a jazz standard. Having the ukulele play both staccato rhythmic chords and a touch of chord melody (including a very cool use of double-stops in the "January, February, June, or July" line) provides the song with a simple and classic jazz-style accompaniment.

 Track 80

Chapter 18, Example 4.

continues

continued

"Tum Balalaika"

If someone only listened to you play this old Russian Jewish folk song without seeing what you were playing, he might think you had taken up the mandolin, bouzouki, or balalaika. This instrumental arrangement makes excellent use of open strings to give your ukulele a light and airy voice perfectly fitting this song.

 Track 81

Chapter 18, Example 5.

"She'll Be Coming 'Round the Mountain"

Deep down, everyone has a bit of rock guitar god in them. This arrangement starts out with some power chords inspired by Pete Townshend of The Who and then goes on to pay tribute to Chuck Berry, Keith Richards, Jimmy Page, and even a little Angus Young of AC/DC.

Track 82

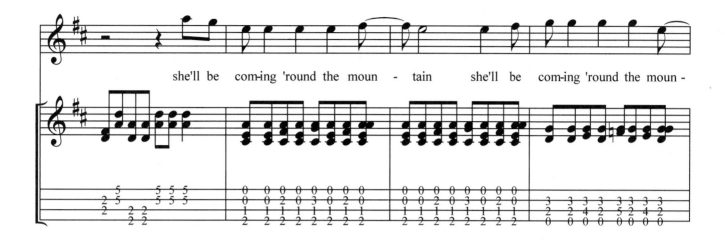

she'll be com-ing 'round the moun - tain   she'll be com-ing 'round the moun -

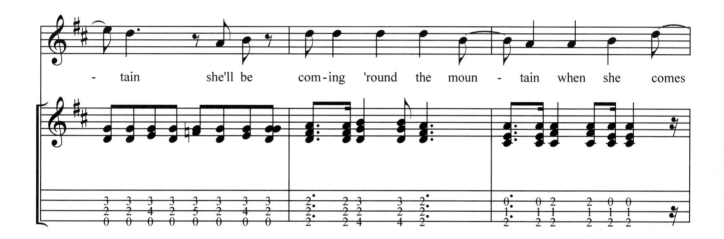

- tain   she'll be com-ing 'round the moun - tain when she comes

Chapter 18, Example 6.

"Aloha Oe"

Hawaiian Queen Lili'uokalani wrote what would be her most famous song while on a horseback trip about Oahu in 1877. This ukulele chord melody arrangement uses an alternative tuning (gCEG) to imitate the style of Hawaiian slack-key guitar playing, where the guitarists use alternative tunings to create mesmerizing finger-picking patterns.

  Track 83

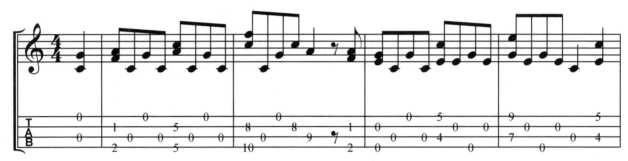

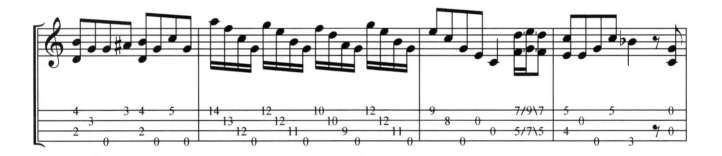

Chapter 18, Example 7.

Practice, Practice

You can read every ukulele tutorial that has ever been printed, watch every tutorial DVD, and take private lessons from the greatest ukulele players in the world, but none of these will matter if you don't practice and play your uke.

Notice *practice* and *play* are two separate words. Practice certainly involved playing your ukulele, but it also focused on learning new material and techniques as well as on reviewing and getting meticulously better at the things you have already learned. Both practice and play are necessary to improve and grow as a ukulele player.

However, sometimes simply finding time to either practice or play seems to be more work than learning! Life is busy, and it is easy for days at a time to slip by between practice sessions. Or worse, when you do manage to get some spare time, you haven't a clue as how to make best use of it to get the most out of your practicing.

The best way to get practice to become a habit in your life is to make an appointment for it. That might seem impossible, but if you think about it, there are probably spots in your day where you can take 15 minutes or so to simply sit and practice and/or play. For most people, the first and last moments of a day tend to work well. The ukulele can be played quietly so you don't have to worry about waking someone. Plus, there are a lot of things you can practice without actually strumming the strings, such as changing chords. If 15 minutes can be stretched into 20 or 25 minutes, that would be even better. Or your practice time could both begin and end your day.

Even if you are hard-pressed to practice on a regular basis, finding 10 minutes here and there is better than nothing. Are you waiting for something to heat up in the microwave? Are you boiling water for tea and letting it steep? Are you waiting for someone to get dressed before going out someplace? Are you watching television for no reason other than it is on, or checking your email or Facebook page for the twentieth time today? Ten minutes a day is more practice time than a single 45-minute or hour-long session in one week. Ten minutes twice a day or even three times a day is obviously better still!

Remember your ukulele is very portable. If you are going to the park or going on a road trip, bring it along. Take it to work and practice during lunch. You might even find yourself getting invitations to play with others and, if that happens, you will be getting some valuable tips for that in the next two chapters.

Whatever time you get to practice, it is important to make the most of it. Before you get started on practicing, take a moment to set some goals for yourself and specific objectives to work on. "Getting better" might seem like a specific goal until you sit down and wonder *how* you are going to get better. "Switching between C, F, and G without pausing" is much more specific. It is also a measurable and attainable goal. Your goals should be both measurable and attainable.

Practice takes place over long periods of time—actually for the rest of your life when you think about it. It is important to make your practice varied and to keep it interesting. A lot of musicians create practice schedules to keep track of the goals they are trying to achieve as well as practice logs to keep a record of what they accomplished during any particular session. Creating a practice schedule allows you to work on several goals concurrently. For example, you might spend Monday focusing on changing chords, Tuesday on maintaining good rhythm, Wednesday on finger picking, Thursday going back over both chords and rhythm together, and then having a review day on Friday.

Having a practice schedule that is varied and tailored to your needs will make you look forward to practicing, and looking forward to practicing makes you create time for it. It is really all very simple: The more you practice and play, the more you learn and the better you get. There is a whole world of music out there waiting for you. Go out and start taking it all in by making time for practice, even if it is just 15–30 minutes a day to begin with.

The Least You Need to Know

- You can play any type of song on your ukulele, but don't expect it to sound just like the original song.
- Through the techniques you have learned, you can make your ukulele sound like other instruments, such as a classical guitar, mandolin, harpsichord, or balalaika.
- You will improve as a uke player only if you make the time to practice and then make the most of your practicing time.
- Try to find time to practice every day. Setting aside a specific time will help you get into a routine of practicing.
- Set practice goals for yourself. Make your goals both attainable and measurable.

Assembling an Ensemble

In This Chapter

* Good reasons to play with others
* Finding ukulele players to jam with
* A quick look at fake sheets and chord sheets
* Creating a second ukulele part for a song
* Adding a baritone ukulele part

Always remember that you don't have to explore the wide and wonderful world of the ukulele all on your own! Throughout its history, the ukulele has inspired a devoted following of both players and fans and, thanks in no small part to the internet, it is easier than ever before to find these people who share your love of this little instrument. Finding them is the first step toward making music with others.

The worldwide community of ukulele players is an incredibly welcoming group. You will find ukulele clubs anywhere from Broken Arrow, Oklahoma, to Oxford, England. There are ukulele clubs in North Queensland (Australia), Madrid (Spain), Dublin (Ireland), Vancouver (Canada), Pago Pago (Samoa), and Kuala Lumpur (Malaysia). You will likely find a community of ukulele players right in your own town!

You know how great it feels when you play your uke? Well, that feeling can become a zillion times stronger when two ukulele players get together! And when you have three, four, or a dozen or more ukuleles making music together, you have the potential for magic like you have never heard! So it is imperative you find other uke players to jam with. In this chapter you will learn just how to find them and how to use the skills you have learned to create some special musical moments in those jams by working together as an ensemble.

The Best Way to Learn

In addition to practicing and playing on your own, playing with others is one of the best ways to make huge leaps of progress in your ukulele playing. Right off the bat you will understand why it is so important to know your basic chords and why being able to keep in rhythm is such a vital part of playing music. Right before a uke get-together, you will probably spend all of your practice time on all the basic chords and rhythms you know, just to make a good impression.

Speaking of rhythm, you will quickly discover from playing with others that rhythm is indeed much more than down and up strokes. You will also confirm that the ability to listen to all that is going on around you is without a doubt the most important skills you can develop as a musician.

Playing with others gives you firsthand experience that no one ever plays without making mistakes. You have to learn to play through them and laugh about them later. Plus, playing with others often exposes you to all sorts of musical styles and genres. You might start out with an old traditional folk song and then play a rock song followed by a country number followed by a jazz standard.

Musical get-togethers are wonderful ways to pick up pointers on all sorts of techniques, from changing chords to using different chord voicings up the neck to fancier rhythm strums to soloing and adding fills. Most musicians (ukulele players in particular for some reason) love to help beginners, so take advantage of the knowledge and experience of more seasoned uke players.

Fair warning, though—most people find making music with others to be highly addictive! Whatever initial worries you might have will soon be replaced by the desire to get together to make more music as soon as possible!

Just Jump In

Do yourself a favor and toss out all the excuses you have already come up with for *not* playing with others. "I'm just a beginner" or "I'm not good enough" or "I'm really shy" are simply ways for you to put off making music in a group. If you know three or four chords, even just the four chords you learned in Chapter 5, then you can play with others.

Remember that all ukulele players start at the same place. When you are in a group, each player brings her own knowledge and experiences and it is like having a roomful of teachers to help you with the rough spots. You won't have to worry if you can't make a chord change quickly enough because someone else will cover it for you. Just try your best to keep the beat steady, and you will get better with each subsequent chord change. The only way to learn to play with others is to play with others, so get out there and do just that!

Above all, try to relax and enjoy yourself and the music you are helping to create!

Fake Sheets

Speaking of music, it is very likely any informal jam you attend will not have music for you to read. Instead of the music being either standard or rhythm notation or ukulele tablature, you will probably find yourself staring at a *fake sheet* or *chord sheet*. Essentially these are simply lines of lyrics with names of chords posted at various places in the lyrics.

 DEFINITION

Fake sheets or **chord sheets** (also occasionally called *cheat sheets*) are simplified written instructions of songs. Fake sheets have the melody line written out in standard music notation (the lyrics are written out as well) with chord names placed at the points in the song where chord changes take place. Chord sheets simply list the lyrics with the chords. There are many styles of chord sheets, so it is good to look one over carefully before you start playing a song.

A typical fake sheet shows a song's melody line written in standard music notation, along with the lyrics and the chords, like this:

A fake sheet of the opening of "Hard Times Come Again No More."

On a fake sheet, you can usually tell where the chord changes occur by seeing where the chords fall over the notes of any given measure. In "Hard Times Come Again No More" (as seen in the previous example), the first measure is four beats of G while the second measure starts with two beats of C and changes back to G on the third beat.

Chord sheets are a lot more like tablature when it comes to information about timing. A chord sheet of the same opening of "Hard Times Come Again No More" usually looks like this:

> G   C G
>
> 'Tis the song the sigh of the wear-y
>
>   A   D7
>
> Hard times hard times come again no more

Here you have chords placed over certain words of the melody. But the location of the chord changes are, more often than not, only approximate. Also, a singer can decide to stretch out a particular word or a syllable while singing, so there are all sorts of potential ways of getting the chord change in the wrong place!

You can see that if you are not at all familiar with a song, having a chord chart is only somewhat helpful. You will know what the chords are, but you are going to be a bit in the dark as to when they change. This is another reason to hold back a bit until you feel more at ease with a new song.

FRET LESS!

Always carry a pencil or pen with you when you take part in a musical get-together. You should take whatever notes necessary to help you understand precisely when any chord changes occur. Plus, you can also draw out chord diagrams of any unfamiliar chords. You can probably stash both blank paper and a pen or pencil in your ukulele case.

Finding Fellow Uke Players

The ukulele is currently riding a huge wave of popularity thanks to the internet and to YouTube in particular. You can find all sorts of websites dedicated to the uke, its history, and its music, as well as videos of uke players.

In numerous forums and chat rooms you can connect with ukulele enthusiasts from all over the world. Some of these sites are the home pages of ukulele clubs; others have lists of various clubs. If you type "ukulele clubs" or "list of ukulele clubs" into your favorite search engine, you will get several thousand places to start!

You can also ask around at your local music store or check your local classified ads (or even Craigslist) for leads on uke groups and clubs. If you take private lessons or go to group ukulele classes, then your teacher or even your classmates may know some local groups. Plus, informal jam sessions among your classmates are great for practicing the material you are covering in class.

One of the easiest ways to find other ukulele players is to carry your ukulele around with you! Take it to work on occasion (and you can use your lunch hour for practicing) or carry it around on your next walk in the park or jaunt around town. You are likely to get chatted up by other musicians, and hopefully they might be (or might know) a uke player who is keen on playing music with someone.

> **SMOOTH STRUMMING**
>
> It is a good idea to hang back a little when you play your first informal jam session. When you don't know a song, listen to the first verse and get a feel for both the chord changes and the rhythm. Keep your strumming simple and concentrate on hitting the new chord at the appropriate beat.
>
> Don't be shy about asking to play a song a second time. Usually everyone benefits from a second go 'round of a song, and it is a great way for the group to work out arrangements.

Throwing Your Own Party

You might even consider hosting your own ukulele hootenanny! Start small by inviting one or two folks and see how things go. Have some songs ready to try out and be sure to ask your guests to bring two or three as well. Ideally you should begin with songs everyone knows and that have just two to five fairly simple chords. It also helps if someone in the group can sing the songs!

Things might go tentatively at first until you and your friends loosen up a bit, but before you know it you will be strumming out some tunes and having a great time. Many larger ukulele groups, even performance groups like the Ukulele Orchestra of Great Britain, began as simple and fun get-togethers.

Making Arrangements

It won't be long until you realize you and the group can do a lot more than just strum chords together. You might hear some of the more experienced players throwing in a few fancy fills here and there or using different forms of chords up the neck.

Just because you are a relative beginner on the ukulele doesn't mean you can't take part in coming up with interesting ways to add to the musical proceedings of your jam. All you need to do is to listen and then apply some of the techniques and ideas you learned in Parts 3 and 4.

> **UKE LORE**
>
> When it comes to ukulele ensembles and the fun and interesting song arrangements they can create, you can't find a better example (or source of inspiration) than the Ukulele Orchestra of Great Britain (UOGB). Founded in 1985, the group consists of eight members playing seven ukuleles of various sizes and one member playing an acoustic bass guitar, which is often jokingly referred to as a "bass ukulele."
>
> The UOGB cover a wide range of musical genres from Tchaikovsky to the Sex Pistols, and their musical arrangements are both imaginative and entertaining. Definitely check out the DVD of the group's 2009 live performance at the Royal Albert Hall where they play selections by David Bowie, Richard Wagner, Talking Heads, and—with the help of a sold-out, standing-room-only audience—have close to a thousand ukuleles belting out "Ode to Joy."

Because we have been using Stephen Foster's "Hard Times Come Again No More" as an example in this chapter, let's take a look and listen to the whole song. This basic arrangement is in the key of G and uses just a single tenor ukulele strumming simple open position chords to accompany the vocal:

Track 84

Chapter 19, Example 1.

continues

continued

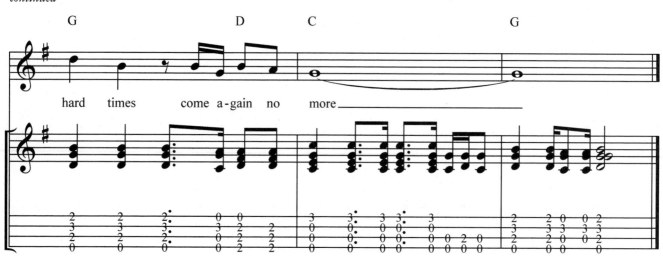

Listen to this last example a few times. It sounds pretty good just on its own, doesn't it? Pay attention to the strumming of the chords and you can hear the rhythm has a distinct pulse, one that gives the song a sense of breathing. Likewise, the melody line being sung has numerous long notes and rests. That means there is space for you to come up with a second or even a third ukulele part if you choose to do so.

Creating More from Less

You definitely need to keep the idea of musical space in mind when you are creating additional ukulele parts for a song. Your goal is to add to the song, making your contribution to it sound organic and not like a distraction. Anyone listening (yourself included) should be taken by how each ukulele part interacts well with one another.

> **SMOOTH STRUMMING**
>
> A good rule of thumb is to remember that the more uke parts added to a song, the less you want to play. For instance, counterbalance the strumming, particularly busy strumming, with single-note arpeggios. If one ukulele is pounding out sixteenth notes, play quarter notes or even half notes.

You might not realize it, but you already know three easy ways to come up with a second ukulele part— picking single-note arpeggios (instead of strumming), playing different chord voicings further up the neck, and adding fills. The following example details a second ukulele part that does a bit of each.

Note how the single notes of the fills at the beginning blend nicely with the strumming of the original ukulele part. Also notice how a lot of the chords are voiced so the note on the A string follows the melody line, especially on the first set of "hard times, hard times" where the chords are played as half notes before cascading into a flourishing fill during the "come again no more" lyric over the A chord.

This is, of course, just one of many possibilities. As an example it is also meant to show you a lot of ideas at once! You probably should start out a bit simpler until you feel comfortable moving between different chord shapes. The idea is to *try something different*—to play a counterpoint to what the other ukulele is doing. Finding out what doesn't work is just as important as discovering what does!

Track 85

Chapter 19, Example 2.

continues

continued

hard   times   come a-gain   no   more_____

> **FRET LESS!**
>
> Be sure to play to your strengths when coming up with additional ukulele parts. If you are worried about staying in rhythm, you can mimic the original strumming using different chord voicings or simplify the strums to quarter notes and half notes.
>
> Likewise, if you are concerned that you don't know where other chord choices might be, you could find it easier to add arpeggios or fills where space allows.

Bringing Up the Lows

Don't forget that because you know where the notes and chords are on the baritone ukulele, you can create a low baritone part for a song, too. The following example, which highlights the baritone ukulele, uses a lot of single notes as well as some fills that involve hammer-ons and pull-offs.

You can hear how the baritone takes advantage of the spaces left by the singer and the other two ukulele players by tossing in some simple but quick fills, like the one after the lyric "lingered."

 Track 86

'Tis the   song   the sigh   of the

Chapter 19, Example 3.

A Fine Ensemble

In some spots it sounds like the baritone ukulele part might be fighting for space with the other ukuleles. But remember you should take into account the fact that the notes of the baritone are lower and not in the same range as the strumming of the original tenor uke and the higher-up-the-neck chords of the concert uke's part.

Let's put all three parts together now, and listen to Track 87.

 Track 87

Doesn't that sound a lot nicer than three ukuleles all strumming the same chords with the same rhythm? Each ukulele plays a distinct part of this trio, and each part complements the other. You have taken what could have been a ukulele chorus in which each player performs the same part and turned it into a ukulele ensemble—and that is what the magic of making music together can be like!

Practice, Practice

Everything you have read about in this chapter is practice (and the result of practice); it is just a bit of a different type of practice than you are used to.

Start with a song you know fairly well—you don't have to be able to play it well, just know what the chords are and when the changes occur. Record yourself playing the basic rhythm of the song, singing along with it if possible, so you have a simple, single ukulele arrangement to work with. Take the time to listen to it, hearing where there might be room for fills or little embellishments. Study the chords and determine where they might be played in other places on the neck with minimal movement between changes. (Be sure to use the online "Quick Guide" performance notes for this chapter as a guideline at www.idiotsguides.com.)

Much of the initial work in creating additional ukulele parts can be hit-or-miss. You might find an idea for a fill sounds great by itself but doesn't ultimately blend in with the other ukulele parts or the vocal line. Starting with fills and embellishments that are short and simple will help you get a good feel for what a song arrangement might allow.

Ultimately through a lot of trial-and-error you will find that you will start to hear secondary ukulele parts in your head. If they are simple parts, you will be able to play them! This is the first major step toward being able to improvise.

Contrary to what you might believe, players who improvise well simply do not just jump in and create their parts by magic. They have spent hours and hours listening to music and tinkering with ideas on their instruments. It might seem like it is all spur of the moment, but the reality is a lot of practice goes into developing the skill set needed to create instantaneous music.

The Least You Need to Know

- Playing with other ukulele players is an excellent way to practice and continue to learn and grow as a musician.
- You can find other players to jam with in many ways—try both the internet and locally.
- Fake sheets and chord sheets are used in jam sessions far more often than regular sheet music or ukulele tablature.
- When you play with others, try to use your knowledge and skills to create additional ukulele parts so everyone isn't just strumming the same chords with identical rhythmic patterns.

Playing Well with Others

In This Chapter

- Jamming with non-ukulele musicians
- Considering amplification
- Playing with guitarists
- Creating a ukulele part for an original song
- Practicing performing

Although jamming with a group of other ukulele players is definitely exhilarating, you should try your hand at jamming with other musicians, too. Being the only ukulele in a group-jamming situation gives you a chance to add your unique voice to a band, whether pitching in to both enhance and keep the rhythm steady or taking your turn in the soloist's spotlight.

Playing in a band situation, whether it is an informal jam or a paying gig, offers up a whole new set of challenges to you both as a ukulele player and musician. When you play with other ukulele players, you already have a general feel for their instruments and what they can do. Pairing your ukulele with a bass guitar, a cello, a flute, a piano, or even an accordion will give you a lot of new musical ideas and take all the skills you have learned to new, higher levels.

It is your firm foundation of those basic skills—listening, keeping rhythm, and knowing what your ukulele is capable of—that will make you a valuable member of any musical group, whether you are the only ukulele player or one of a dozen.

Can You Hear Me Now?

When you start playing with others, one of the first things you notice is there is more music to listen to. You all might be playing the same song, but, as you learned in the last chapter, you might be playing different parts. Part of the listening, by necessity, becomes listening for your own part to make sure you are playing it to the best of your abilities. Making music with other ukulele players can be difficult sometimes because you might not always be able to distinguish your ukulele from that of another player. But thankfully, this is not often the case.

After you begin to jam with instruments other than ukuleles, you encounter a different scenario. In a group setting your ukulele will maintain its unique voice, but that voice might be somewhat on the quiet side—especially compared to instruments like the piano or an electric guitar. Add in a bass guitar and drums and you are likely to think your uke doesn't have any voice at all!

A lot depends on the situation and set up. If you are taking part in an all-acoustic get-together you might be able to hear your uke (and all the other instruments) just fine. But if you are sitting directly next to a grand piano, it might not be the case. So don't hesitate to change seats to better hear yourself as well as all the other musicians in the group.

> **SMOOTH STRUMMING**
>
> Whenever you play with others, always try to position yourself in a seat where you can see and hear as many of your fellow musicians as possible. Remember your ears are your musical guide so you should give them every possible advantage.

You are also going to learn it is a simple fact of life that when musicians get more and more into the music being made they tend to get louder (faster, too, sometimes!). Eventually, you are going to find yourself considering just how to make your ukulele be heard as part of the group instead of being seen as a prop no one realizes you are actually playing.

A Pickup for Your Ukulele

There are essentially three ways to amplify your ukulele. The most obvious is to use a microphone plugged into a PA system or a dedicated amplifier. This solution might seem a bit quaint and anti-quated, but many people feel it still is the best way to present the purest ukulele sound to the world. Because better microphones tend to deliver better sound quality, this can become pricey. But if you're asked to play with a band and they have their own PA and vocal microphones, dedicating a mic to your ukulele is usually an easy and painless task.

Because many ukulele players want to be heard in group situations, ukulele manufacturers are responding by producing electric/acoustic instruments. These ukuleles are regular acoustic ukuleles equipped with a "pickup"—either a miniature microphone or a transducer placed inside the uke's body under the saddle. An output jack, which allows you to plug a cable directly from your ukulele into either an amplifier or a PA system, is also built in to the body of your ukulele.

If you would prefer not to buy another ukulele, you have the option of having a luthier or guitar tech install a pickup into your current ukulele. This does involve drilling holes into your instrument, so you will need to talk over the procedure with the tech and get any questions you might have answered first.

Still another option is to use a stick-on–style pickup. Basically this is a small microphone (usually smaller than a quarter in diameter) that you stick onto your ukulele. The wire from the microphone has a jack on one end where you plug the cable that runs to your amplifier or PA.

Adding an Amp

Of course, the ability to be plugged in is totally useless without something to plug in to, and that would be an amplifier. Unless you are specifically looking to cover up the natural sound of your ukulele, use an amplifier specifically geared toward acoustic instruments, such as an acoustic guitar. These amps should help keep your ukulele sounding clean and clear.

> **SMOOTH STRUMMING**
>
> Having a ukulele you can plug in to an amplifier means you also can run your uke through any effects box or a series of them. This means you can essentially give your ukulele the same kind of sounds usually reserved for the electric guitar. Do you want some crunchy heavy metal distortion? No problem! How about a bit of chorus and echo to emulate Andy Summers of the Police? Some Mark Knopfler–style delay? It is all yours to explore after you have electrified your ukulele.

All this discussion about amplifying your ukulele might boil down to one question—are you planning on playing your ukulele in a situation where it might benefit from being amplified? For most players, the answer is usually no. But you could possibly change your mind in the future. Playing at open mics or sitting in with friends who play electric instruments is certainly within your capabilities at this point. It doesn't hurt to consider that one day you might indeed find yourself wanting to take your ukulele to a bigger stage.

Then the question becomes does your amplified ukulele sound the way you want it to sound? There are all sorts of options for you to explore when it comes to giving your uke a bigger voice. Take your time and get the amplification solution that best fits your needs.

Finding Space in a Group

Whatever other musicians you end up playing with, remember all songs have the same basic parts—a melody, harmony, and rhythm. Your task as a group member is to help give a song the best possible presentation. Because the ukulele blends in well with almost any other instrument, you can find yourself dealing with any musical aspect of a song.

For example, the melody usually falls to the singer, but if you are playing an instrumental version of a song, any instrument can be given the task of carrying the melody. As you read in Chapter 17, playing the melody line of a song is also a safe bet when it comes to taking a solo. A bit of tremolo picking can help bring out the melody lines when a number of other instruments are playing at the same time.

The chords of a song are the harmony, and you can add interesting layers to a song by using chord voicings different from those being played by other members of the group. Your ukulele has a unique musical voice, and where you play any given chord can help add layers to the harmonies. Listen to the overall balance of a song to hear whether most of the notes are in the high, middle, or lower range. Because the ukulele's range of notes tends to be in the middle to high area, you will usually find space there to play your standard chords. Occasionally, though, you might find a song needs a bit of a high punch, and playing your chords farther up the neck will help you provide that.

As far as rhythm goes, it is easy to have so many different strums and pulses jockeying for space that a song loses its groove and sounds disjointed. Listen to the feel of the song before you join in. Hear how the drummer or bass player (or whomever) is laying down the basic groove and start out either by copying it or strumming simple additions. If the drums are coming down hard on the second beat, for example, try a light upstroke on the offbeat between the second and third beats. Don't be shy about talking out rhythm parts with the others in your group and doing a short trial run to hear if they work. Initially it might be hit-or-miss, but with practice you will be a contributing member to the rhythm section.

The Uke and the Guitar

It is fairly safe to say most of the musicians you are more likely to meet will be guitarists (some of whom might be your fellow ukulele players). Playing with guitarists can be a challenge because the ukulele and the guitar are very much alike, both in terms of sound and playing techniques. And if you are playing with a group of guitar players, you are likely to feel like a fifth wheel.

But you can deal with multiple guitars with the same logic you apply to playing with multiple ukulele players. Use your ears to hear where the spaces in the music are and where short fills can be used to embellish a song. If the guitarists are primarily strumming, try using arpeggios and finger-picking patterns to create new layers, which will help make the song more interesting.

You need to use your eyes as well as your ears when playing with a guitar player. The ukulele doesn't have anywhere close to the range of notes available to the guitar, but guitarists rarely make use of their instruments' full capabilities in a single song. With its re-entrant tuning, the majority of the notes between the ukulele's first and fifth frets (including those of the open strings) fall into the same range as the notes between the third and tenth frets of the guitar. So if you are playing with a guitarist who primarily plays open position chords close to the headstock, you should find that both of you have a lot of room to jam in.

"It's Not a Love Song"

To give you an example of how you might go about integrating your ukulele into a group situation, here is an original song by Nick Torres (yes, that is the same Nick who has been singing the song examples in this book). I have chosen his song for a number of reasons, but the main one being that you are likely to find yourself playing original music when you play in a band, so using Nick's song is a great way for you to deal with a totally unfamiliar song. Although the song itself might be new, its two four-chord progressions (one in the verse and one in the chorus) are used in many songs.

The band you will be playing with consists of two acoustic guitars, an electric guitar, a bass guitar, and two percussionists. Here is a fake sheet for you to follow along with:

Track 88

Chapter 20, Example 1.

Making Adjustments

The first thing you probably noticed were the song's chords: A, F#m, D, and E. These are hardly the most ukulele-friendly chords. But think a minute about some of the things you have learned in this book. In Chapter 13 you learned about D tuning. If you were to use D tuning here and transpose accordingly, you would find yourself playing the following chords:

Original Chord	D Tuning Chord
A	G
F#m	Em
D	C
E	D

That is certainly a lot more inviting! And you might find the D tuning gives your instrument a sweeter tone, especially if you are playing a soprano ukulele or a concert ukulele. That will also help you stand out in contrast to the guitars.

Look again at the fake sheet for this song and listen to the CD as you do. You can hear the band has conveniently left you a lot of space. You could easily come up with some call-and-response fills during the vocal pauses, like this:

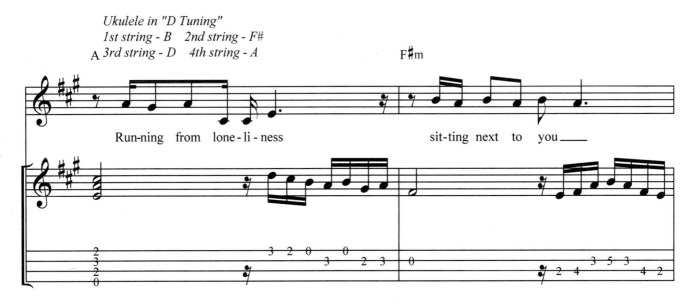

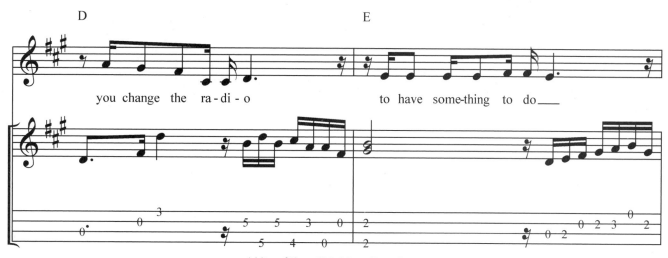

Adding fills to "It's Not a Love Song."

Another approach might be to come up with a finger-style pattern to counterbalance all the strumming of the various guitars. This is where being in D tuning truly pays off because you can come up with a pattern like this for the introduction and verse section (played on a concert ukulele, by the way):

Track 89

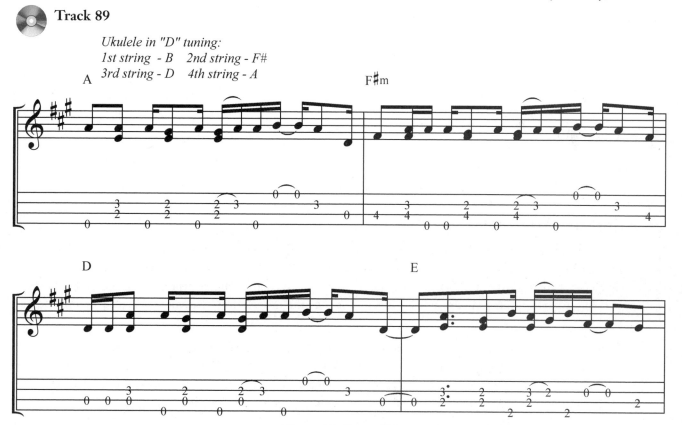

Chapter 20, Example 2.

This picking pattern repeatedly uses the notes at the second and third frets of the E string (which, because it is now tuned to F♯, are A and G♯) and creates some interesting harmonies as those notes are played over each of the four chords. The laidback rhythm of this picking pattern also mirrors that of the acoustic guitars, and the choice of not adding call-and-response fills gives the song breathing space.

That gives you the chance to create a different picking pattern for the chorus, such as this one:

 Track 90

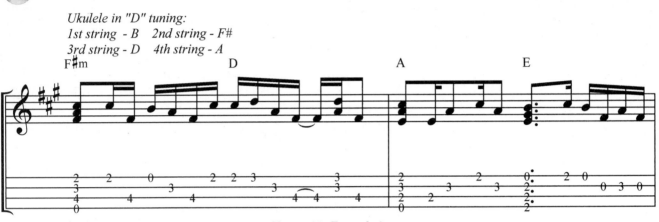

Chapter 20, Example 3.

It is important to note that you don't necessarily need to play these patterns exactly the same each time. Playing around with the rhythm a bit, as you learned in the finger-picking examples in Chapter 10, will make the ukulele sound more natural. In addition, you can hear that the other instruments don't play a single pattern throughout the song either!

 Track 91

Track 91 on the CD gives you a good demonstration of how to take these basic ideas for patterns and vary them a bit as you play.

Putting the Song First

You can hear how the ukulele adds a lot of character to this arrangement without being the center of attention. In fact, if you had not known in advance there was a ukulele in this song you might have mistaken it for a guitar or another string instrument. In the song's chorus, the uke has a quality that is part harp, part guitar, and part banjo—it is almost beyond description, and yet it perfectly complements the song.

Coming up with the best ukulele part for a song should always be your goal. Sometimes that part might be simple strumming to assist with keeping the rhythm; sometimes you might add little fills, much in the way a guitarist, pianist, or saxophone player might; and sometimes you might be the soloist for a song. Quite often, though, you will probably find yourself doing a bit of each.

Practice, Practice

It is kind of amazing how many musicians will practice scales or changing chords or keeping good rhythm for hours and hours on end, but seldom think twice about practicing performing!

Suppose you decide to play at an open mic and put together three songs to play. You have undoubtedly practiced the songs numerous times, but have you thought about practicing how you are actually going to perform them? Have you practiced with your ukulele amplified and plugged in to an amp or a PA? Have you practiced playing your ukulele with the aid of a microphone? Have you practiced singing with a microphone?

An even more important question would be have you practiced how to play through your mistakes? Mistakes are part of the game—everyone makes them. It is close to impossible to perform without making at least one, so you need to be able to count on your ability to continue on with a song regardless of whatever mistakes you happen to make.

FRET LESS!

In case you didn't know, there is one and only one guaranteed way to not make a mistake—don't ever play! Fortunately, no musicians see that as a viable option.

The truth is most of the times you make a mistake few of your listeners will know that you did unless you make a big deal out of it. A missed note or chord here or there doesn't usually garner a lot of attention. So just keep playing, and try not to make that mistake again next time.

Practicing a performance is by necessity a different type of practice than practicing to learn a song or to play a tricky chord change or rhythm. When you are practicing a song, you have the luxury to go over a part again and again, breaking it down into small sections to work through the tricky parts.

Ideally you should practice a performance in as close to a manner as you will be performing—same equipment, same players (if you are playing in a group), same song list. You should stand as you would on stage or wherever you will be playing. And, if possible, it doesn't hurt to have an audience to play to and from whom you can elicit feedback.

In a practice performance you can work out any anxieties you might have about a particular song or concentrate on being relaxed and natural when playing. Try to make rehearsals as real as possible, and your real performance should benefit greatly.

The Least You Need to Know

- When playing with other musicians, your biggest challenge might be hearing your own ukulele!
- Besides playing with a microphone, you have the option of having a pickup installed in your ukulele or buying an electric/acoustic uke.
- If you decide to buy an amplifier, your best bet is to get one made specifically for an acoustic instrument.
- Always try to have your ukulele add to the mood and personality of a song. Work out different parts and see which one best fits the song you are working on.
- Practice actual performances whenever you can, preferably with an audience you trust to give you honest and constructive feedback.

The Adventure Continues

In the following chapters, you'll find the details on how to shop for and find the right uke for you, how to properly clean and store it, and the all-important task of how to change its strings. You'll also learn about how to use your local music store to help you with all these tasks. Finally, you'll learn how to make a practice plan for yourself to keep progressing on what will, hopefully, be a lifelong journey of making and sharing music using your uke.

Smart Shopping

In This Chapter

- Finding the right ukulele for you
- Shopping and utilizing a local music store
- Buying a uke online
- Extras you will need

Many a would-be uke player's first instrument is a gift, or a hand-me-down, or something serendipitously found in a closet or yard sale. Maybe you have a uke that belonged to your great-great-great grandmother or to a sibling who decided to take up drums instead.

Keep in mind that your first ukulele is, wherever it came from, quite often just that—your *first* ukulele. Sooner or later you're going to want an instrument of your own choosing, or perhaps it might be more accurate to say you're going to want a uke to choose you.

Maybe you don't have a ukulele at all yet and are trying to work out which type you want to get. There are all sorts of ukes to choose from—hundreds, maybe thousands. But don't let that overwhelm you. More choices mean lots of ukes you can tinker with to find the one to call your own. But don't think that there's only one "right" uke for you; otherwise, you're likely to miss out on other ukes that will also make beautiful music with you.

Hopefully you've been thinking about the types of music you like (and like to play) and about which styles and techniques you enjoy. The more you know about what you want to do, music-wise, the more information you have about the kind of ukulele(s) you want.

What to Keep in Mind

You want your ukulele to fit you like a shoe does (or should). *Fit* here refers to both size and personality. Be sure to read the Quick Guide, "Choosing the Ukulele That is Right for You" at idiotsguides.com/ukulele for more about picking the ukulele that fits you best. And regardless of what size ukulele you choose, remember it's a musical instrument you're buying, neither a toy nor a wall decoration. Plenty of ukuleles are *meant* to be toys or decorative keepsakes. Don't get one of those to learn to play on. It will only frustrate you and could cause you to give up playing all together.

Solidify the idea that you're buying a musical instrument, particularly when it comes to considering how much you want to spend on a ukulele. You can spend between $30 and $50 (U.S.) on a "starter" ukulele. Then if it inspires you to keep playing, you can sell it (or give it away or trade it in) and *then* spend more money on a better ukulele. Or, you could spend between $75 and $125 on a decent yet still reasonably inexpensive uke from the start and play it the rest of your life because it's well-made and should, barring any unfortunate accidents, play well for decades.

Look at your potential ukulele as you would examine a fine shoe or suit or even a piece of furniture. If it looks like it has been sloppily assembled, with bits of glue showing on the seams or the inside of the body, or if the frets protrude from the sides of the neck, it probably was made carelessly. But a ukulele doesn't have to be expensive to be a great instrument.

Most players prefer ukuleles with solid wood tops, as opposed to wood laminates (a top made of thin sheets of wood pressed together). Ukes can and do come in a wide variety of woods. You'll find ukes with mahogany tops, as well as those constructed out of various types of spruce and cedar, both of which are used quite a bit for the tops of guitar bodies. Spruce tops tend to produce a very boom-y sound, while cedar (which can be found on many classical guitars and acoustic guitars marketed to finger-picking players) has a warmer and more complex tone. Cedar is also softer (less hard, as well as less loud) than spruce and scratches very easily.

You'll also find ukuleles made out of koa, which is a native tree of Hawaii. These days, though, koa is very scarce, so you're bound to pay a steep price for an instrument made of this exotic wood. That's why one of these ukes probably isn't the best choice for a beginner.

Buying Local

Your choice of ukulele, or any musical instrument for that matter, is an extremely personal, hands-on decision. You truly can't judge a uke's feel and playability without holding it in your hands. Thankfully, more and more music stores, from the huge corporate ones to the local mom-and-pop shops, are stocking ukuleles these days.

UKE LORE

You can often find good used ukuleles for good prices at consignment or vintage shops, yard/garage sales, and estate sales.

There are many advantages to buying your instrument locally. First, most of the people who work in music stores are incredibly friendly. They know that playing music is one of the coolest things one can do in life, and they want you to be able to make that magic for yourself. Talk with the salespeople (or the owner) and get a feel for which staff member might best be able to help you when it comes to questions about ukuleles.

SMOOTH STRUMMING

When you go to a music store or as you look online, take notes about what you're seeing and hearing. You're never going to be able to remember half the things you've learned and heard in your research, so make it easier for yourself by keeping a small notebook handy while you seek out your ukulele.

Also, don't be afraid to ask questions. Most music store workers love to talk shop and will do their best to answer whatever questions you have. Ask politely to try a few ukuleles and for their personal recommendations.

When you try a uke, handle it as carefully as you can. Take off your watch or any jewelry you're wearing that could accidentally ding or dent it.

If at all possible, bring a friend who plays uke along with you when you shop. Initially, you should try whichever instruments strike your fancy. If you are able to pare down your choices to a handful, then have your friend play each one while you listen. Don't even look at the ukulele while it's being played; just listen to what it sounds like because this is what you're going to sound like. It's important to remember that, when you play ukulele, you aren't hearing what your audience is hearing. They are sitting in a better place than you when it comes to listening to the music. So put yourself in that same place as a future listener.

Likewise, make sure your friend (or the store salesperson if you're on your own) plays what you'll be playing—simple strummed chords for a start. If your friend plays something very fancy, you won't listen to the uke; you'll just hear how your friend sounds fantastic and won't even notice how different each ukulele sounds compared to the others.

Another advantage to buying locally is that you'll often get a good warranty on your uke. Plus, you can more easily deal with returns or repairs.

Even if you end up buying your ukulele online, you can, and should, still develop a good working relationship with your local music store. If you ever run into an emergency situation and need a repair done quickly, the local store is where you're probably going to go.

Online Awareness

For the ukulele player, the internet is both a godsend and a snare. There is certainly no lack of ukuleles to choose from online. But you have no way of knowing whether any of them are meant for you until you have one in your hands.

This is why you owe it to yourself to get your hands on as many different types of ukuleles as you can first, just to see and feel what works for you in terms of the instrument's size. Then when you begin to search for ukuleles online, you will have a good idea (or several good ideas) of what you're looking for in terms of manufacturers and models.

The internet is very helpful for checking out reviews, especially of the ukes you tried and liked. But be sure to keep in mind that what you'll be reading is not from professional reviewers but rather with ordinary people. This isn't to say that ordinary people can't give unbiased reviews, but you never know whether a person is giving a ukulele a good (or bad) review because he actually knows something about ukes or because he wants to feel that he made a good purchase. With careful reading, you can spot trends. If an issue, good or bad, pops up over and over again, such as "cheap tuning pegs" or "great full sound," you should note it and look into it further.

Taking part in a community forum can help, too. There are many ukulele discussion groups where the members pitch in to answer questions from beginners. And though some of this will certainly be biased, overall you can usually get a balanced overview.

Finally, if you do buy your uke online, be sure to check out the return policy of the seller you buy it from. This is important because it's not until you have the uke in your hands and can see it and play with it that you will know if it's a good one for you.

Extras, Extras

Your new ukulele is likely going to be only *part* of your purchase. You should also get a case to go with it. Cases often, but not always, come with a uke and are already included in the price, but make certain before you buy whether (pardon the pun) this is the case.

Gig bags are soft cases that are lightweight and good for carrying your ukulele; nowadays they come in all sorts of styles and varying levels of durability. Some are little more than nylon sheaths with zippers, while others are constructed with dense foam to protect your instrument.

Hard shell cases are another option. They usually cost more but offer your instrument a very durable and safe mode of transportation. You can spend almost as much time choosing a case as you can a ukulele!

Of course, a tuner is essential and it will last you a lifetime if you treat it well. However, you will need to replace the batteries from time to time.

SMOOTH STRUMMING

Be sure to pick up a spare set of strings. You never know when you might break one! Also, grab at least one set that has a low G string if you think you might like to explore playing in low G tuning at some point. Some stores sell individual strings so you could just pick up a single low G string without purchasing a whole set.

If you buy your ukulele at a store, be sure to have it "set up" before it leaves the shop. A setup for a uke is a bit like a tuneup for a car. The music tech will check your instrument's action (the height of the strings from the frets) and intonation, as well as make sure it has no fretting problems. Often you'll get a cleaning and a fresh set of strings as well (although you might have to pay for the strings). Many stores include a setup as part of the cost when buying a new instrument from them, but double-check to be certain.

Even if you buy your uke online, be prepared to take it into your local shop to get it set up after you get it. The setup will put your uke in the best possible condition for you to start playing it.

You should also take your ukulele in for a setup on a somewhat regular basis. If you live somewhere quite dry, getting an annual setup is a good idea. If you live in more regular seasonal conditions, then every two years should be fine.

The Least You Need to Know

- When you buy a ukulele, remember that you're purchasing a musical instrument and not a toy.
- Take notes during every phase of your ukulele search. They will help you remember what and which ones you liked best.
- Get to know the people at your local music store. They will be an ongoing resource for you whether you buy a uke from them or not.
- If you buy a ukulele online, do your research first on what you like and know the return policy.
- A case and a tuner are essential extras you should purchase to go with your ukulele.

Taking Care of Your Ukulele

In This Chapter

- Keeping your ukulele clean and sounding its best
- Matching your uke to the right strings
- Learning how to change your strings
- Storing your uke safely when you're not playing it
- Dealing with changes in temperature and humidity

Your ukulele is an important part of you. It helps you create music and bring that music to your audience. Any bad day becomes better when you sit and play. When you and your uke are in sync, you're pretty much on top of the world.

Like people, ukuleles need their share of care and attention. Without it, they get a little worn and tired and don't always sound their best. You could pick up your uke and play a note and hear a bit of buzz that wasn't there before. Or maybe you notice that the fretboard feels a little gritty when you slide your fingers along the neck.

Fortunately, many of the things you can do to keep your uke at its best don't involve a lot of effort or work. They are simple things that take moments at most and go a long way toward making both you and your ukulele happy.

Keeping it Clean

As a ukulele player, you make your instrument sing. And you also make it dirty. Sure, it can collect dust all on its own, but just as you want your music to make its mark on the world, you're constantly leaving your own mark(s) on your ukulele.

Handling Your Hands

Your hands obviously have the most contact with your ukulele. Your strings, along with the fretboard and neck, have the most contact with your hands. But don't forget your picking hand and arm also make a lot of contact with both the strings and the body of the uke. If you happen to sweat a lot when playing, guess where some of that sweat's going to end up?

FRET LESS!

Your uke is at the mercy of its environment. Aside from dust, it will collect lint; pet hair (if you have them); or anything at all in the air, like cigarette smoke (if you smoke, play with people who do, or play in smoky places like bars) or sawdust (if you play in a garage or basement). Keep your uke stored in a case when you're not playing it to keep it as clean as possible.

The first thing you can do to keep your ukulele happy is to make sure your hands are clean each time you play. This might not always be possible, but you can certainly make a point of not picking up your uke right after eating a handful of potato chips or fried chicken. After all, you wouldn't want someone else to handle your ukulele if her hands were greasy, would you?

FRET LESS!

You can avoid giving your uke some major dings by taking off watches or jewelry, especially on your strumming hand. Dangling bracelets, cufflinks, and even heavy buttons on the cuffs of shirts will bang against the top of the ukulele's body when you strum, causing dings and scratches in the surface.

A Good Rub Down

Remember, too, that your hands naturally contain oil (and sweat), so you also need to make a point of giving your instrument a light cleaning after each time you play it. Take a clean, dry, lint-free cloth (your local music store is bound to have "guitar cleaning cloths" that will work fine on your uke) and give the body, including the back and sides, a good rubdown, wiping off the sweat and smudges that have accumulated while playing.

Then be sure to wipe the neck clean. When you're done with that, and if your cloth is thin enough, slip it between the strings and fingerboard. Going one string at a time, pinch a bit of cloth around the string between your thumb and fingers and give the string a good rubbing along the entire length of the neck.

Finally, give the headstock a bit of a wipe, again carefully fitting the cloth under the strings to get rid of the dust that tends to settle there.

This daily wipedown doesn't have to be all that extensive, and it certainly won't take a great deal of time. Plus, if you stick with this routine, you probably won't have to worry about doing a major fretboard cleaning the next time you change your strings.

Some Things About Strings

Your ukulele strings are the heart of your instrument. Without them, your uke can't play. Your strings get the brunt of all the playing you do, and all that strumming, finger picking, picking, bending, hammering, pulling, and sliding takes its toll after a while. Taking good care of your strings, keeping them clean and changing them when needed, will help keep your ukulele sounding its best.

UKE LORE

Strings for the ukulele used to be made from gut but now are made out of nylon. Some string manufacturers have created synthetic materials (such as "nylgut" by Aquila) that have more of the warm acoustic qualities of gut strings.

Strings can come in a variety of colors, but translucent and black are the most common.

Time for a Change

Your eyes, ears, and fingers are the best judges of when it's time to change your strings. If they look very dull, sound kind of lackluster, or feel dirty, or any combination of those symptoms, then get a new set. The unwritten rule is that if you can't remember the last time you changed your uke's strings, then it's time to change them. The unwritten corollary to this rule is even if you *can* remember, it's still probably time to change them.

When to change strings depends a lot on how much you play and practice. If you play your ukulele a lot, more than ten hours a week, you probably should change strings every four to six months. The casual player, someone who plays between five and ten hours a week, can probably get by with changing strings every six to nine months. Some folks make a habit of changing their strings when they change the clocks ahead an hour in the spring and then again when they change back an hour in the fall—that's certainly one way to remember to do it!

Checking the Package

Getting the right type of strings for your uke isn't all that hard. But getting familiar with all the different brands of strings can take a lot of time, especially if you don't change them all that often. Listen to other ukulele players and ask their opinions about string brands, especially if you happen to like the sound of their strings. It's funny, but whenever you ask someone what the best strings for your ukulele may be, they will almost invariably give you the name of the brand they last bought. When you start hearing a brand of strings repeated by numerous players, you should investigate that brand further.

You might, at first, find yourself overwhelmed with the choices facing you, but you really should look at it as a chance to further explore the sounds of your ukulele. Different strings will give you a slightly different sound. Each time you change your strings, at least for the first few times, make a point of trying a different type or brand and see which gives you the sound you like most.

SMOOTH STRUMMING

Whenever you buy a new set of strings, consider buying two packs. That way you have a ready replacement should one string break unexpectedly. You can buy single strings as well as full sets as long as you know what gauge your strings are. In fact, if you use low G tuning, it's a smart idea to have two or even three single low G strings on hand. Always keep the packet of the last set of strings you buy handy (in your ukulele's case is a good place) so you know which gauges your strings are without guessing.

Be sure to match your string purchase to your specific ukulele size. Strings generally come in "Soprano/Concert," "Tenor," and "Baritone" sizes. Sometimes they will be labeled "Hawaiian" instead of "Soprano." Either way, these strings will fit either the soprano or the concert ukulele. The main thing to avoid if you have either a soprano or concert ukulele is buying tenor or baritone strings. These strings are simply too long for the smaller two ukes.

The strings package should also indicate whether the fourth string is a high G or low G. Be sure you get the correct one for what you want!

Don't worry if the package says that the strings are for "jazz tuning" or "D tuning." As you read in Chapter 13, there's not a lot of difference between standard and D tuning so either strings will do.

All at Once or One at a Time

Uke players often argue about whether it's best to change strings one at a time or to change all four at once. The main debate concerns whether removing all the strings at the same time changes the tension in the neck enough to damage it. The major advantage to changing all four strings at once is that you can give your fretboard a thorough cleaning with all of the strings off.

> **SMOOTH STRUMMING**
>
> Before you even start to change your strings, notice first how the strings are wound onto the tuning poles and approximately how many wraps each string is getting. Take time especially to examine how the strings have been braided on the bridge. Paying attention to how it was done by the manufacturer will give you a clear idea of how it should look after you have changed the strings yourself.

There are good arguments for either side, but most uke players change all the strings at once. If you're truly worried about changing your strings correctly, ask a musician friend to show you how or take your ukulele to your local music store and ask if they could change the strings for you. And then ask if you can watch as it's done. Unless things are especially busy, they're usually more than glad to let you watch and give you pointers. Also don't be afraid to ask questions.

Out with the Old Strings

Changing strings involves two basic steps—removing the old strings and then putting on new ones. First, double-check your tuning knobs and make certain you know which direction you need to turn your tuners to either tighten or loosen the strings.

Then, loosen a string to the point that it has a fair amount of slack. You can then simply unravel the string from its tuning post or use a pair of wire cutters (or even kitchen scissors) to cut the string between the nut and the tuning mechanism. You do this so that you can carefully remove the longer piece of string from the body of the guitar. You don't want to just pull the string through the bottom in a hurry because you might cause the string to scratch the finish of the uke—that is often the case when you're dealing with the end of the string that has been wrapped around the tuning post.

After you've cut the string and taken off the long piece, unravel the short end of the string from the tuning post and pull it loose. Discard both pieces of string.

While the Strings Are Off

After you've removed all the strings, give the fretboard a good wiping with a dry clean cloth. A small amount of fingerboard polish or lemon oil applied to the cloth, and *not* directly onto the fretboard, can help keep it from drying out. Also be sure you apply the liquid to the cloth and not directly onto the ukulele's body and neck, and use as little as possible.

> **FRET LESS!**
>
> Unless you go to a store that specializes in ukuleles (and there are some out there), any polish or cleaner you'll find is usually going to be labeled as a "guitar polish," "guitar cleaner," or "guitar fretboard oil." This is fine because the guitar and the ukulele are practically cousins. What works with one will, quite often, be more than okay with the other.

If you have a particularly dirty buildup, get right up close to the fretboard and breathe on it, using the moisture from your breath along with a clean, dry cloth or a paper towel to lift dirt and grime and wipe it away.

For exceptionally bad buildups of dirt and oil on the fingerboard, you can use a hard plastic surface, like a credit card or even a guitar pick, to *gently* scrape off the worst spots.

On with the New Strings

To put on your new strings, start by tying the strings onto the saddle, as shown here:

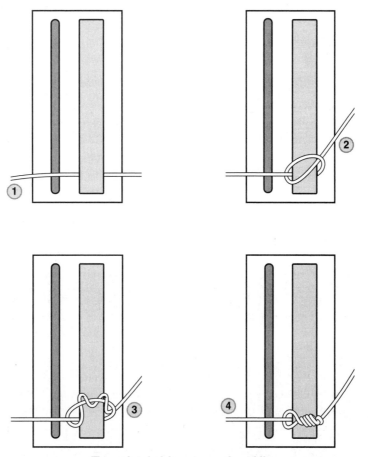

Tying the ukulele string to the saddle.

First, slip the string into its appropriate hole in the bridge (it's a lot easier to push it in toward the bottom of the ukulele than toward the headstock). Then pull it about three to four inches out through the bottom of the bridge, as shown in the first panel (1) of the above illustration.

Loop the string around itself back at the top of the bridge (2), and then braid the loose end around the portion of the string sitting on top of the bridge (3). Be sure to hold the longer section of the string (the side that's going up the neck) tight as you do so. You don't have to wrap it around a lot. Two or three times will do fine. The last pass should place the end of the string at the bottom of the bridge. Give the longer end a tug (4) while holding the braided end to tighten the braid a bit.

Take the loose end of the string, guide it through the appropriate slot in the nut, and then thread it through the post hole of appropriate tuner. After pulling the string taut, give it enough slack so that the string will be able to wrap about four or five times around the tuner—this will be between an inch-and-a-half to two inches.

When you've given the string just enough slack, make a kink in the string on the far side of the tuning post (the side it came out of when you put it through the post hole) in the direction opposite of how you're going to wind the tuner. You want the string to be wrapping around the posts from the center of the neck to the outer edge. That means the g and C strings will be wrapping counterclockwise while the E and A strings should be wrapping clockwise.

Start turning the tuner peg in the proper direction while, with your free hand, holding onto the string to keep even tension as the string wraps around the tuner. Make sure that the string is still in its proper slot in the nut while you do this.

FRET LESS!

Winding your string around the tuning post is a bit of an art and will take some practice and patience on your part. Too many windings produces overlap and unevenness and will cause the string to not wind onto and unwind from the post smoothly as one tunes. This leads to sudden jumps in pitch while tuning and sometimes while playing. Too few windings do not afford sufficient friction (grip) and will permit slippage.

Pulling Up the Slack

It often takes a while for your new strings to stretch out and settle into tuning. But there's no reason you can't help them along with the process a bit.

As you wind the string, pluck it from time to time as you tighten it and check it against your tuner. You still want to stretch out the string a bit, so tune the string slightly higher than the target note. For instance, if you're tuning the G string, tune it so that it's about halfway between G and G#. This will help stretch out the string, but it's just the first step.

After you have all four strings tuned to a slightly higher pitch than normal, gently but firmly pull on the string with your fingers, directly up from the fretboard as if you were drawing an arrow on a bow. Check the tuning again. You should have gone lower than the string's normal note. Retune the string, this time tuning it to the proper standard pitch. Then do the same with the other strings.

When you have all four tuned slightly higher again, repeat the "bow and arrow" pull, check the tuning again, and retune. This time around, tune each string to its proper pitch. Stretching out the string during the initial tuning process after changing the strings will keep it from slipping out of tune after you've gotten it into tune. Usually three "bow and arrow" pulls does the trick.

Keeping Things Cool and Consistent

If you play your uke a lot (or if you're trying to!), you may prefer keeping it out in the open as opposed to in its case. This is tricky as there are no real "ukulele stands," at least not at the time of this writing. Most items passing off as such are actually mandolin or violin stands being marketed to the ukulele crowd. Until someone comes up with a stand specifically designed for the ukulele, you're taking your chances with a stand.

So you have to be smart about where you put your ukulele. Keep it out of high traffic areas—places where people and pets are constantly moving around and might accidentally knock it over. Some people find that hanging their uke on wall hangers is a great solution to avoid such mishaps. But, like stands, some wall hangers are not meant to hold a uke. So before you buy one, make certain it will safely hold yours.

You also shouldn't hang or place your ukulele someplace where it can get overexposed to the elements. *Always* keep it away from heaters, radiators, air conditioners, and even out of any constant direct sunlight.

Remember that your ukulele, just like you, wants to be comfortable. Not too hot, not too cool. Sometimes things are unavoidable—you may have to transport it in the trunk of your car, for instance. If it's really hot or cold outside, a few hours in the car or trunk shouldn't hurt it, but all day or night certainly could.

SMOOTH STRUMMING

Having your ukulele out where you can see it can give you more of a nudge when it comes to practicing, especially if it's somewhere you can't help but see it! Putting it right by the television, for instance, might lead to more playing and practicing instead of watching a few hours of television. Or you could practice while you watch!

Also, help your uke avoid dramatic changes in climate whenever possible. After transporting it in the heat or cold, let it sit in its case and adjust to the stability of room temperature for a while before taking it out to play.

If your home can get very dry, invest in a humidifier (a violin or a small guitar humidifier will do) to keep the wood of your uke from drying out. The folks at your local music shop can show you the many options available.

Likewise, if the conditions are damp and humid, it would be a good idea to invest in some silica packs that you can keep in your ukulele case.

When the weather is either on the dry side or on the humid side, put your ukulele in its case (with its silica packs or humidifier as the case may be) at the end of the day. And if you know you're not going to be playing for a much longer period of time than usual, keep the case in a cool, dry spot. Preferably keep it someplace inside your house, where it will get neither too hot nor too cold.

Practice, Practice

When you make taking care of your ukulele part of your daily practice routine, you'll find that you don't even think of cleaning and maintenance as a "chore." Plus, your instrument will be in top working condition whenever and wherever you play. You'll also probably be the envy of your other uke-playing friends!

Speaking of friends, be sure that you all practice good habits when using each other's instruments. Don't play someone else's uke (or guitar or any instrument) before cleaning your hands first and taking off your watch or bracelets. Be especially careful of anything that can really scratch the back of the body of a ukulele, like a zipper or long necklace. Treat someone else's uke better than you treat your own.

Finally, you owe it to yourself and your ukulele to learn how to change your strings, so practice this as well. Luck often dictates that you'll need to do so at a performance! So it's good to know that you can effortlessly change a string when the need arises.

The Least You Need to Know

- It's important to keep your ukulele clean and stored at a comfortable temperature.
- Learn how to change your strings yourself, and do it on a regular basis.
- Be sure to get the right strings for whatever size ukulele you have. Read the string packages to be certain you get what you want.
- Be careful about where you leave your ukulele when you're not playing it so it doesn't get damaged.
- Avoid subjecting your ukulele to rapid changes or extremes of temperature, humidity, and dryness.

Making Music Forever

In This Chapter

- Making a practice plan
- Listening as practicing
- The importance of playing with and for others

You should give yourself a standing ovation at this point. You've come a long way and learned a lot over the course of these pages. You've learned a lot of chords and rhythms, how to strum in a wide variety of ways and styles, how to finger pick, and how to use your skills to play with others.

And you're just getting started! Much of your future learning will come from your own playing, whether on your own or with others. You will discover more ways to use the basic information and techniques learned in this book to grow and evolve both as a ukulele player and as a musician.

Good Practice Habits

Growth will only come from playing and practicing. You can theorize and analyze music all you want to, but eventually all that knowledge and all those ideas have to get into your fingers so they can make music. This happens with practice. Every step forward comes down to practice. It's *always* about practice. The only way you'll get better at the ukulele is by playing and practicing on your ukulele. It truly is that simple.

Make a Plan

An effective practice strategy is to create a plan for yourself with your ukulele. Not something like "I want to get better," but rather a specific practice plan with reasonable and measurable goals. It will help you to become a better and better ukulele player. Your goals will change over time as you progress as a musician, but the important point is to always have a practice plan with specific goals.

Strive to play every day, even if it's only for a short period of time. If you play every day, you will see, hear, and feel your progress; this will inspire you to keep practicing, and you will look forward to it. Set aside a minimum length of time to practice every day. If you go longer, great! But practice the minimum amount at least. When you get a rhythm going with your practice time each day, you'll probably find that you end up playing a lot more than your daily minimum! The daily aspect of practicing is, initially, more important than the length. Practicing 15 minutes a day will do you more good (and get you more practice time) than practicing one full hour once a week.

> **SMOOTH STRUMMING**
>
> Be realistic about setting practice time, but also be practical. One hour a day is a great place to start, but so is 10 to 15 minutes a day. And if you can come up with a few times in your day to practice for 10 to 15 minutes, you'll find yourself practicing an hour each day!

Your practice plan should not try to cover everything at once. When you're first starting out, focus your practice on basic techniques. Warm up your fingers of both hands with some "one finger one fret" exercises, and maybe do some basic chord changes and rhythm strumming.

In your practice plan, you can map out which exercises, chords, and strums you want to work on over the course of a week or month, and just work on those and wherever that may take you. After you have those down, move on to a new set, all the while still practicing what you learned already. Use the practice songs in this book or any songs you know not only to have some fun, but also to give you a practical application of the skills you're practicing.

Try to start your practice each time with new material and challenges to keep pushing yourself forward into new musical territory. You'll surprise yourself how quickly you will learn new things, even when they seem impossible at first. Be sure to have fun when you practice. Give yourself time to explore your ukulele, experiment, and be creative. Come up with some fills or riffs, do a little improvising with one of the solo practice tracks on this book's CD, or play along with one of your favorite CDs. Every minute you spend practicing is a minute your fingers are developing more skill and dexterity.

Listen Actively

Remember, too, that you can do a lot of practicing even when you don't have your uke at hand. Listen to music to develop your ear training. Try to hear whether you're listening to a major chord or a minor chord. Can you pick that out? Can you hear the difference between a dominant seventh and a major seventh? If not, it's okay—just notice the music and remember the things you hear that you'd like to try.

Listen as well for chord progressions. First, try just to hear the changing of the chords; then attempt to work out what the progression is and how many beats each chord of the progression gets. Practicing these skills will help you figure out songs you want to play just by listening to them.

Always carry some music with you when you can. Whenever you find a spare moment or two, you can practice reading either notation or tablature.

When you go to a concert or even an open mic, watch and listen to the other musicians, no matter what instrument they're playing. If they play ukulele or guitar, watch their hands on the neck. Do they play a lot of chords with open strings or a lot of barre chords? Is it straight strumming or broken chord / arpeggio / partial chord playing? Do they do a lot of finger picking? Or do they blend finger picking and strumming together in a style all their own? By just actively observing you are learning.

You can practice rhythm, that incredibly important aspect of music, almost anytime you have a song in your head. Tap out rhythms with your strumming hand while you listen to music. Or work out a strumming pattern on paper using notation from a songbook.

If you can get yourself in the habit of thinking about music and how it all relates back to the ukulele, then you will almost always be practicing in your head. And then when you get your uke back into your hands, you'll have a lot to catch up on!

The Ultimate Learning Experience

Never turn down the chance to play music with other people. You can do this once you know just four or five basic chords. Don't worry about not being "good enough" to play along with other musicians. They all started the same way you did and went through the same anxieties. Just sit down and play and listen and learn because there is always going to be more to learn!

Also, playing with others gives you a *reason* to practice. Knowing that you're going to be playing and that you're going to want to be able to contribute positively to the group is great incentive to practice.

When you play with others, remember that music is about communication, not competition. Whatever your skill level, there will always be someone "better" than you, but all that really means is that he has just been playing *longer* than you. You will find that most musicians are more than happy to help you when it comes to improving both your individual and your group playing skills. There usually is someone to whom you can teach something, too.

Whatever your musical dreams and desires may be—whether playing with others or simply for your own pleasure—be sure that, first and foremost, you are having fun. The more you enjoy it, the more you'll want to play. Not only does the fun really begin now, it never stops, and it also just keeps getting better.

Play every chance you get!

"... and the dreams that you dare to dream really do come true ..."

And before you go, here's a "good luck" gift—a finger-style chord melody–based arrangement of "Over the Rainbow," by Harold Arlen and E. Y. Harburg.

Way back in Part 3, you had all the tools you needed to be able to do a strumming version of this song, much in the style of Israel "IZ" Kamakawiwo'ole's version. All you had to do was find the chords and play them with a simple strumming pattern.

This arrangement, though simple enough for you to play with a bit of practice, incorporates just about all the various techniques and musical ideas you've learned. Hopefully you'll like it so much that you'll play it for your friends and family. After all, while it's fun to play music, it's even *more* fun to share it.

Track 92

OVER THE RAINBOW

Music by HAROLD ARLEN   Lyrics by E.Y. HARBURG   Arranged by David Hodge

find me   some - where_____ o - ver the rain-bow

blue-birds fly   birds fly   o-ver the rain-bow

why then oh why   can't I   if hap - py lit - tle blue-birds fly be-

The Least You Need to Know

- Make a practice plan, and practice every chance you get.
- Actively listening to music and identifying chords and rhythms is great practice you can do anytime.
- Playing with others is one of the best ways to improve your skills and grow as a musician.
- Always have fun playing your uke, and share your music with your family and friends.

Track Guide to the CD

Track 1:   Chapter 1, Ukulele Comparison

Track 2:   Chapter 2, Tuning

Track 3:   Chapter 3, Example 1

Track 4:   Chapter 3, Example 2 (0:00)
Chapter 3, Example 3 (0:18)

Track 5:   Chapter 4, Example 1 (0:00)
Chapter 4, Example 2 (0:18)
Chapter 4, Example 3 (0:37)

Track 6:   Chapter 4, Example 4

Track 7:   Chapter 5, Example 1 (0:00)
Chapter 5, Example 2 (0:13)

Track 8:   Chapter 5, Example 3

Track 9:   Chapter 5, Example 4

Track 10: Chapter 5, Example 5

Track 11: Chapter 5, Example 6

Track 12: Chapter 5, Example 7
"It's Raining, It's Pouring"

Track 13: Chapter 6, Example 1

Track 14: Chapter 6, Example 2
"Kum Ba Yah" in key of C

Track 15: Chapter 6, Example 3
"Kum Ba Yah" in key of G

Track 16: Chapter 7, Example 1 (0:00)
Chapter 7, Example 2 (0:12)
Chapter 7, Example 3 (0:24)

Track 17: Chapter 7, Example 4

Track 18: Chapter 7, Example 5

Track 19: Chapter 7, Example 6

Track 20: Chapter 7, Example 7 "Polly Wolly Doodle"

Track 21: Chapter 7, Example 8

Track 22: Chapter 8, Example 1

Track 23: Chapter 8, Example 2

Track 24: Chapter 8, Example 3 "After the Ball"

Track 25: Chapter 9, Example 1 (0:00)
Chapter 9, Example 2 (0:14)

Track 26: Chapter 9, Example 3
"He's Got the Whole World in His Hands"

Track 27: Chapter 9, Example 4

Track 28: Chapter 9, Example 5 (0:00)
Chapter 9, Example 6 (0:16)

Track 29: Chapter 9, Example 7 (0:00)
Chapter 9, Example 8 (0:14)

Track 30: Chapter 9, Example 9
"My Bonnie Lies Over the Ocean"

Track 31: Chapter 9, Example 10 (0:00)
Chapter 9, Example 11 (0:15)
Chapter 9, Example 12 (0:36)

Track 32: Chapter 9, Example 13 "Red River Valley"

Track 33: Chapter 9, Example 14

Track 34: Chapter 9, Example 15 "Alberta"

Track 35: Chapter 10, Example 1 (0:00)
Chapter 10, Example 2 (0:20)
Chapter 10, Example 3 (0:32)

Track 36: Chapter 10, Example 4

Track 37: Chapter 10, Example 5 (0:00)
Chapter 10, Example 6 (0:16)

Track 38: Chapter 10, Example 7

Track 39: Chapter 10, Example 8 "Three Pattern Song"

Track 40: Chapter 10, Example 9

Track 41: Chapter 10, Example 10

Track 42: Chapter 10, Example 11
"What Child Is This?"

Track 43: Chapter 11, Example 1 (0:00)
Chapter 11, Example 2 (0:05)
Chapter 11, Example 3 (0:11)
Chapter 11, Example 4 (0:18)

Track 44: Chapter 11, Example 5

Track 45: Chapter 11, Example 6

Track 46: Chapter 11, Example 7

Track 47: Chapter 11, Example 8

Track 48: Chapter 12, Example 1 (0:00)
Chapter 12, Example 2 (0:15)
Chapter 12, Example 3 (0:29)

Track 49: Chapter 12, Example 4
"Sometimes I Feel Like a Motherless Child"

Track 50: Chapter 12, Example 5

Track 51: Chapter 12, Example 6 (0:00)
Chapter 12, Example 7 (0:29)

Track 52: Chapter 12, Example 8 "Sloop John B"

Track 53: Chapter 12, Example 9

Track 54: Chapter 12, Example 10 "Dry Bones"

Track 55: Chapter 13, Example 1

Track 56: Chapter 13, Example 2 (0:00)
Chapter 13, Example 3 (0:21)

Track 57: Chapter 13, Example 4
"Swing Low, Sweet Chariot"

Track 58: Chapter 14, Example 1
"Star of the County Down"

Track 59: Chapter 14, Example 2
"Sloop John B" baritone ukulele

Track 60: Chapter 14, Example 3
"Sloop John B" baritone and tenor ukuleles

Track 61: Chapter 15, Example 1 (0:00)
Chapter 15, Example 2 (0:14)
Chapter 15, Example 3 (0:35)
"Twinkle, Twinkle, Little Star"

Track 62: Chapter 15, Example 4 (0:00)
Chapter 15, Example 5 (0:32) "Ode to Joy"

Track 63: Chapter 15, Example 6 "Amazing Grace"

Track 64: Chapter 16, Example 1

Track 65: Chapter 16, Example 2
"Sloop John B" in key of C

Track 66: Chapter 16, Example 3
"Man of Constant Sorrow"

Track 67: Chapter 16, Example 4 (0:00)
Chapter 16, Example 5 (0:12)
Chapter 16, Example 6 (0:27)

Track 68: Chapter 16, Example 7

Track 69: Chapter 16, Example 8

Track 70: Chapter 17, Example 1 (0:00)
Chapter 17, Example 2 (0:17)
Chapter 17, Example 3 (0:48)

Track 71: Chapter 17, Example 4

Track 72: Chapter 17, Example 5
"Blues Soloing Backing Track"

Track 73: Chapter 17, Example 6

Track 74: Chapter 17, Example 7
"Minor Key Soloing Backing Track"

Track 75: Chapter 17, Example 8

Track 76: Chapter 17, Example 9
"Major Key Soloing Backing Track"

Track 77: Chapter 18, Example 1 "Blue Uke"

Track 78: Chapter 18, Example 2 "Brahms' Lullaby"

Track 79: Chapter 18, Example 3
"Old Time Mountain Uke"

Track 80: Chapter 18, Example 4
"Shine On, Harvest Moon"

Track 81: Chapter 18, Example 5 "Tum Balalaika"

Track 82: Chapter 18, Example 6
"She'll Be Coming 'Round the Mountain"

Track 83: Chapter 18, Example 7 "Aloha Oe"

Track 84: Chapter 19, Example 1
"Hard Times" vocal and tenor ukulele

Track 85: Chapter 19, Example 2
"Hard Times" featuring concert ukulele

Track 86: Chapter 19, Example 3
"Hard Times" featuring baritone ukulele

Track 87: Chapter 19, Example 4
"Hard Times" vocal and ukulele trio

Track 88: Chapter 20, Example 1
"It's Not a Love Song" band without ukulele

Track 89: Chapter 20, Example 2

Track 90: Chapter 20, Example 3

Track 91: Chapter 20, Example 4
"It's Not a Love Song" band with ukulele

Track 92: Chapter 23, Example 1
"Over the Rainbow"

Chord Charts

Here are chord charts for the chords you'll most likely run across when playing ukulele.

First are the major and minor chords, plus their various seventh chords:

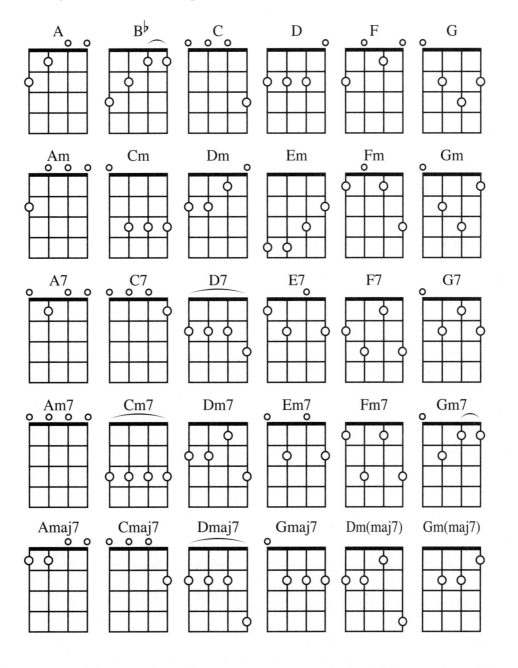

Next are the embellished chords—the various augmented, sus4, power chords (also called 5 chords), sixths, ninths, diminished sevenths, and so on:

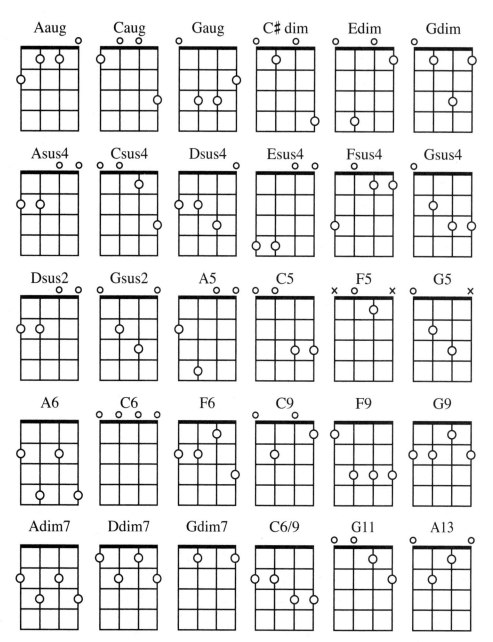

Finally, here are some interesting voicings of chords that work very well on the ukulele:

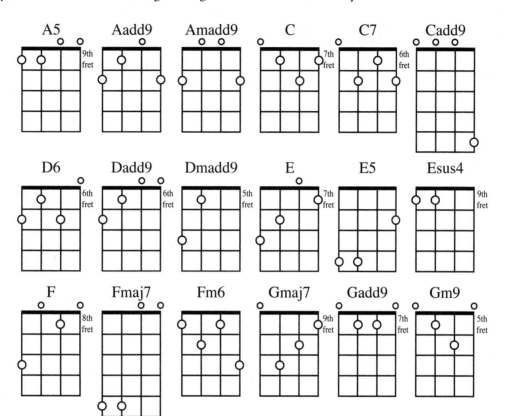

A Quick Guide to Music Notation and Tablature

Both standard music notation and ukulele tablature are used in most of the examples you'll find in this book. This appendix serves as a quick reference on various terms and symbols found in music notation and tablature. The basics of reading ukulele tablature can be found in Chapter 3.

Notes in notation are identified by their location on the musical staff, which is a set of five horizontal lines. The notes can appear on any of the lines or in the spaces between the lines. They can also appear on ledger lines above or below the staff or in the spaces between those ledger lines.

Ukulele tablature uses a set of four horizontal lines with each line representing one of the ukulele's strings. The bottom line is the g string (which is the string closest to you as you look down while holding your ukulele in a playing position) and, going upward on the tablature lines, the next line represents the C string. The second line from the top represents the E string, and the top line represents the A string. Numbers placed on these tablature lines indicate which fret to play on any particular string.

Most ukuleles (not counting the baritone) use the following range of notes, which are also shown with their ukulele tablature counterparts:

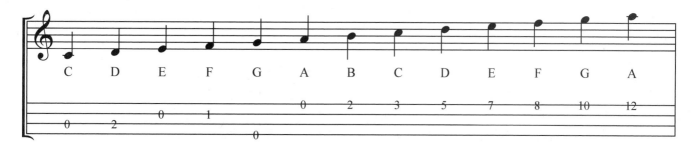

In addition to these notes, there are also accidentals, where the note is either sharp (raised a half-step in pitch), indicated by the symbol ♯, or flat (lowered a half-step in pitch), which is indicated by the symbol ♭. A natural sign, indicated by the symbol ♮, placed before a note negates any sharp or flat.

In standard notation, the key signature appears at the beginning of the first line of music and indicates which notes will be flat or sharp throughout the given piece (unless negated by a natural sign). An accidental added before a note indicates that specific note will be either flat or sharp for the entire measure where the accidental occurs, unless negated by a natural sign (♮).

In both standard notation and tablature, music is divided into measures (also called *bars*), which have a set number of beats. The number of beats is indicated by the top number of the time signature, which is most often a 4 or a 3. The lower number indicates which type of note—usually a quarter note (4) or an eighth note (8)—receives the rhythmic value of one beat.

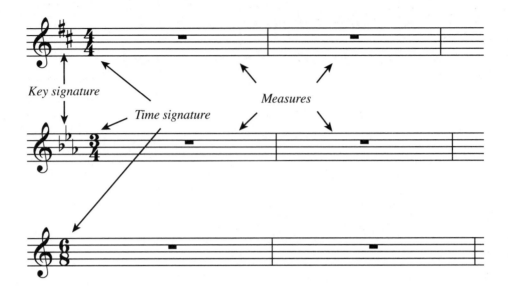

Notes are given rhythmic values, which are identified by the shape of the note head and flag. Notes can also be *tied*, which creates a rhythmic value of the combined notes in a tie. *Rests*, which are rhythmic pauses, also have identifiable shapes:

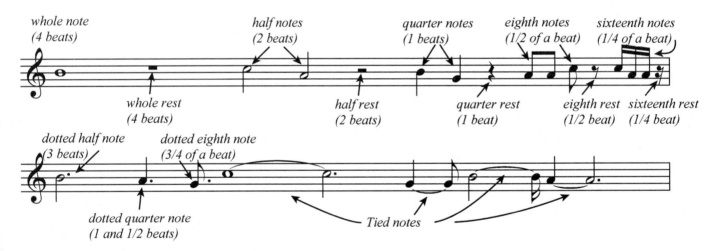

Rhythm notation, which uses a combination of note head shapes and slashes, indicates the rhythm with which to strum chords. This saves you the time and trouble of having to read the notes (or tablature of the notes) of any given chord to determine which chord it is. Rhythm notation uses the same rest shapes as standard notation:

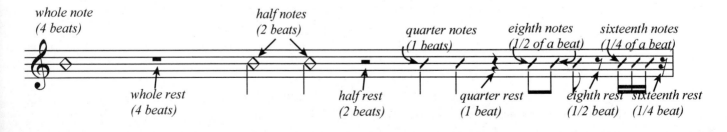

There are four common ukulele slurs—hammer-ons, pull-offs, slides, and bends—each of which is described in detail in Chapter 11. Slurs are often connected in the same way that tied notes are. However, tied notes are notes of the same pitch value (two C notes, for example), while slurred notes are notes of different pitches:

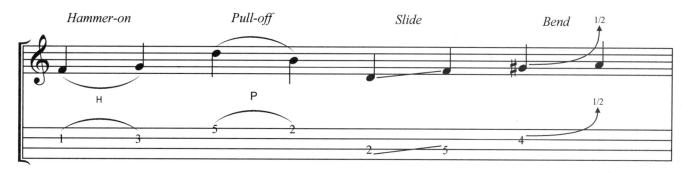

Written music also usually contains directions, particularly when it comes to repeating a particular passage of music. Usually this involves the use of repeat symbols that are placed at the beginning and end of the passage in question:

When the music requires a different ending for a repeat, first and second endings are used. The end of any given song is usually a double bar line:

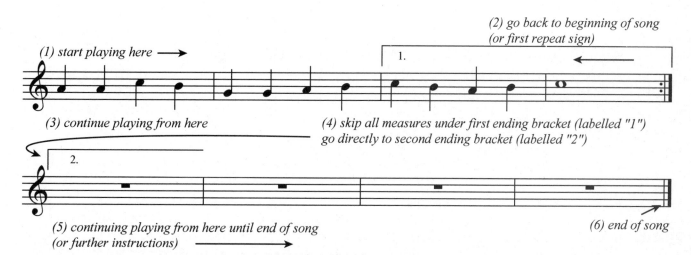

For Further Reading and Study

The Complete Idiot's Guide to Playing the Ukulele was specifically designed and written to start you on a lifelong musical journey. Hopefully you have found that this book has given you a solid grasp of the basics (chords and strumming) as well as a healthy sampling of more advanced beginner and intermediate techniques that you will use each time you play your uke. But even with the knowledge you've learned here, there are whole other worlds for you and your ukulele to explore.

Fortunately, the aspiring ukulele player has a huge wealth of resources to assist in that exploration. In addition to hundreds of books, videos, and CD and DVD tutorials on ukulele instruction, an ever-growing number of tutorial websites exist on the internet—and that's not even including the thousands of YouTube videos you can find.

If you're looking for history of both the ukulele and the cultural impact of this little instrument, author Jim Beloff's book *The Ukulele—A Visual History* (Backbeat Books, Second Edition, 2003) is a delight to read and look at. It is chock-full of great information and stories of ukuleles as well as the major uke players and manufacturers.

Mr. Beloff is also a great source when it comes to finding material for songs and styles. To date, he has written more than two dozen ukulele song books (most in the "fake book" style mentioned in Chapters 19 and 20), and you'll find that he has a book covering just about any musical style you can think of from classical to Disney to Elvis to Rodgers and Hammerstein. You might find his *The Daily Ukulele—365 Songs for Better Living* (Hal Leonard, spiral bound edition, 2010), co-written with his wife Liz, a great way to keep up your daily practice regimen.

Mr. Beloff has also teamed with the nationally renowned teacher Fred Sokolow to produce *Fretboard Roadmaps—Ukulele: The Essential Patterns That All the Pros Know and Use* (Hal Leonard, 2000), which is a great book to help you master the layout of the ukulele's fretboard. This a great book if you're especially interested in soloing and improvising.

When you've gotten to a more advanced stage of playing, you'll definitely want to check out Mr. Sokolow's *Blues Ukulele: A Jumpin' Jim's Songbook* (Flea Market Music, 2008) and *Bluegrass Ukulele: A Jumpin' Jim's Songbook* (Flea Market Music, 2010) for a more detailed study of these two musical genres.

If you're a classic rock fan, you might want to try *The Complete Idiot's Guide to Rock Hits for Ukulele* (Alfred, 2010). It contains 25 songs from the likes of the Allman Brothers, Cream, Led Zeppelin, Pink Floyd, and more.

And you certainly should explore your ukulele's Hawaiian roots! Try Michael Preston's *Let's Kanikapila! Ten Steps to Learn Ukulele the Hawaiian Way* (Mutual Publishing, 2006) to get you started. Then you can move on to *Hawaiian Style Ukulele Volume 1* (Ukulele PuaPua, 2009) to play some incredibly beautiful traditional Hawaiian music.

If you want to explore finger-style ukulele playing as well as alternate tunings, I highly recommend Mark Kailana Nelson's *The Uke Buke ... Learn to Play Slack Key Style Ukulele* (Acme Arts/CreateSpace Publishing, 2010). Mark has created beautiful ukulele arrangements of traditional Hawaiian songs (and others) done in various alternate tunings usually associated with Hawaiian guitar playing. You'll definitely want to have a low G string handy if you work through this book!

As you've read over and over (and over) again in this book, practicing is an essential part of improving, both as a ukulele player and as a musician. While neither of the following two books are specifically geared toward the ukulele, I still recommend them highly when it comes to helping any musician practice: *The Musician's Way: A Guide to Practice, Performance and Wellness* by Gerald Klickstein (Oxford University Press, 2009) and *The Principles of Correct Practice for Guitar* by Jamie Andreas (Jamey World, Inc., Second Edition, 2005). Both of these books will give you the mindset you need to make the most of your practice as well as the awareness of what goes into physically playing your instrument. You cannot help but get better simply by reading both of these books.

Finally, for learning more about music theory, check out Michael Miller's *The Complete Idiot's Guide to Music Theory* (Alpha Books, 2002). For good measure, also look through his *The Complete Idiot's Guide to Soloing and Improvisation* (Alpha Books, 2004) to help you with your own soloing.

Even though countless books, DVDs, and websites are available, you still probably want to think about getting a teacher. A lot of places offer group ukulele lessons; you can also find one-on-one instruction if you look around. Either will give you instant feedback as well as encouragement and support.

Finally, please feel free to write and ask me any questions you may have. My email address is dhodgeguitar@aol.com. Or you can contact me through my blog www.davidhodge.com. I try to answer every email I get. I spend my days teaching, so please don't worry if I don't respond immediately.

Index

Numbers

A

B

C

D

E

F

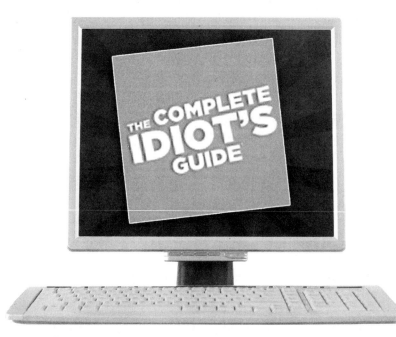